Rzym antyczny
Polityka i pieniądz

The Ancient Rome
Politics and Money

IV

PRACE
NAUKOWE

UNIWERSYTETU
ŚLĄSKIEGO
W KATOWICACH

NR 2558

40 LAT
UNIWERSYTETU
ŚLĄSKIEGO

Rzym antyczny
Polityka i pieniądz

The Ancient Rome
Politics and Money

IV

pod redakcją
Wiesława Kaczanowicza

Wydawnictwo Uniwersytetu Śląskiego

Katowice 2008

Redaktor serii: Historia
SYLWESTER FERTACZ

Recenzent
LESZEK MROZEWICZ

Contents

Contents

Introduction

We give the fourth volume of the cycle *The Ancient Rome. Politics and Money* to the Readers. The first publication of the series came out in 1993 and the next one — in 1997. Both publications were edited by Professor Andrzej Kunisz, for many years a lecturer of ancient history, as well as the director of the Department of Ancient and Medieval History in the Institute of History at the University of Silesia in Katowice, well-known and highly valued researcher, particularly in the field of numismatics of the Roman Empire. Professor Kunisz died after a long and serious illness on 25 November, 1998.

At the beginning of 1999 the Department of Ancient and Medieval History was divided into two organizational units. One of them is the Department of Ancient History, which is under my supervision. The research profile of the Department has not undergone any essential changes. It was reflected in the contents of the articles published both in the third of the series *The Ancient Rome. Politics and Money* (which come out in 1999), as well as in this volume.

The research of research workers and PhD students of the Department concern therefore mainly the issues related to the history of Rome in the period of the Empire. The primary field of our interest are the issues connected with the history of *Imperium Romanum* in the third century AD. The research is mainly focussed on the issues of ideology and propaganda, realised through coins by the authorities of that time.

Numismatic sources are therefore the basis for the research carried out in the Department of Ancient History at the University of Silesia. The most important publications, which are currently prepared and designed, will concern, among other things, comparative questions with reference to the ideas promoted on the issues of coins from the second and third century AD (A.A. Kluczek), the propaganda activity of emperor Aurelian (A.A. Kluczek) as well as the issue concerning ideological aspects on the coins of Roman empresses in

the period of the crisis of the Empire in the third century AD (W. Kaczanowicz). A catalogue of the finds of Roman coins in the Great Poland area is
also prepared (W. Kaczanowicz).

Another topic of research work carried out in the Department is the
research on broadly based political issues from the period of the fall of the
Roman Republic. A monograph regarding the third consulate of Gneius
Pompeius in 52 BC is only one of many undertakings planned in this field
(N. Rogosz).

Wiesław Kaczanowicz

TOMASZ ŁADOŃ

The Process of Romanization in the Spanish Provinces at the Time of the Sertorian War

The beginnings of organization of the province on the Iberian Peninsula date back to the threshold of the second century.[1] In 197 the Senate decided that two provinces would be created there: Hispania Ulterior (Farther Spain) and Hispania Citerior (Nearer Spain) and that praetors would be sent there to govern them.[2] The peoples living on the peninsula did not, however, give up easily to the Roman administration, and above all they resisted to the exploitation by the Roman governors. As a consequence, almost throughout the entire second century the Republic was forced to conduct difficult wars in Spain.[3] The conquer of Numantia in 133 is generally considered to be the turning point ending these conflicts, yet armed encounters continued in the following years.[4]

---

[1] The dates in the paper refer to the times before the birth of Christ.

[2] Liv. XXXII, 27, 6; 28, 2. See also: C.H.V. Sutherland: *The Romans in Spain*. London 1939, p. 47; J.S. Richardson: *Hispaniae. Spain and the Development of Roman Imperialism 218—82 B.C.* Cambridge 1986, p. 75; Idem: *The Romans in Spain*. Cambridge 1996, p. 45; L.A. Curchin: *Roman Spain. Conquest and Assimilation*. London—New York 1991, p. 29.

[3] T. Rice Holmes: *The Roman Republic and the Founder of the Empire*. Vol. 1. Oxford 1923, p. 9; C.H.V. Sutherland: *The Romans...*, pp. 64—87; W.V. Harris: *War and Imperialism in Republican Rome 327—70 B.C.* Oxford 1979, p. 209 f.; J.S. Richardson: *The Romans...*, p. 41—82.

[4] M. Cary, H.H. Scullard: *Dzieje Rzymu*. T. 2. Warszawa 1992, p. 283 f.

The Roman conquest was followed by a gradual romanization[5] of Spanish provinces.[6] The process had a different course in various parts of the peninsula. Romanization was much faster in the eastern and southern parts, where a more significant flow of Roman people was taking place. Since Latin was there the language used in administration, religion and commerce, it goes without saying that the powerful locals were forced to start using it. It also turned out that, besides the above-mentioned factors, Latin over the years began to make communication between Iberian tribes using various languages easier.[7] Drafting barbarians by Roman governors also facilitated romanization.[8] Natives fighting under the Roman rule adopted Roman customs, language, and after returning from the army they propagated them among their fellow tribesmen.[9] Romanization was also an effect of migration of Iberian peoples, both mandatory — from mountain settlements to valleys,[10] and voluntary — e.g. to seaside towns, where, due to a multinational population, Latin became the dominant language.[11] Initially in the towns Italian immigrants lived in separate districts, over the years, however, the population blended.[12]

The romanization transformation had an entirely different course in the West, North and center of the Iberian Peninsula. In republican times there still existed a tribal system in those regions, local law was in force, Iberian language in speaking and writing was used. The Romans were treated as intruders, autochtonic inhabitants refused to serve under their command, which lead to imposing high taxes on entire tribes by the Roman governors. At the end of 2nd century, after the constant fighting ceased, the process of romanization began also in that part of the peninsula, yet it was much slower than in the Ebro valley, and it flourished only in the time of the Empire.[13]

---

[5] The term is used in historiography in different contexts. This results, among others, from the difficulty to unambiguously define the term "romanization". About the discussion on that topic: L. M r o z e w i c z: *Rozwój ustroju municypalnego a postępy romanizacji w Mezji Dolnej.* Poznań 1982, pp. 104—109. This researcher ventured to create his own definition. According to him "[...] stosując określenie 'romanizacja', należy pod tym rozumieć nasycanie świadomości jednostek i całych grup społecznych rzymskim modelem kulturowym" ("[...] using the term 'romanization', one should understand saturating individuals and entire social groups with the Roman cultural model"). See: Ibidem, p. 109. This definition was used by the author of this paper as being in force.

[6] On this subject see: L.A. C u r c h i n: *The Romanization of Central Spain.* Routledge 2004. Also there the newest literature on the subject.

[7] J.B. T s i r k i n: *Two Ways of Romanization of Spain.* "Klio", Bd. 70 (1988), p. 479.

[8] See: A. B a l i l: *Un factor de la romanisatión: las tropas hispánicas al servicio de Roma.* "Emerita", nr 24 (1956), pp. 108—134.

[9] *Fontes Hispaniae Antiquae.* Vol. 4. Ed. A. S c h u l t e n. Barcelona 1937, pp. 154—156.

[10] App., *Ib.* 99; Strab. III, 3, 5; Flor. II, 33.

[11] J.B. T s i r k i n: *Two Ways...*, p. 479.

[12] As it was for example, in Corduba or Carthago Nova. See: Ibidem, p. 480.

[13] Ibidem, pp. 480—484.

In the beginning of 1st-century romanization of the Iberian Peninsula was speeded up more. Undoubtedly the war fought there between Sertorius and Rome in the seventies contributed to that. However, that process is reflected relatively poorly in the sources. Very weak numismatic sources[14] and a small number of inscriptions preserved from the time of the Sertorian war[15] cause that the study of the subject of this article must be based first of all on the analysis of the preserved literary texts.[16]

Because of such weak source base, the influence of the sertorian conflict on the process of romanization escapes unequivocal assessments and the historians still argue about that matter. Some see Sertorius as the creator of a new style of proceeding in the provinces, which in a perspective aimed to allow representatives of the natives to participate in governing the country, or even a propagtor of a *römisch-iberisches Reich*.[17] Others stress that Sertorius's concessions and privileges for the barbarians were of tentative nature and were caused solely by the will to pull them to his side in the fight with the Sullans.[18] To a smaller degree the importance for the development of romanization in the Spanish provinces of the activities of Metellus Pius and Pompeius is perceived, who, while fighting the war against Sertorius, were trying to use the local tribes in the fight on their side.[19] Besides tentative effects, those actions had also long-term effects, by tying the Iberian community stronger to the Roman authorities of the peninsula.

---

[14] M.H. Crawford does not identify any coins with the period of the Sertorian war, he only notes the coinmaking of Gaius Annius, the Sullan governor of Spanish provinces in 82—81. See: M.H. C r a w f o r d: *Roman Republican Coinage*. Vol. 1. Cambridge 1974, pp. 381—386.

[15] There are few preserved inscriptions related to Sertorius's actions, and the authenticity of the preserved ones is questionable: P.O. S p a n n: *Quintus Sertorius...*, p. 140. Some more inscription material can be related to the actions of Metellus and Pompeius, although in the case of the latter there is additional difficulty in identifying the period they refer to.

[16] The antic authors of course were not interested in the issue of romanization of Spanish provinces. Describing the story of the conflict, on numerous occasions they refer to it, in a more or less consciouss way. Cicero's, Sallust's, Plutarch's of Chaeronea and Appian's of Alexandria notes are of exceptional value here.

[17] V. E h r e n b e r g: *Sertorius*. In: I d e m: *Ost und West. Studien zur Geschichtlichen Problematik der Antike*. Brünn—Prag—Leipzig—Wien 1935, pp. 190, 192; A. S c h u l t e n: *Sertorius*. Leipzig 1926, p. 80; C.H.V. S u t h e r l a n d: *The Romans...*, pp. 94—96. The inhabitants of Spain in the following centuries appreciated the merits of the Marian governor in the work of romanization of the Iberian Peninsula. An expression of this was naming after Sertorius the university founded in 14th century AD in Osca, the town where at the beginning of the war against the Sullans Sertorius founded the school for the children of Iberian aristocrats. This college, called "Sertoriana Universidad" or "Sertoriana Academia", survived until 19th century AD. See: P.O. S p a n n: *Quintus Sertorius and the Legacy of Sulla*. Fayetteville 1987, p. 168.

[18] P.O. S p a n n: *Quintus Sertorius...*, p. 168.

[19] Researchers focus more on relating the actions of the commanders during the war. See: J. Van O o t e g h e m: *Lucius Marcius Philippus et sa famille*. Namur 1961, pp. 188—215; R. S e a g e r: *Pompey. A Political Biography*. Berkeley—Los Angeles 1979, pp. 17—21.

Undoubtedly, the relationship with the Iberian tribes was a priority for Sertorius from the very beginning of the war. Immediately upon receiving the governorship of the Spanish provinces, he took actions which signalled abandoning the hitherto prevailing, restrictive policy of the Roman governors towards the tribes inhabiting the Iberian Peninsula. He caused the change of status of Spanish towns from *civitates stipendiariae* to *civitates liberae*, perhaps even *liberae et immunes*.[20] That was connected with introducing inner autonomy and releasing some of the taxes for Rome. Besides that, one of Sertorius's best moves was to free the local tribes from the duty of giving winter quarters for the Roman legionnaires.[21] He set the example himself, by setting his camps outside the borders of the Iberian towns.[22] Removing that burdensome and inconvenient duty from the inhabitants of the Iberian towns, assured him a huge popularity among them.

The above-mentioned actions of the governor were greeted with significant support from the Iberian people. The fact that after an almost two years-long absence on the peninsula Sertorius returned there on an explicit request of an envoy of one of the tribes is a proof of that.

Plutarch of Chaeronea is giving the details: "As he [Sertorius — T.Ł.] was deliberating whether to turn his efforts next, the Lusitanians sent ambassadors and invited him to be their leader. They were altogether lacking in a commander of great reputation and experience as they faced the terror of the Roman arms, and they entrusted themselves to him, and to him alone, when they learned about his character from those who had been with him".[23]

One wonders why the request to Sertorius was sent by the Lusitanians, a tribe, which inhabited the territory of present-day Portugal and was known at that time for a relentless attitude towards Roman efforts to dominate the Iberian Peninsula.[24] Some of the researches are of the opinion that the reason of the proposal was the will to make Sertorius lead an anti-Rome in-

---

[20] Plutarch (*Sert.* 6, 4) does not specify those changes, we can however guess that they were reflected in *lex Antonia de Termessibus*, published later. See: F.F. Abbott, A.C. Johnson: *Municipal Administration in the Roman Empire*. New York 1968, pp. 42—45, 279—282; J.R. Hawthorne: *The Republican Empire*. London 1963, p. 10 f.

[21] Plut., *Sert.* 6, 4.

[22] Ibidem.

[23] Plut., *Sert.* 10, 1.

[24] Strab. III, 152—153: "And yet the country north of the Tagus, Lusitania, is the greatest of the Iberian nations, and is the nation against which the Romans waged war for the longest times. The boundaries of this country are: on the southern side, the Tagus; on the western and northern, the ocean; and on the eastern, the countries of the Carpetanians, Vettonians, Vaccaeans, and Callaicans, the well-known tribes; it is not worth while to name the rest, because of their smallness and lack of repute. Contrary to the men of to-day, however, some call also these peoples Lusitanians."

surgency.[25] This opinion was, according to me, completely disproved by P.O. Spann.[26] The presence of Romans in Spain dates back as far as more than a century before Sertorius appeared on the Iberian Peninsula and local peoples must have realized that it was impossible to dislodge the intruders. An anti-Rome rebellion would not have had any chance of success. The only thing the locals could count on was a change in the policy of the Roman governors, who had been until that time famous for brutality and ruthlessness towards the inhabitants of the peninsula. Sertorius, on the other hand, during his short reign proved that a change in the policy towards the local people was possible. Yet after he was driven away from Spain in 81, another Sullan governor, Gaius Annius, came to power, who, as we can assume, went back to the old restrictive policy. Lusitanians and other tribes centered around them could have made a sort of an alliance with Sertorius: in return for the support given him in his fight against the Sullans, after his prospective return to power in the Republic by his party, a more liberal policy would be in force, similiar to the one the Marian governor began in 82.[27]

If we look this way at the genesis of Sertorius's co-operation with the Lusitanians, then the Spanish rebellion, lead by the Marian, appears not anti-Rome, but more as anti-Sullan. Just as for the Lusitanians and other Iberian peoples supporting the Marian governorship was the only chance to improve their own situation under the Roman rule, so for Sertorius, given his

---

[25] In connection with that in some studies Sertorius is even accused of treason, and L. Wickert (*Sertorius*. In: *Rastloses Schaffen: Festschrift für Friedrich Lammert*. Stuttgart 1954, p. 98) directly calls Sertorius *imperator Lusitanicus*. A. Schulten is of the opinion that Sertorius supported Lusitanians in their urge to revolt: A. S c h u l t e n: *Sertorius...*, p. 53. See also: H. B e r v e: *Sertorius*. "Hermes", Vol. 64 (1929), p. 221.

[26] P.O. S p a n n: *Quintus Sertorius...*, pp. 58—62. The American researcher right underlines that accepting the proposal to lead the anti-Roman riot would have been a political suicide for Sertorius. He would have lost any chance to negotiate with the capital authorities the amnesty and return to Italy. His constant exposing the legality of his post in Spain also are a proof against a potential "treason" (see: C.F. K o n r a d: *Plutarch's Sertorius. A Historical Commentary*. Chapel Hill—London 1994, p. 116), so is the fact of approval of the alliance with Lusitanians by the Romans accompanying Sertorius. It is well known that Romans scorned the peoples living in the provinces (in that topic: D.B. S a d d i n g t o n: *Roman Attitudes to the "Externae Gentes" of the North*. AC 4 (1961), p. 92 f.; P.O. S p a n n: *Quintus Sertorius...*, p. 61). Even if Sertorius was an exception, it is difficult to assume, that his companions would have applauded their leader yielding to persuasions of barbarians.

[27] Such understanding of the alliance between Sertorius and Lusitanians is only a hypothesis, since Plutarch was too laconic in giving information about this topic. See: Plut., *Sert.* 10, 1; 11, 1. It is, however, worth stressing that in the changing political situation of that time, when during only seven years the government of the Republic changed three times, leaders of Lusitanians and other nations, who supported Sertorius, could not have foreseen that they tied their fate to a party that had already lost. In that topic: P.O. S p a n n: *Quintus Sertorius...*, p. 60; C.F. K o n r a d: *Plutarch's Sertorius...*, p. 116.

situation at the time, the alliance with the barbarians seemed the only way to reach the ultimate success, that is to conquer the Sullans.[28]

The support Sertorius received from the Iberian tribes spread very quickly in the western part of the Iberian Peninsula and soon reached also the eastern part. It is known that at the beginning of the rebellion only twenty towns pronounced for the Marian governor, while during the following several months he succeeded in subjugating the Vaccaeans, Vettonians neighbouring the Lusitanians and still later the Arevacs living further east and probably Illergets.[29]

It is very difficult to explain the phenomenon of Sertorius's popularity and the fact of the numerous tribes switching to his side. Plutarch in *Life of Sertorius* justifies that with the leaders nature, reportedly inspiring awe among the barbarians and knowingly using their superstitious belief in the super-natural.[30] It seems that Sertorius did indeed master the ability of imposing his charisma on large masses of native Iberians. In fact, however, the support for the Marian governor could not have been based solely on awe and fear. What convinced the simple barbarians to Sertorius, the biographer from Chaeronea thinks, did not for sure impress those of their leaders, who made the decision to support the rebellion started by the leader. They were probably convinced by what Plutarch wrote about in *Life of Sertorius* a few chapter earlier, that is the continuation of the liberal policy towards the natives, tax exemptions, giving up staying within their towns for winter quarters and — what seems not without importance — Sertorius's actions towards stronger romanization of the Spanish provinces.

One of these actions by Sertorius was to organize the Iberian troops in the Roman manner. If Sertorius was to match the Senate troops in fight, he had to

---

[28] See: P.O. S p a n n: *Quintus Sertorius...*, p. 60: "Clearly, for the Lusitani, the only plausible course was to support Roman governor whose victory in the civil war would give them a livable relationship with Rome. For Sertorius and his followers, only a Lusitanian offer to support their *Roman* political cause, to operate as allies, was acceptable." On the other hand, it is hard to define Sertorius's political goes at this stage of the war. The only thing he could count on was the hope that stirring the Iberian tribes against the Sullans will make the position of the latter in the country and in a longer perspective — to change the configuration in the government, which will allow him to reach an agreement with the capital authorities and return to Italy.

[29] Plut., *Sert.* 11, 1; 12, 2; Liv., fr. XCI. About spreading Sertorius's authority on Iberian Peninsula see: C.F. K o n r a d: *Plutarch's Sertorius...*, p. 150 f.

[30] The best known example of using the credulity of the barbarians was using a white doe by Sertorius. A unique specimen of that animal accidentally got into the hands of the leader. He explained the barbarians that the doe was given to him as a gift from the goddes Diana and that it was able to tell the future. Many times later he used the animal's presumed ability to manipulate his Iberian subordinates. The history of the white doe was very popular in the ancient times and survived in many records. See: Plut., *Sert.* 11; 20; Val. Max. I, 2, 4; Front., *Strat.* I, 9, 13; Gell. 15, 22; App., BC I, 110, 514. See also: W.O. M o e l l e r: *Once More the One — Eyed Man Against Rome.* "Historia", Bd. 24 (1975), pp. 405—408; J.S. R i c h a r d s o n: *The Romans...*, pp. 96—97.

train the barbarians. He probably turned some part of the units into heavy infantry, the majority however remained light formations, which were perfect for guerilla warfare tactics and fighting in the difficult Spanish landscape. He also introduced in his units the Roman customs, discipline and arms.[31] Thanks to that he "converted their forces into an army, instead of a huge band of robbers".[32] Both the Lusitanian tribes and the ones that supported Sertorius later, that is Celtiberian and the inhabitants of Ebro valley, were included in the training.[33] Of course, the above-mentioned Sertorius's actions were caused by the necessity of the moment and resulted from preparing the troops to fight against the Sullans. This, however, does not diminish the fact that introducing the Roman in Sertorius's barbarian army contributed to instilling there new patterns and popularization of Roman ideas.[34]

The creation of a Roman school in the town of Osca[35] for the children of the Iberian tribe leaders, was also a very important action by Sertorius, which can be seen as a step towards deepening the romanization of the Spanish provinces. Plutarch says that Sertorius "set over them teachers of Greek and Roman learning; thus in reality he made hostages of them, while ostensibly he was educating them, with the assurance that when they became men, he would give them a share in administration and authority. So the fathers were greatly pleased to see their sons, in purple-bordered togas, very decorously going to their schools, and Sertorius paying their fees for them, holding frequent examinations, distributing prizes to the deserving, and presenting them with the golden necklaces which the Romans call bullae."[36]

The words of the biographer from Chaeronea do not tell us, when Sertorius created this school. P.O. Spann supposes that it took place in 77, when Lepidus's riot had already been quenched in Rome and the decision to send Pompeius to Spain had been made.[37] Accepting this date seems reasonable, I do not, however, suppose that the proceedings in Italy influenced Sertorius's decision.[38] It is even possible that Sertorius considered setting up the school even before Lepidus's defeat, and one of the main reasons behind its creation

---

[31] Plut., *Sert.* 14, 1.

[32] Ibidem.

[33] See: App., BC I, 108, 506. More: C.F. K o n r a d: *Plutarch's Sertorius...*, p. 140.

[34] Army had a very strong influence on speeding up the process of romanizations of provinces. See.: L. M r o z e w i c z: *Rozwój...*, p. 110.

[35] Osca at the feet of Pyrenees, one of the main towns of Illergets, is meant here. In this topic see: Strab. III, 4, 10; Ptol., *Geogr.* II, 6, 67—68; Plin., *N.H.* III, 24. Szerzej: A. S c h u l t e n: *Osca.* In: RE, Hlb. 36. Stuttgart 1942, col. 1536; C.F. K o n r a d: *Plutarch's Sertorius...*, pp. 141—142.

[36] Plut., *Sert.* 14, 2—3. See: App., BC I, 114, 533.

[37] P.O. S p a n n: *Quintus Sertorius...*, p. 167. See: A. S c h u l t e n: *Sertorius...*, p. 80.

[38] Sertorius could not have created the school earlier, since he only appeared in Near Spain around the beginning of 77. See: C.F. K o n r a d: *A New Chronology of the Sertorian War.* "Athenaeum", Vol. 83 (1995), p. 186.

was his intent to bring to the side of the Marians — who were represented in Spain by Sertorius — as many of the Nearer Spain tribes as possible. Perhaps even in Lepidus's camp the possibility of using Spanish contingents in the fight to control Rome was considered.[39] After the defeat and death of that leader, Sertorius continued to strive for the support of the people inhabiting the Nearer Spain, so one can suppose that he did not give up the school either; since that moment, however, it played a different part — besides the goals of educating and spreading Roman culture and science, it was a peculiar safeguard against the possibility of betrayal of the Iberian tribes. Exactly those intentions of Sertorius are stressed by Plutarch.[40] According to the biographer from Chaeronea, the facility in Osca was supposed to gather all the children of Iberian aristocrats in one place, which allowed the governor to keep their faithfulness and unity in the fight against the Sullans. Undoubtedly not all the fathers of the children educated in Osca were fully devoted to Sertorius's case. This is also confirmed by the later fates of the hostages: at the end of the rebellion, when more and more tribes went over to the Sullan side, the Marian governor ordered a part of the children in Osca to be executed.[41]

Sertorius, in creating and maintaining the school for the powerful Iberians, was probably guided first of all by political cunning. As a matter of fact, it is difficult to assume that in the times of a difficult war against the Sullans, the Marian leader found the time to make far-reaching, visionary plans to unify the Republic with the provinces.[42] The search for the answer for reasons behind the creation of the Osca school can not, however, obscure the influence this decision, and its later completion, had on the history of the country on the Tiber, since creation of such facility was the first attempt, confirmed by sources, to romanize the barbarian elite in a province. The idea gave birth to the later actions of Roman politicians aiming to integrate the inhabitants of the provinces with the country.[43]

Besides a conciliatory policy towards the Iberian tribes, Sertorius tried to seek their support also in another way. He probably promised the most emi-

---

[39] If such idea had ever been born — and there is no such information in the sources — he must have relied on using troops from the tribes of Near Spain. Lusitanians would have been very difficult to convince to leave their own settlements and march to Italy.

[40] Plut., *Sert.* 14, 2.

[41] Plut., *Sert.* 25, 4.

[42] P.O. S p a n n: *Quintus Sertorius...*, p. 167; C.F. K o n r a d: *Plutarch's Sertorius...*, pp. 143—144. See: V. E h r e n b e r g: *Sertorius...*, pp. 190—192, 198—201; A. S c h u l t e n: *Sertorius...*, pp. 82—83, 156—158.

[43] Similiar action several years later will be taken in the East by Marc Anthony, and on a larger scale an integration policy following Sertorius's will be applied by emperor August. See: C.F. K o n r a d: *Plutarch's Sertorius...*, p. 142. Also there literature on the subject.

nent of them to give them Roman citizenship after the war.[44] The authors of the sources do not, in fact, confirm that directly[45]; traces of such actions by Sertorius are perhaps the few inscriptions with his name.[46] This could not, however, have happened on a large scale — lavishing this privilege would not for sure have been greeted with acceptance of the Roman Senate. If Sertorius had hoped to reach an agreement with the capital authorities by negotiations, he must have realized that giving citizenship to members of Iberian aristocracy diminished the chance of agreement with the Sullans. It is, however, undeniable that this aspect of the leader's actions was of immense importance for the inhabitants of the peninsula. The status of Roman citizen raised the prestige to a much larger degree, it also protected from the possibility of misuse by Roman governors.[47] These actions were also an important factor in romanization of the Iberian Peninsula.

The romanization transformation in the Spanish provinces was not only caused by Sertorius's actions — it was also a result of the conduct of Roman commanders sent by the capital authorities to quench the rebellion. Still in 80 Sulla delegated to Farther Spain Quintus Caecilius Metellus Pius. That commander in the first stage of the war against Setorius could not count on support from the Iberian peoples inhabiting Farther Spain, since the majority of local tribes were on Sertorius's side. So Metellus, right after arriving to the province assigned to him by the Senate, began devastating the territories inhabited by Sertorius's allies, wishing to discourage them this way.[48] The result he achieved, however, was reverse than intended — the hatred towards Sullans among the inhabitants of Farther Spain only strengthened, and its consequence was an even stronger bond of the local tribes with the Marian governor. As a result of this the Sullan commander built a network of fortifications alongside the Anas river in the direction of Tag, which was supposed to serve two purposes: as a base for sorties into the enemy territory and as a protection against potential retaliatory actions of Sertorius and his Spanish

---

[44] It is possible that Sertorius, as a proconsul, gave citizenship to the powerful Iberians. It would not have been unprecendented — Pompeius Strabo had such authority already in 89. P.O. Spann (*Quintus Sertorius...*, p. 195, footnote 46) suspects that in a crisis situation in the country after Sulla's landing in Italy, the Marians could have given him extraordinary powers. See: ILS 8888; E. Badian: *Foreign Clientelae (264—70 B.C.)*. Oxford 1958, p. 278; J.P.V.D. Balsdon: *Romans and Aliens*. London 1979, pp. 83, 91. See also: H. Berve: *Sertorius...*, p. 225.

[45] See in that context: Plut., *Sert.* 14, 3 and remarks of C.F. Konrad: *Plutarch's Sertorius...*, p. 142.

[46] CIL II, 16; 254; 3752; 3786. See: I.G. Gurin: *Rimlanie i warwary w Sertorianskom dwiżenii*. AMA 11 (2002), p. 56.

[47] P.O. Spann: *Quintus Sertorius...*, p. 80.

[48] Sall., *Hist.* I, 112: "illo profectus vicos castellaque incendere et fuga cultorum deserta igni vastare, neque late aut securus nimis, metu gentis ad furta belli peridonei". See: L.A. Curchin: *Roman Spain...*, p. 43.

allies. Probably Metellinum (present-day Medellin) on the Anas river was the first of such military camps and governor's headquarter at the same time.[49] Then he began extending the network of camps towards North, West and finally South-West. North of Metellinum Castra was created, behind the river Tag — Vicus Caecilius,[50] to the West — Caeciliana, several kilometers away from Olisipo[51] (present-day Lisbon). Perhaps from this very camp Metellus conducted the warfare, as a result of which he conquered two cities: Dipo and Conistorgis, located somewhere between the rivers Anas and Tag.[52] Metellus's penetration reached probably even further North, as far as the river Durius.[53] Metellus's actions described above, although forced by Lusitanians' resistance, turned out to be a foundation for romanization of the territory of present-day Portugal. The road from Emerity to Bracary was later built alongside the route of the camps of the Sullan commander.[54]

After Sertorius's defeat in the battle of Segontia Metellus changed his attitude towards the Iberian people. It became visible first of all in the big scale propaganda, which was aimed to cast doubt among the until then allies of Sertorius and as a consequence — to make them go over to the Sullan commander's side. Plutarch of Chaeronea mentions that Metellus "moreover, after a victory which he once won over Sertorius he was so elated and delighted with his success that his soldiers saluted him as Imperator and the cities celebrated his visits to them with altars and sacrifices. Nay, it is said that he suffered wreaths to be bound upon his head and accepted invitations to stately banquets, at which he wore a triumphal robe as he drank his wine, while Victories, made to move by machinery, descended and distributed golden trophies and wreaths, and choirs of boys and women sang hymns of victory in his praise."[55] Splendor, commonly displayed by the Sullan had surely a huge psychological meaning. Showing the power of Rome, served mainly pulling more and more tribes to Metellus's side (or at least discouraging them from further supporting Sertorius), at the same time, however, it filled the consciousness of individuals

---

[49] A. S c h u l t e n: *Sertorius...*, p. 66; P.O. S p a n n: *Quintus Sertorius: Citizen, Soldier, Exile.* (Dissertation). Texas at Austin 1976, p. 82; M. B i e r n a c k a - L u b a ń s k a: *Śladami Rzymian po Hiszpanii. Przewodnik archeologiczny.* Wrocław 1983, p. 55.

[50] The precise location of those camps is unknown. About hypotheses on that subject: A. T o v a r: *Iberische Landeskunde.* Bd. 2. Baden-Baden 1976, pp. 237—244; P.O. S p a n n: *Quintus Sertorius...*, p. 67 f.

[51] C.F. K o n r a d: *Plutarch's Sertorius...*, p. 137.

[52] Sall., *Hist.* I, 113; I, 119. See: P.O. S p a n n: *Quintus Sertorius...*, p. 68.

[53] C.F. K o n r a d: *Plutarch's Sertorius...*, p. 138.

[54] See: C.H.V. S u t h e r l a n d: *The Romans...*, p. 92. In the time of the Empire most of the Roman roads in Spain crossed in Metellinum. See: *De Hispania Antiqua (roman period).* Excerpts and translation H. G e s z t o f t. Warszawa 1990, p. 101, map number 2.

[55] Plut., *Sert.* 22, 2.

and society groups with Roman culture, so it was a manifestation of romanization.[56]

Giving the Roman citizenship to the local potentates by Metellus was also a sign of his new policy. The Sullan commander did perform that on a large scale, as Cicero's words imply.[57] Such actions undoubtedly won new allies in Spain for Metellus. At the same time the governor imposed heavy taxes on those who did not surrender to him on time. This burden was lifted by Caesar only ten years later.[58]

Another material proof of Metellus's actions in Lusitania are inscriptions. On the territory between the rivers Anas and Tag seventeen inscriptions were found, which the historians connect with activities of Quintus Caecilius Metellus Pius in this region.[59] Apart from that a few inscriptions were found in the town of Corduba.[60] Some of them may be linked with the above-mentioned practice of giving Roman citizenship to the powerful Iberians.

The other Sullan commander, who battled Sertorius — Cn. Pompeius — must have realised, when he was setting out in 77 for the Iberian Peninsula, that the key to victory in the war in Spain is, among others, succeeding in breaking the alliance between the Marian governor and the natives of the province. Some Iberian tribes supported Pompeius already when he was crossing the Pyrenees, that is why the Senate commander did not meet any significant resistance there. Indicctens and Lacetans, living south of the Pyrenees Passes, went over to Pompeius's side,[61] and the negotiations with them were conducted by Berons and Autrigons.[62] Furthermore, many Spanish towns pronounced themselves for Pompeius. Sertorius tried to stop those dealings, cruelly punishing the traitors,[63] but the circle of Pompeius's Iberian

---

[56] I follow here the above-mentioned definition of romanization from the book by L. M r o - z e w i c z: *Rozwój...*, p. 109 f.

[57] Cic., *Arch.* 26: "[...] a Q. Metello Pio, familiarissimo suo, qui civitate multos donavit". Probably Metellus did that based on *lex Gellia — Cornelia* (Cic., *Balb.*, 50—51), but it is possible that these were actions on his own accord. According to A.M. W a r d: *M. Crassus and the Late Roman Republic*. Columbia—London 1977, 24 f. Metellus had that right already before *lex Gellia — Cornelia* of 72.

[58] [Caes.], *Bell. Hisp.* 42, 2.

[59] S.L. D y s o n: *The Distribution of Roman Republican Family Names in the Iberian Peninsula*. AS, Vol. 11/12 (1980/1981), pp. 284—285.

[60] CIL II, 2263; 2264; 2272.

[61] Sall., *Hist.* II, 98, 5.

[62] Liv., fr. XCI.

[63] Contrebia, which after declaring itself on Pompeius's side was captured and severly punished by Sertorius, can be an example of this. See Liv., fr. XCI. About identifying this town see: G. F a t a s: *El Bronce de Botorrita*. BRAH, t. 176 (1979), p. 421; J.S. R i c h a r d s o n: *The Tabula Contrebiensis: Roman Law in Spain in the Early First Century B.C.* JRS, 73 (1983), pp. 33—41; P.O. S p a n n: *Saguntum vs. Segontia. A Note on the Topography of the Sertorian War*. "Historia", Bd. 33 (1984), pp. 116—119.

followers kept growing larger. On the North of the peninsula Vascons went over to the Sullan side and Pompeius set up the military camp Pompaelo (present-day Pamplona) on their territory, in the place of a pre-roman settlement.[64]

The support given to Pompeius by a large part of Iberian peoples was caused, I suppose, by two factors: the large force, which the Sullan governor had brought to Iberian Peninsula, but also perhaps the new policy, which he started using towards the Iberian people. Pompeius probably followed the route set a few years earlier by Sertorius and continued his liberal policy towards the local peoples.[65] Despite that during the Sertorian war Pompeius was not able to get such strong support from the Iberian people as Sertorius did. Even if they did declare themselves on the Sullan side, they supported him neither in a military nor in a financial way.[66] It is therefore difficult to call them "allies" in the full meaning of the word — the attitude of those Iberian peoples can be rather described as waiting and "friendly neutral".

The relations between the Iberian nations and Pompeius improved further after the attack on Sertorius in Osca in 73. Plutarch stresses that most of the Iberians refused at that time to continue fighting under M. Perperna's command and sent envoys to the Sullan commanders to discuss the terms of surrender.[67] Pompeius did not execute reprise, on the contrary — he took actions, which won him much popularity on the Iberian Peninsula. It survived until the following civil wars in Rome, and even Pompeius's sons took advantage of it.

Among the mentioned undertakings to win allies, and in the future those who could be helpful in romanizing the Spanish provinces, were numerous acts of giving Roman citizenship to members of Iberian tribes. The best known new

---

[64] Sall., *Hist.* II, 93. See: Strab. III, 4, 10. See also: I. Modrzewska-Pianetti: *Zarys archeologii Hiszpanii rzymskiej.* Warszawa 2002, p. 75.

[65] Plut., *Sert.* 18, 2: "[...] many of the cities which were subject to Sertorius turned their eyes towards Pompey and felt inclined to change their allegiance". Also mentions about Pompeius's winter quarters prove that he did not try to use the old custom of imposing his presence on the Iberian towns. See: Sall., *Hist.* II, 94; II, 98, 5; Plut., *Sert.* 21, 5; App., *BC* I, 110, 512. Pompey's complaints on lack of resources to continue the war and his sharp correspondence with the Senate about that (See: Sall., *Hist.* II, 98) can also confirm the fact that he did not try to financially exploit the Iberian tribes that went over to his side.

[66] At least there is no such information in the sources. More: J.S. Richardson: *The Romans...*, p. 101.

[67] Plut., *Sert.* 27, 1. A handful of towns however continued the resistance. They were: celtiberian Clunia, Uxama Argaela and Termes (all of them were Arevac towns). The Vascons town of Calagurris Nasica, where there were act of cannibalism, defended itself fanatically (since Vascons went over to Pompeius's side, it is suspected that there was a celtiberian garrison in the town). On the east coast Tarraco and Dianium were defending themselves. Sources and commentary on that: C.F. Konrad: *Plutarch's Sertorius...*, p. 216 f.

citizen was Lucius Cornelius Balbus of Gades.[68] It is worth mentioning that the above-mentioned acts of giving citizenship, although they were Pompeius's individual initiative, were approved in 72, when the consuls L. Gellius Publicola and Cn. Cornelius Lentulus Clodianus passed the famous act in that matter.[69]

It is known that Pompeius, having conquered Perperna's army, carried out a settlement action in Spain. Probably the settlers, however, did not come from Pompeius's ranks,[70] they were rather the remains of Sertorian troops, which surrendered to him after the last battle.[71] In Valencia region this action was directed by Pompeius's legate, Lucius Afranius.[72] It is possible that some of the former Sertorians also settled around Osca and Tarraco.[73] Since that time they were a group of Pompeius's faithful allies in Near Spain.[74]

Besides that Pompeius also regulated the relations with the Iberian tribes. Not much is known about his actions: he rewarded the allies and punished the enemies. The fact is, that more than twenty years later the commander's actions were still perfectly remembered.[75] Above that he tried to eliminate the

---

[68] Cic., *Balb.* 5; 11; 19; 38; 40. See also: E. B a d i a n: *Foreign Clientelae...*, p. 303; E.S. G r u - e n: *The Last Generation of the Roman Republic.* Berkeley—Los Angeles—London 1974, p. 64. There are however very few inscriptions confirming the fact of giving Roman citizenship to members of local tribes. About reasons of such situation: S.L. D y s o n: *Roman Names...*, p. 289.

[69] Cic., *Balb.* 19; 32—33; see 38. See: J.P.V.D. B a l s d o n: *Romans...*, p. 83; E.S. G r u e n: *The Last Generation...*, p. 36—37.

[70] In face of an unclear situation in Italy in the end of the seventies, Pompeius could not afford disbanding even part of his own army. It can be suspected that after a few years of a hard war the legionnaires expected more from their commander than parcels of land in Spain. See: A.J.N. W i l s o n: *Emigration from Italy in the Republican Age of Rome.* New York 1966, pp. 40—42.

[71] P.O. S p a n n (*Quintus Sertorius...*, p. 137) rightly argues that some Sertorians and Lepidans after ten years of fighting in the Iberian Peninsula had no reason to go back to Italy. They would have gladly accepted land in the province. It is unknown how many stayed. Some for sure returned to Italy. In 70 the tribune of the people Plautius introduced a resolution (*lex Plautia de reditu Lepidanorum*), which brought them back to public life. About that: T.R.S. B r o u g h - t o n: *The Magistrates...*, Vol. 2, pp. 128, 130 (concerning the sources and dating), and also D.H. K e l l y: *Evidence for Legislation by Tribunes 81—70 B.C.* In: *Auckland Classical Essays Presented to E.M. Blaiklock.* Dunedin 1970, p. 133 f.

[72] CIL IX, 5275. See: T.R.S. B r o u g h t o n: *The Magistrates...*, Vol. 3, pp. 12—13. About him: B. B a r t s c h: *Die Legaten der römischen Republik vom Tode Sullas bis zum Ausbruche des zweiten Bürgerkrieges.* Breslau 1908, p. 10.

[73] See the remarks of P.O. S p a n n: *Quintus Sertorius...*, pp. 210—211, annotation 83.

[74] Caes., *Bell. civ.* I, 61, 3; II, 18, 7. See also: A.J.N. W i l s o n: *Emigration...*, p. 32: "Pompeius took a personal attitude to his defeated enemies, making it quite clear that their best hope for the future lay in becoming his *clientes*, and his later influence in Citerior must have been largely based on Roman survivors of Sertorius' armies who saw their future in Italy as uncertain, and preferred to stay in the land of their long exile, under his protection."

[75] Caes. *Bell. civ.* I, 61, 3: "Huic consilio suffragabatur etiam illa res, quod ex duobus contrariis generibus, quae superiore bello cum Sertorio steterant civitates, victae nomen atque imperium absentis Pompei timebant, quae in amicitia manserant, magnis affectae beneficiis eum diligebant."

threat of the dangerous Iberian peoples, resettling them from the inaccessible mountain seats to the valleys.[76]

The influence of Sertorius's war against the Sullans on speeding up the process of romanization of the Spanish provinces can be therefore seen very clearly. It was among others a consequence of the fact that for more than ten years Iberian tribes were involved in an internal Roman conflict. It must be stressed that the war against Sertorius was — as J. Richardson rightly wrote — "war between Romans, not between Romans and Spaniards".[77] Iberian tribes were not, as it used to be until that time, a side of the conflict, they were rather an ally of one of the sides. To involve the local peoples in an internal Roman conflict, one had to offer them something. Sertorius used the fact that the inhabitants of the peninsula strived above all to improve their situation under Roman rule, so he offered them to apply a more liberal policy towards the residents of the province. He went even further, however — he imposed Roman cultural patterns on his supporters, an example of which was training the Iberian army in the Roman fashion or carrying out educational action among a part of Iberian youth. Even if in the beginning these attempts had no marks of purposeful romanization of Spanish provinces, they certainly speeded the process up. Pompeius and Metellus were not able — confronted with such attitude of Sertorius — to continue their old style policy, based on exploitation and reluctance of the locals in the Spanish provinces. The actions taken by those commanders, as much as Sertorius's deeds, influenced romanization transformation in the Spanish provinces. The real initiator of the new course on the Iberian Peninsula, however, was Sertorius. The governors who followed him — whatever politcal option they represented — were not able to retreat from the path of changes which he proposed, which in the following decades will lead to an even stronger romanization of the Spanish provinces.

---

[76] That is what he did for example with the Vascons. Isid., *etymol.* IX, 2, 107: "idem et Vascones [...] quos Cnaeus Pompeius edomita Hispania et ad triumphum venire festinas de Pyrenaei iugis deposuit et in unum oppidum congregavit. Unde et Convenarum urbs nomen accepit."

[77] J.S. Richardson: *Romans...*, p. 101.

Translated by Marcin Janus

Tomasz Ładoń

PROCES ROMANIZACJI W PROWINCJACH HISZPAŃSKICH
W OKRESIE WOJNY SERTORIAŃSKIEJ

Streszczenie

Romanizacja prowincji hiszpańskich w okresie Republiki Rzymskiej następowała stopniowo. Przez pierwsze stulecie istnienia prowincji hiszpańskich był to proces raczej powolny, a na pewno nierównomierny — bardziej ulegała mu bowiem wschodnia część Półwyspu Iberyjskiego, znacznie wolniej — część zachodnia. Jednocześnie plemiona iberyjskie stawiały duży opór rzymskim rządom w Hiszpanii, wynikiem czego były liczne bunty i wojny z rzymskimi namiestnikami.

Istotnym wydarzeniem, które — zdaniem autora niniejszego artykułu — w znaczącym stopniu przyspieszyło proces romanizacji na Półwyspie Iberyjskim, była wojna sertoriańska (80—72 przed Chr.). Sertoriusz — namiestnik prowincji hiszpańskich z ramienia władz mariańskich — prowadził ją z Metellusem Piusem i Pompejuszem — sullańskimi namiestnikami przysłanymi na półwysep przez władze w Rzymie. W konflikt ów aktywnie włączyły się plemiona iberyjskie. Zdecydowana większość z nich poparła Sertoriusza w nadziei na to, że po zwycięstwie poprawi się ich sytuacja pod rzymskim panowaniem.

Autor niniejszego artykułu starał się ukazać przykłady działań zarówno Sertoriusza, jak i wodzów sullańskich, których konsekwencją było wzmożenie procesu romanizacji prowincji hiszpańskich. Wśród inicjatyw Sertoriusza wymienia: założenie szkoły w Osce dla dzieci iberyjskich możnych, organizację oddziałów iberyjskich na wzór rzymski, liberalną politykę wobec miejscowych, sprzyjającą rozprzestrzenianiu się wpływów rzymskich wśród Iberów Nie mniej istotne były działania sullańczyków: założyli oni wiele obozów i baz wojskowych, które stały się później zalążkami przyszłych osad i miast. Starali się również przeciągać na swoją stronę plemiona iberyjskie, hojną ręką rozdzielając obywatelstwo rzymskie. Po zakończeniu wojny Pompejusz przeprowadził także na Półwyspie Iberyjskim zakrojoną na szeroką skalę akcję osadniczą.

Przemiany romanizacyjne, następujące w okresie wojny sertoriańskiej i bezpośrednio po jej zakończeniu, wytyczyły więc nowy szlak w polityce władz w Rzymie wobec prowincji hiszpańskich.

Tomasz Ładoń

LE PROCESSUS DE ROMANISATION DANS LES PROVINCES HISPANIQUES
PENDANT LA GUERRE CONTRE SERTORIUS

Résumé

La romanisation des provinces hispaniques à l'époque de la république romaine se produisait successivement. Pendant les premiers siècles de l'existence des provinces hispaniques ce processus était plutôt lent, et sûrement inéquitable — la partie Est de la Péninsule Ibérique s'y soumettait plus facilement que la partie Ouest. Également les tribus ibériques résistaient fortement au gouvernement romain en Espagne, ce qui provoquait de nombreuses révoltes et guerres contre des proconsuls romains.

L'évènement principal, qui selon l'auteur de cette étude a intensifié le processus de la romanisation de la Péninsule Ibérique, étaient les guerres contre Sertorius (80—72 av. J-Ch.). Sertorius — proconsul des provinces hispaniques nommé par les gens de Marius — l'a menée contre Metellus Pius et Pompée, des proconsuls de Sylla, envoyés en Espagne par le pouvoir de Rome. Les tribus ibériques se sont engagées activement dans le conflit, en soutenant surtout Sertorius en vue d'une amélioration de leur situation sous l'emprise romaine.

L'auteur de cette étude essayait de démontrer des exemples d'agissements de même de Sertorius que des chefs de Sylla, dont les conséquences étaient d'intensifier la romanisation des provinces hispaniques. Parmi des initiatives de Sertorius il compte: la fondation de l'école à Osca pour les enfants de principales familles locales, la formation des troupes hispaniques sur le modèle romain, une politique libérale envers le peuple qui facilitait l'influence romaine sur les Ibères. Les agissements des syllaniens n'étaient pas moins importants: ils ont fondé de nombreux camps militaires, qui sont devenus des origines des villes. Ils essayaient également de gagner l'appuie des tribus ibériques en promettant la citoyenneté romaine. Après la guerre, Pompée a exécuté sur la Péninsule Ibérique une grande action de colonisation.

Les changements de romanisation au cours de la guerre contre Sertorius et directement après cette période ont tracé un nouveau chemin dans la politique de Rome envers les provinces hispaniques.

NORBERT ROGOSZ

An Assessment of the Political Role of the Senate in the Roman Republic in the Years 59—55*

In the years 59—55, the position of the Roman Senate — one of the most important institutions of the Republic — was challenged, and then severely weakened. As a result, we observe, particularly in comparison with the late 60s, a fall in its importance. This manifested itself in its being deprived of direct rule, that is in its being made to retreat into the background of the political life, and in the lessening of its influence on national affairs. This was not the result of a legal limitation of the Senate's rights, for the diminishing of its role was neither formal, nor legal. In this respect, the situation of this institution, in relation to the previous years, did not change. The reduction of its importance in the early 50s resulted from the unfortunate, from the point of view of the Senate's defenders, outcome of the political rivalry that took place during that period in Rome.[1]

---

* The present text summarises my reflections included in the paper *Polityczna rola senatu w Republice Rzymskiej w latach 59—55* ("The Political Role of the Senate of the Roman Republic in the years 59—55 BC"). Katowice 2004. In that paper, it functioned as the Conclusion. As it is now presented separately in an English language version, it has been provided with more extensive footnotes supporting and documenting the author's argument. The dates refer to the times before the birth of Christ.

[1] The above statement refers to the final results, sometimes, for example from the spring of 57 to the beginning of April 56 inclusive, the results of that rivalry were favourable for the Senate. But this did not affect the final outcome.

All the then enemies of the Senate contributed to this effect. But chiefly, this was the work of the main enemies, first of all, of the triumvirs. Caius Julius Caesar, Cnaeus Pompeius, and Marcus Licinius Crassus were intent on achieving this result from the very beginning of their alliance, as this was a fundamental condition for carrying out their strategic plans.[2] For similar reasons, and also for some other ones, Publius Clodius, the tribune of the people for 58, also contributed the weakening of the Senate's position in the Republic.[3]

The *optimates* — identifying themselves with the Senate, heading it, and defending it — refused to reconcile themselves to the shrinking of that institution's importance. This is why, they launched, in so far as they could make use of favourable circumstances, a campaign against the enemies of the Senate so as to restore it to its former importance, and give it a position proper to its high status in the state. Therefore, the role of the Senate, in the period in question, was not stable and varied in keeping with the course of the political conflict.

For the first time, the Senate lost its rule, and even the power to influence significantly the matters of the state in 59, in favour of the triumvirs. This happened after C. Julius Caesar had forced through the *lex Iulia agraria*, as a result of the *optimates'* losing their political fight with him, and with Pompey and Crassus, at the time when the law in question was being passed.[4] All this was also the result of the wrong strategy adopted by the defenders of the Senate, and particularly by their leader, M. Calpurnius Bibulus, who limited his actions, and those of the senators supporting him, to actions remaining within the law, actions that failed to go beyond the Senate's competence, and that had the nature of passive, though spectacular, protests.[5] As a result of the

---

[2] Cf.: Cic., Ad Att. I, 14, 1; 17, 9—10; 18, 2; 6—7; 19, 4; II, 1, 6—8; Liv., per. CIII; Vell. Pat. II, 40, 5; 44, 1—5; Suet., Iul. 18, 2—20; 22, 1; Plut., Caes. 13, 1—14, 7; Crass. 14, 1—4; Pomp. 46, 1—48, 3; Cat. Min. 31, 1—33, 3; App., BC II, 8, 28—13, 49; Cass. Dio XXXVII, 49—50; 54—58; XXXVIII, 1—8; J. van O o t e g h e m: *Pompée le Grand, bâtisseur d'Empire*. Namur 1954, pp. 299—310; H. G e s c h e: *Caesar*. Darmstadt 1976, pp. 41—42, 45—46.

[3] On the motivation Clodius's hostility towards the Senate, see: Cic., Ad Att. I, 12, 3; 13, 3; 14, 5; 16, 1—11; 18, 3; II, 1, 4—5; Liv., per. CIII; Vell. Pat. II, 45, 1; Plut., Cic. 28—30, 1; App., BC II, 14, 52—53; Cass. Dio XXXVII, 45—46, 3; cf.: Suet., Iul. 6, 2; 20, 4; Plut., Caes. 9, 3—10, 7; 14, 9; T. Ł o p o s z k o: *Trybunat Publiusza Klodiusza w świetle źródeł i historiografii*. Warszawa 1974, pp. 193—195; W.J. T a t u m: *The Patrician Tribune. Publius Clodius Pulcher*. Chapel Hill—London 1999, pp. 63—86.

[4] Cic., Ad Att. II, 9, 2; 14, 1; 18, 1—2; 19, 3; Flac. 2, 4; Liv., per. CIII; Vell. Pat. II, 44, 4—5; Suet., Iul. 20, 1—2; 4; Plut., Caes. 14, 1—3; 6—7; Pomp. 47, 3—48, 4; Cat. Min. 31, 4—32, 6; App., BC II, 10, 34—12, 42; Cass. Dio XXXVIII, 1—8; Ch. M e i e r: *Untersuchungen zur römischen Innenpolitik zwischen 63 und 56 v. Chr*. Heidelberg 1956, pp. 172—191 (in typescript); L. C a n f o r a: *Giulio Cesare*. Roma-Bari 1999, pp. 89—91.

[5] On Bibulus's attitude and policy, in that period, see: Cic., Ad Att. II, 9, 1; 15, 2; 20, 4; 6; 21, 4—5; Liv., per. CIII; Vell. Pat. II, 44, 5; Suet., Iul. 20, 1; Plut., Caes. 14, 2—3; 5—7; Pomp. 47, 4; 48, 1; 4; Cat. Min. 31, 5—32, 2; App., BC II, 10, 35; 11, 37—41; 12, 45; Cass. Dio XXXVIII, 2—4,

illegal actions of Caesar and the other triumvirs, the position of the Senate in the Republic was seriously undermined.

The above statements are in keeping with the opinion of most historians, who suggest that it was the triumvirs that initiated the process of diminishing the Senate's importance.[6] Some researchers, however, claim, and L. Piotrowicz is the most uncompromising about it, that this did not happen in the first months of the year 59, after Caesar's *lex Iulia agraria* had been forced through, but earlier. It was, namely, supposed to be an immediate consequence of the establishment of the, so-called, first triumvirate.[7] In the light, however, of the source texts referring to the said question, and of the conclusions drawn from them,[8] it is difficult to second this opinion.

The undermining of the Senate's position, in 59, took place because, after the above-mentioned, victorious for the triumvirs, political campaign, the Senate found itself in a very difficult situation. Several factors were at play. First of all, the limitation of the Senate's actions meant that it was effectively excluded active participation in public life.[9] A negative influence on the Senate's situation was also exerted by the capital's inhabitants, especially the lower classes, who — particularly in the beginning — strongly supported the triumvirs, and the same is true of the *equites*, and of Pompey's veterans.[10] The Senate's position was also affected by the efficient activity of the anti-senate opposition on the political scene, and by the latter's being dominated by the supporters of Caesar, Pompey, and Crassus. All the above-mentioned factors led even, in the period in question, to the Senate's isolation, and to the isolation of the politicians who came to its defence.

The situation was made worse by the reshuffle that took place at that time among the senators. Some of them, namely, changed their orientation, and

---

1; 6—7; M.J.G. G r e y - F o w: *The Mental Breakdown of a Roman Senator: M. Calpurnius Bibulus.* GR, 37 (1990), pp. 180—181; I. H o f m a n n - L ö b l: *Die Calpurnii.* Frankfurt a/M 1996, pp. 189—190; F.X. R y a n: *Bibulus as President of the Senate.* „Latomus", Vol. 55 (1996), pp. 384—388.

    [6] See: N. R o g o s z: *Polityczna rola senatu w Republice Rzymskiej w latach 59—55.* Katowice 2004, pp. 25—30.

    [7] L. P i o t r o w i c z: *Dzieje rzymskie* ["Roman History"]. In: WHP. T. 3. Warszawa 1934, p. 416. See also e.g.: R.E. S m i t h: *The Failure of the Roman Republic.* Cambridge 1955, pp. 123—124; Ch. M e i e r: *Zur Chronologie und Politik in Caesars erstem Konsulat.* "Historia", Bd. 10 (1961), p. 68; K. C h r i s t: *Krise und Untergang der römischen Republik.* Darmstadt 1979, p. 290.

    [8] N. R o g o s z: *Polityczna rola senatu...*, pp. 14—15, 90—91.

    [9] Cic., Ad Att. II, 9, 2; Flac. 2, 4; Vat. 15, 35—36; Suet., Iul. 20, 1; 4; 21—22, 1; Plut., Caes. 14, 2; 7—8; Pomp. 48, 4; Cat. Min. 33, 1—2; App., BC II, 11, 37; 12, 42; 13, 48; Cass. Dio XXXVIII, 6, 4—5; 8, 2; P. S t e i n: *Die Senatssitzungen der Ciceronischen Zeit (68—43).* Münster 1930, pp. 25—28.

    [10] These questions are discussed in greater detail by: N. R o g o s z: *Rzymskie grupy społeczne a przemiany polityczne w Republice na przełomie lat sześćdziesiątych i pięćdziesiątych I wieku przed Chrystusem.* In: *Electrum.* T. 4. Red. E. D ą b r o w a. Kraków 2000, pp. 59—72.

started to collaborate actively with the triumvirs, joining their traditional supporters. Even taken together, however, they formed a rather small group of politicians. Because of their small number, they could not exert decisive influence on the Senate's actions, its political attitude, and on the line-up of parties existing in it.[11] The reason for it was also the isolation of the triumvirs supporters in the Senate cased by the clearly hostile attitude of the majority of the senatorial aristocracy towards Caesar, Pompey, and Crassus. In spite of all this, the senators connected with the triumvirs could be very dangerous for the Senate and its defenders,[12] as they received support from their patrons, the greatest potentates of the state, who, as could be expected, knew how to discipline them.

Among the senators supporting the triumvirs, we find, first of all, the politicians connected with Pompey and Crassus. There were, however, some, albeit a minority, who had, usually recent, links with Caesar, who was a consul at that time.[13] Only a few of the senators sympathising with the triumvirs belonged to the elitist group of former consuls,[14] most of them were relatively new senators who had lower ranks and smaller experience. This limited severely the possibilities for this group to do harm to the Senate. It should be remembered, however, that some of them had functions that were very useful in carrying on intense political intrigues. They could then use their functions against the Senate and cause serious harm to it.[15]

The defenders of the Senate were definitely more numerous. Most of them were the *optimates* — sworn enemies of the triumvirs and supporters of the

---

[11] The triumvirs' supporters did, however, influence decisively the political situation in the Republic, but it happened outside the Senate: Cic., Ad Att. II, 4, 2; 5, 2; 6, 2; 7, 2—4; 8, 1; 9, 1; 18, 1; 3; 19, 2; 4; 23, 2.

[12] In this context see: Cic., Ad Att. II, 5, 2; 6, 2; 9, 2; 15, 2; 19, 1—2; 4; 22, 1; 23, 2; 24, 2—4; Q. fr. I, 2, 5; Vat. 6, 14—7, 18; 9, 21—11, 28; 15, 35—36; Vell. Pat. II, 45, 1; Suet., Iul. 20, 1; 4—5; Plut., Caes. 14, 6; 8—9; Pomp. 47, 4—5; 48, 1; Cat. Min. 32, 1—2; 33, 3—4; App., BC II, 10, 36; 11, 38—12, 45; Cass. Dio XXXVIII, 3, 1—2; 4—5; 6, 3; 6; 7, 2; A.W. L i n t o t t: *Violence in Republican Rome*. Oxford 1968, pp. 159—160, 213.

[13] The senators in question became his supporters because, in 59, he could launch them on successful careers: Cic., Ad Att. II, 6, 2; 7, 3—4; 16, 1; 19, 4; 24, 2; Vell. Pat. II, 44, 4; Suet., Iul. 20, 4; 21—22, 1; Plut., Caes. 14; Pomp. 47, 6; 48, 3; Cat. Min. 31, 3; 33, 4; App., BC II, 10, 35; 13, 47—48; 14, 50—52; Cass. Dio XXXVIII, 1, 1; 6, 3; 9, 1; 12, 1. They were fewer than the partisans of Pompey and Crassus because, at that time, Caesar's influence was not yet so strong as theirs.

[14] They were only the following: M. Pupius Piso Frugi Calpurnianus and L. Afranius, consuls in 61 and 60. On them read in: M. M a l a v o l t a: *La carriera di L. Afranio* (cos. 60 a. C.). MGR, 5 (1977), pp. 251—303; I. H o f m a n n - L ö b l: *Die Calpurnii...*, pp. 130—143.

[15] Such practices could be exemplified by the actions of P.Vatinius, a tribune of people in 59, who was connected with Caesar: Cic., Sest. 63, 132; Vat. 7, 17—18; 9, 21; 11, 26; 12, 29; 15, 35—36; App., BC II, 14, 52; Cass. Dio XXXVIII, 6, 6; cf.: Cic., Ad Att. II, 6, 2; 7, 3. More on his activity: G. N i c c o l i n i: *I fasti dei tribuni della plebe*. Milano 1934, pp. 279—285; G. B e l l a r d i: *Un "mostro" partorito dalla parola: P. Vatinio nella interrogatia di Cicerone*. AR, 17 (1972), pp. 5—10.

traditional *libera res publica*. The senators of that persuasion formed the most dynamic and the most active faction in the Senate. Their leaders were very conservatively minded, and belonged to the Senate's aristocratic elite. Their aim was to make the senate dominate the political scene, and regain its supreme position in the Republic.[16] Other senators, of less determined views, did not show signs of similar activity. In the intrigues carried on in Rome at that time their position was clearly lower. At the time of violent conflicts, particularly frequent in the early months of 59, they usually backed up the *optimates*, and closely cooperated with them. As a result, the senators acting in the Senate's defence had an overwhelming superiority over its enemies. Owing to the above-mentioned cooperation and a sense of solidarity, they constituted, at the time of great political tensions, a solid block, wholeheartedly supporting the actions of their actual leader, the consul M. Calpurnius Bibulus.[17]

In 59, the senators were divided into a numerically weak group of the triumvirs' supporters, and the *optimates*, dominant in the Senate, with their supporters. An overwhelming majority of the members of the Senate were then firmly against the triumvirs, and particularly against Caesar, who represented the triumvirs at that time. That majority, however, found themselves in a no-win situation owing to Caesar's, and his main collaborators', consistent actions, and owing to the above-mentioned faulty strategy, chosen by Bibulus. The power in the Republic was seized by Caesar, who — making use of the support of some, allied to him, officials, and of the *concilium plebis*, dominated by the triumvirs' supporters — continued to reign supreme, also in the name of his partners, until the end of his consulship.[18]

---

[16] The portraits of the leaders of the then *optimates* can be found in: R. S y m e: *The Roman Revolution*. Oxford 1960, pp. 21—27; A.M. W a r d: *Marcus Crassus and the Late Roman Republic*. Columbia—London 1977, pp. 14—19, 20—34. See also: P.J.J. V a n d e r b r o c c k: *Popular Leadership and Collective Behavior in the Late Roman Republic (ca. 80—50 BC)*. Amsterdam 1987, pp. 210—217.

[17] Liv., per. CIII; Suet., Iul. 20, 4; Plut., Caes. 14; Pomp. 47, 4; 48, 1—2; 4; Cat. Min. 31, 5—32, 1; App., BC II, 10, 34—11, 37; 12, 42; Cass. Dio XXXVIII, 2—3; 6, 4; P. S t e i n: *Die Senatssitzungen...*, pp. 25—26; L.A. B u r c k h a r d t: *Politische Strategien der Optimaten in der späten römischen Republik*. Stuttgart 1988 ("Historia Einzelschriften", H. 57), pp. 196—198; L. de L i b e r o: *Obstruktion. Politische Praktiken im Senat und in der Volksversammlung der ausgehenden römischen Republik*. Stuttgart 1922 ("Hermes Einzelschriften", H. 59), pp. 19, 39—40, 61—63, 72—76.

[18] Cic., Ad Att. II, 9, 1—2; 13, 2; 17, 1; 18, 1—2; 19, 1; 20, 3; 21, 1; 22, 6; 25, 2; Q. fr. I, 2, 5; Vat. 15, 35—36; Vell. Pat. II, 44, 4—5; Suet., Iul. 20, 1—2; 4; Plut., Caes. 14, 6—8; Pomp. 47, 3—48, 4; Cat. Min. 31, 4—33, 3; App., BC II, 10, 34—12, 45; Cass. Dio XXXVIII, 1—8; E. M e y e r: *Caesars Monarchie und das Principat des Pompejus*. Stuttgart—Berlin 1922, pp. 71—94; J. D i c k i n s o n: *Death of a Republic. Politics and Political Thought at Rome 59—44 BC*. New York—London 1963, pp. 73—92; Ch. M e i e r: *"Res publica amissa". Eine Studie zu Verfassung und Geschichte der späten römischen Republik*. Wiesbaden 1966, pp. 282—286.

Caesar, Pompey, and Crassus certainly wanted to prolong this situation, as it gave them, until the end of the year 59, ascendancy over the Senate, a dominant position on the political scene, and direct rule in the Roman state. Some of the measures they took indicate, however, that they wanted to extend their influence also over the following years. How far ahead they were planning is hard to say. That they had long-rage plans is evidenced by such facts as Caesar's making the *optimates* swear that they shall not attack his agrarian laws, which were of foremost importance in securing the triumvirs' position, power, and influence in the Republic,[19] the so-called dynastic marriages of Caesar and Pompey,[20] forcing through — their protégés, L. Calpurnius Piso and A. Gabinius, as consuls in 58, which guaranteed the permanence of the political order established by Caesar,[21] or Caesar's being appointed, for five years, the governor of the provinces bordering directly on Italy, or close to it, and the commander of the four legions stationed there.[22] This question cannot be solved decisively on the basis of the available sources, and we are confined here to more or less suggestive speculations. In spite of this, however, it is possible to argue that, in 59, after Caesar's forcing through the above-mentioned agrarian laws, when the political situation became clear and favourable for the triumvirs, they did intend to marginalise the Senate for a longer — hard to say how long — period of time.[23]

---

[19] This is strongly emphasised by Cicero: Ad fam. I, 9, 8. In this context, see also: Plut., Caes. 14, 6; Pomp. 48, 2—4; App., BC II, 12, 42; Cass. Dio XXXVIII, 6, 4—7, 4.

[20] This suggestion is definitely confirmed by the opinions attributed to Marcus Porcius Cato, the Younger: Plut., Caes. 14, 4—6; Cat. Min. 31, 4—5; 33, 3; App., BC II, 14, 50—51. See also: Cic., Ad Att. II, 17, 1; Vell. Pat. II, 44, 3; Suet., Iul. 21—22, 1; Plut., Pomp, 47, 5—6; Cass. Dio XXXVIII, 9, 1—2; J. C a r c o p i n o: *Jules César*. Paris 1968, pp. 213—214; M. G e l z e r: *Caesar. Der Politiker und Staatsmann*. Wiesbaden 1960, p. 72.

[21] Suet., Iul. 20, 1—22, 1; Plut., Caes. 14, 5; Pomp. 48, 3; Cat. Min. 33, 4; App., BC II, 14, 50—51; Cass. Dio XXXVIII, 9, 1—2. See also: Cic., Ad Att. II, 5, 2; 9, 2; E. M a t t h e w s - -S a n f o r d: *The Career of Aulus Gabinius*. TAPhA, 70 (1939), pp. 74—76; B. E n g l i s c h: *L. Calpurnius Piso Caesoninus, ein Zeitgenosse Ciceros*. München 1979, pp. 23—27.

[22] This made it possible for the triumvirs to intimidate their opponents (they did so already in 59: Cic., Ad Att. II, 16, 2; C.H. O l d f a t h e r: *Caesar's Army in May 59 BC*. CJ, 25 (1930), pp. 299—301), and to use Caesar's army as an instrument of political pressure (which took place in the following years, during elections: Plut., Crass. 14, 6; Pomp. 51, 4; H. K o w a l s k i: *Armia a wybory w Rzymie w okresie schyłku Republiki*. W: *Antiquitas*. T. 14. Red. A. Ł a d o m i r s k i. Wrocław 1988, p. 118), or to expand further their influences (Suet., Iul. 22, 1; Plut., Pomp. 51, 1—2; Cat. Min. 33, 3). According to M. G e l z e r (*Caesar...*, p. 78) Caesar's army could also be used in the prospective military intervention in Italy. In the light of the later events, particularly in view of the course of the campaign in Gaul, this was rather unlikely.

[23] Such an intention, after the optimates and the Senate were deprived of direct rule, and when the triumvirs' domination in Rome was complete (Cic., Ad Att. II, 6, 2; 9, 1—2; 13, 2; 18, 1—2; 20, 3; 22, 6; 25, 2; Q. fr. I, 2, 5; Suet., Iul. 20, 1—2; App., BC II, 12, 42—45; Cass. Dio XXXVIII, 6—9, 2; see also: Plut., Caes. 14, 6; Pomp. 48, 1—4; Cat. Min. 31, 4—33, 3), could be regarded as quite realistic.

Caesar's having made the two agrarian bills become law meant that he captured the whole political power in the Republic, which decisively undermined the Senate's position.[24] In spite, however, of what some scholars suggest, this weakening and marginalising of the Senate's position on the political scene did not have to be permanent.[25] On the other hand, the supremacy of the triumvirs and their supporters in political life, and Caesar's uncommon energy, industriousness, and practical skills in the art of governing made the hopes for the Senate's quick change of its position look unrealistic.[26] This position could improve only if there was a major change in the balance of political forces. However, for the above-mentioned reasons, no significant transformations in this respect were possible before the lapse of Caesar's consulship. Then Caesar had to leave Rome and go to his provinces, while the rule of the city was to be transferred to L. Calpurnius Piso and A. Gabinius. In connection with this circumstance, the *optimates* could count on enhancing the Senate's status. Their hopes were raised by several circumstances. First of all, it Pompey and Crassus did not fulfil any public functions, so to control the situation in the city they had to rely on the consuls. Pompey's experiences in the years 61—60 indicated, however, that this way of influencing the course of political life could end in a failure.[27] Such expectations were well grounded also because, in 60, Pompey and Crassus, without Caesar's help, could not overcome the differences between each other, and fully cooperate.[28]

The *optimates'* hopes for restoring the Senate to its proper place and position in the Republic were also boosted by other circumstances. For example, the agrarian reforms, and, to some extent, also other legislative proposals

---

[24] Cic., Ad Att. II, 9, 2; 15, 2; 24, 4; Q. fr. I, 2, 5; Suet., Iul. 20, 1—4; Plut., Caes. 14; Pomp. 48, 1—4; Cat. Min. 32, 2—33, 3; App., BC II, 12, 42—45; Cass. Dio XXXVIII, 6, 4—7, 4; 8, 2—4; P. Stein: *Die Senatssitzungen...*, pp. 26—28; J. Dickinson: *Death...*, p. 79; Ch. Meier: *Res publica...*, pp. 282—286; S.L. Utczenko: *Kryzys i upadek republiki w starożytnym Rzymie.* Warszawa 1973, pp. 98—100.

[25] See, for example, L. Piotrowicz's suggestions (*Dzieje...*, p. 416).

[26] Cic., Ad Att. II, 5, 2; 7, 3—4; 9, 1; 16, 1; 17, 1; 18, 1—3; 19, 1; 21, 3; 24, 2—4; Liv., per. CIII; Suet., Iul. 20, 1—22, 1; Plut., Caes. 14; Pomp. 47, 3—48, 4; Cat. Min. 31, 4—33, 3; App., BC II, 10, 34—14, 53; Cass. Dio XXXVIII, 1—12, 1. Cicero sometimes voiced groundless hopes for a change in the political situation in Rome: Ad Att. II, 14, 1; 15, 1; 16, 1; cf.: 8, 1; 12, 2; 13, 2; 19, 2—3; 20, 4; 21, 1—5; 23, 2; Q. fr. I, 2, 5.

[27] Cic., Ad Att. I, 13, 4; 14, 1—2; 6; 16, 12—13; 18, 3; 5; 19, 4; 20, 5; II, 1, 6; Vell. Pat. II, 40, 5; Suet., Iul. 19, 2; Plut., Pomp. 46, 3—4; Cat. Min. 31, 1—2; App., BC II, 9, 31—32; Cass. Dio XXXVII, 49—50; J. Leach: *Pompey the Great.* London 1978, pp. 114—122; P. Greenhalgh: *Pompey the Roman Alexander.* London 1980, pp. 167—204.

[28] Cic., Ad Att. II, 3, 3; Liv., per. CIII; Suet., Iul. 19, 2; Plut., Caes. 13, 2; Crass. 14, 1—2; Pomp. 47, 1—2; App., BC II, 9, 32—33; Cass. Dio XXXVII, 44, 3—4; M. Gelzer: *Pompeius.* München 1949, pp. 129, 131, 138—142; B.A. Marshall: *Crassus. A Political Biography.* Amsterdam 1976, pp. 91—102; Ch. Meier: *Caesar.* München 1986, pp. 239—240.

implemented by Caesar constituted an infringement of standard procedure, of some religious norms, and, in particular, would not have become law without a use of force.[29] This could make it easier for them to attack and criticise the triumvirs, and, consequently, to fight with them so as to regain the control over the state.[30] Apart from that, the *lex Iulia agraria Campana*, by means of which Caesar won the support of the Roman proletariat, gave allotments of land only to 20 000 of the poorest Romans.[31] There were, however, several times more of the *proletarii* in the capital.[32] Most of them did not get then any land, and neither did they obtain any other benefits from Caesar, Pompey, or Crassus. This is why the *optimates* could expect that the support of the *proletarii* for the triumvirs would diminish, and that, with a passage of time, they would become disappointed, and, eventually, dissatisfied with Caesar's policy.[33] They had a chance then to win the support of a large part of lower class Romans, and to use it in the renewed fight with the triumvirs.

However, after C. Julius Caesar's leaving of the consul's office, the expectations of the defenders of the Senate for an improvement of its position were not fulfilled. This was the work of P. Clodius who, on 10 December, 59, took the office of the tribune of the people. Owing to the conflict between him and the senators belonging to the senatorial elite, which took place during the lawsuit brought against him in 61,[34] he used his office to attack the Senate and to make its position even more unfavourable. He achieved this by forcing through several bills, during the first months of his tribunate, which were

---

[29] See: Cic., Ad Att. II, 9, 1; 18, 2; 20, 6; 21, 4—5; 24, 2—4; Q. fr. I, 2, 5; Dom. 15, 40; Har. resp. 23, 48; Liv., per. CIII; Vell. Pat. II, 44, 5; Suet., Iul. 20, 1; 3—4; Plut., Caes. 14; Pomp. 47, 4—48, 4; Cat. Min. 31, 4—33, 3; App., BC II, 10, 34—12, 42; Cass. Dio XXXVIII, 1—8; J.W. H e a t o n: *Mob Violence in the Late Roman Republic, 133—49 BC*. Urbana 1939, p. 65; A.W. L i n t o t t: *Violence...*, pp. 189—190.

[30] The *optimates'* first such actions were undertaken already under Caesar's consulship: Cic., Ad. Att. II, 15, 2; cf.: T. Ł o p o s z k o: *Attempts at Rescinding Caesar's Bills of 59 BC*. AUMC-S, Sect. F, Vol. 32 (1977), pp. 1—28.

[31] Vell. Pat. II, 44, 4; Suet., Iul. 20, 3; App., BC. II, 10, 35; cf.: Plut., Caes. 14, 1; Pomp. 47, 3; Cat. Min. 31, 4; 33, 1; Cass. Dio XXXVIII, 1, 1—3; see also: M. C a r y: *The Land Legislation of Julius Caesar First Consulship*. JPh, 35 (1920), p. 178; G. R o t o n d i: *Leges publicae populi Romani*. Hildesheim 1962, pp. 387—388. S.L. U t c z e n k o: *Kryzys...*, p. 99; T. Ł o p o s z k o: *Historia społeczna republikańskiego Rzymu*. Warszawa 1987, p. 297.

[32] See e.g.: I d e m: *Trybunat...*, p. 141; B. K ü h n e r t: *Die plebs urbana der späten römischen Republik*. Berlin 1991 ASAWL, Phil.-hist. Kl., Bd. 73, H. 3, pp. 27—29.

[33] Cic., Ad Att. II, 16, 1. A change in mood, unfavourable for the triumvirs, among the Romans of the lower social strata, took place in July 59. (Cic., Ad Att. II, 19, 2—3; 20, 4; 21, 1—5; T. Ł o p o s z k o: *Trybunat...*, pp. 207—212). But this did not bring about the expected changes on the political scene.

[34] Cic., Ad Att. I, 13, 3; 14, 1—2; 5; 16, 1—11; 18, 2—3; Har. resp. 21, 44—45; Vell. Pat. II, 45, 1; Plut., Cic. 28—30, 1; App., BC II, 14, 51—53; Cass. Dio XXXVII, 3, 1—2; cf.: Ph. M o - r e a u: *Clodiana religio. Un procès politique en 61 av. J.-C.* Paris 1982.

favourable for the Roman *proletarii*.[35] As a result, he became their unquestioned spokesman and leader. Consequently, he was able to reactivate and develop, on a so far unheard of scale, the movement of the *populares*, to become its leader, and to dominate the *concilium plebis*, and to make of it — of course at the cost of the Senate — the most important political institution in Rome.[36] Eventually, P. Clodius strengthened his position so much that he became a fully independent politician, in the capital. This enabled him to attack the directly the Senate, and to banish from Rome some of its leaders, namely Marcus Tullius Cicero, and Marcus Porcius Cato.[37] In this way, he deprived the Senate of the support of the politicians who, owing to their connections, position, and personal qualities had, in propitious circumstances, the greatest chances to initiate an efficient struggle against the Senate's enemies, so as to restore it to its proper place in the Republic.

In spring 58, the bills unfavourable to the Senate having been approved, Cicero and M. Cato having been expelled from Rome, the Senate's position was even worse than during Caesar's consulship. All this happened also owing to the fact that P. Clodius managed to win over the consuls of the time — Piso, and Gabinius.[38] It seemed then that any hopes for a reasonably quick change, especially for an improvement of that situation, were completely groundless, especially because, in the first months of 58, the relations between the main enemies of the Senate, that is P. Clodius and the triumvirs, were amicable enough.[39]

In spite of this sad, for the Senate, state of affairs, and unfavourable tendencies, the unhappy situation did not prove permanent. At the end of the first half of the year 58, some gradual transformations, on the Roman political

---

[35] These were particularly *lex Clodia frumentaria and lex Clodia de collegis*. Indirectly also *lex Clodia de iure et tempore legum rogandarum*. Cf.: G. R o t o n d i: *Leges...*, pp. 393, 397—398; T. Ł o p o s z k o: *Trybunat...*, pp. 140—145; W. W i l l: *Der römische Mob*. Darmstadt 1991, pp. 70—74.

[36] Plut., Cic. 30, 1; Cass. Dio XXXVIII, 12, 4; 13, 1; cf.: 2—6; T. Ł o p o s z k o: *Trybunat...*, pp. 162—173; H. B e n n e r: *Die Politik des P. Clodius Pulcher*. Stuttgart 1987 ("Historia Einzelschriften", H. 50), pp. 53, 58—61, 83—89; W.J. T a t u m: *The Patrician Tribune...*, pp. 135, 141—148.

[37] Liv., per. CIII; Vell. Pat. II, 45, 1—2; 4; Plut., Caes 14, 3; Pomp. 48, 5—6; Cat. Min. 34, 1—2; Cic. 30—31; App., BC II, 14, 53—15, 58; Cass. Dio XXXVIII; 12, 4—16, 6; 22, 1; R. F e h r l e: *Cato Uticensis*. Darmstadt 1983, pp. 139—146; K. K u m a n i e c k i: *Cyceron i jego współcześni*. Warszawa 1989, pp. 266—269.

[38] Cic., Or. sen. gr. eg. 2, 3; 4, 10; 7, 16; Or. pop. gr. eg. 5, 11; 13; 9, 21; Dom. 9, 23—24; 21, 55; 23, 60; 51, 131; Sest. 7, 16; 10, 24—25; 25, 55; Plut., Cic. 30, 1; 31, 1; 4; E. M a t t h e w s - S a n f o r d: *The Career...*, pp. 76—79; B. E n g l i s c h: *L. Calpurnius Piso...*, pp. 30, 34—36.

[39] Cic., Ad Att. III, 7, 3; 8, 3; Or. sen. gr. eg. 13, 32; Dom. 3, 5; 9, 22; 50, 131; Sest. 17, 39—41; Har. resp. 22, 47; Plut., Cic. 30, 2—4; 31, 2—4; Cass. Dio XXXVIII, 12, 3—4; 13, 1—14, 1; 15, 1—16, 1; 17, 1—3; cf.: Plut., Caes. 14, 8; App., BC II, 15, 54; T. Ł o p o s z k o: *Trybunat...*, pp. 221—255.

scene, began,[40] which some of the actors of the Roman political life did not expect, and which, in the following months, brought about a radical change of the situation, and, a little later, a far-reaching rearrangement of the balance of forces between the most important politicians and political groupings. These changes led, in the first place, to the undermining of the triumvirs' position in the capital, which made it impossible for them to control the course of events in the Republic, and, in the long run, to impose any efficient rule on it.[41]

The said political transformations took place without the Senate, or the *optimates* dominant in it, being in any way involved in them, even though they were very favourable and propitious both for the institution itself, and for the *optimates*, as a political faction. They should be estimated as such because they weakened the Senate's and the *optimates*' main enemies. If those changes continued, they could have enabled those political forces to resume their struggle of the recovery of the power and influence which they had lost in the previous year.

The above described changes were caused by the conflicts that developed at that time in the triumvirs' surroundings. They were provoked by P. Clodius, who so far cooperated with the triumvirs and was on good terms with them. Having taken the above-mentioned measures, which strengthened greatly his position in Rome, he pursued his activities in such a degree that he threatened the balance of forces achieved by the triumvirs in the previous year.[42] Moreover, having won the support of a great majority of the Roman *proletarii*, and having organised them as the political faction of the *populares*, which he reconstructed and turned against the Senate, and the *optimates*, he created out of them a formidable political force that had no counterbalance in the city.[43] As a result, he took control of the city, and pushed the triumvirs and their

---

[40] Cic., Ad Att. III, 8, 3; 10, 1; cf.: Ad Att. III, 11; 12, 1; 14, 1; Dom. 25, 66; Plut., Pomp. 48, 5—6; Cic. 33, 1; App., BC II, 15, 58; R. S e a g e r: *Pompey. A Political Biography*. Berkeley—Los Angeles 1979, pp. 105—106, 108; H. B e n n e r: *Die Politik...*, pp. 56—57; W.J. T a t u m: *The Patrician Tribune...*, pp. 167—170.

[41] Cic., Ad Att. III, 13, 1; Dom. 25, 66—67; 50, 129; Sest. 32, 69; Plut., Pomp. 48, 5—49, 2; Cic. 33, 1; App., BC II, 15, 58; Cass. Dio XXXVIII, 30, 1—2; M. G e l z e r: *Pompeius...*, pp. 153—154; J. L é a c h: *Pompey...*, p. 131; H. B e n n e r: *Die Politik...*, pp. 57—58, 62—63.

[42] In the first place, as a result of his intervention in the Eastern affairs, he jeopardized the interests of Cn. Pompeius: Liv., per. CI—CII; Vell. Pat. II, 37, 5; 40, 1; Plut., Pomp. 31—42 passim; App., BC II, 1, 2; Mith. 114—115; Syr. 49—51; Cass. Dio XXXVII, 20, 1—3; A.N. S h e r - w i n - W h i t e: *Roman Foreign Policy in the East, 168 BC. to A.D. 1*. Duckworth 1984, pp. 186—234; R.D. S u l l i v a n: *Near Eastern Royalty and Rome, 100—30 BC*. Toronto—Buffalo—London 1990, pp. 153—303, passim.

[43] Cic., Ad. Q. fr. I, 4, 3—4; Or. sen. gr. eg. 13, 33; Sest. 15, 34—35; 25, 55; Plut., Cic. 30, 1; 33, 1; Cass. Dio XXXVIII, 12, 4; 13, 1—2; see also: J. L i n d e r s k i: *Państwo a kolegia. Ze studiów nad historią rzymskich stowarzyszeń u schyłku republiki*. Kraków 1961, p. 53; T. Ł o p o s z k o: *Trybunat...*, pp. 96—115, 142—143; H. B e n n e r: *Die Politik...*, pp. 58—61, 63—71. W. W i l l: *Der römische Mob...*, p. 72.

supporters into the background. As he undertook his actions independently, failing to consult either Cn. Pompeius or M. Licinius Crassus, he became the most influential politician in the Republic.[44]

Clodius, emboldened by the success of his actions, turned, without delay, against the triumvirs, and put them on the defensive. He managed to completely marginalise Pompey,[45] while Crassus held himself aloof, leaving his two partners, and particularly Pompey, without the necessary support. This meant that the alliance of the triumvirs was hit by a deep crisis, their mutual links turned out to be rather weak, and their cooperation insufficient. In such conditions, any effective action of the three against P. Clodius was impossible.

Even though the antagonism between Clodius (and the movement of the *populares*, of which he was the head, was aggravating and the involved parties were more and more absorbed in it) and the triumvirs its immediate results did not influence at first the position of the Senate. For several reasons, however, it was advantageous to it. First of all, with the passage of time, the main opponents of the *optimates*, under whose sway the Senate remained, were fighting against each other with ever increasing intensity, so they did not attack the Senate the way they used to,[46] so they did not make the position of the Senate worse. Since it looked as though the conflict would be resolved in Clodius's favour,[47] the triumvirs were forced to look for the means that would allow them to regain the lost position on the political scene, and the control over the Republic. They had to do so quickly and intensely, for their situation was steadily getting worse. They could hardly count on the consuls, who became Clodius's supporters.[48] They themselves had almost no chance to carry out aggressive actions because — with the exception of Caesar, absent from Rome, they did

---

[44] This is confirmed by many sources of information: Cic., Ad Att. III, 7, 3; 8, 3; Q. fr. I, 3, 5; Att. III, 12, 1; 13, 1; Q. fr. I, 4, 3—4; Or. sen. gr. eg. 2, 3—4; 13, 33; Or. pop. gr. eg. 6, 14; Dom.-passim; Sest.-passim, particularly, however: 15, 34—35; 25, 55—56; 30, 66; Har. resp. 18, 39; 27, 58; Plut., Pomp. 48, 5—6; Cic. 30, 1; 33, 1; Cass. Dio XXXVIII, 13, 1—6; 16, 4—6; 17, 6—7; 30, 1—2.

[45] Cic., Or. sen. gr. eg. 2, 4; 11, 29; Or. pop. gr. eg. 6, 14; Dom. 25, 67; Sest. 32, 69; Har. resp. 23, 49; Plut., Pomp. 49, 2; Cass. Dio XXXVIII, 30, 2; J. van O o t e g h e m: *Pompée...*, pp. 350—353; R. S e a g e r: *Pompey...*, pp. 108—109; P. G r e e n h a l g h: *Pompey the Republican Prince*. London 1981, pp. 13—16.

[46] See, in this context, the sources concerning the development of the political situation in Rome in the second half of 58: Cic., Ad Att. III, 12, 1; 13, 1; 15, 6; 19, 1; 23, 1; Sest. 30, 66—31, 67; Plut., Pomp. 48, 6—49, 2; Cic. 33, 1; App., BC II, 15, 58; Cass. Dio XXXVIII, 30, 1—4.

[47] Plut., Pomp. 48, 6; 49, 2; Cic. 33, 1; Cass. Dio XXXVIII, 30, 2; cf.: T. Ł o p o s z k o: *Trybunat...*, pp. 6, 255, 259—260; H. B e n n e r: *Die Politik...*, pp. 62—63; W. W i l l: *Der römische Mob...*, pp. 82—84; W.J. T a t u m: *The Patrician Tribune...*, pp. 170—175.

[48] See: Cic., Or. sen. gr. eg. 5, 11—12; 7, 16; 12, 31; 13, 32; Or. pop. gr. eg. 5, 11; 13; Dom. 24, 62; 25, 66; 43, 113; Sest. 12, 28—29; 14, 32—33; 15, 35; 32, 69; Plut; Cic. 31, 1; 4; Cass. Dio XXXVIII, 16, 2—6; E. M a t h e w s - S a n f o r d: *The Career...*, pp. 76—79; B. E n g l i s c h: *L. Calpurnius Piso...*, pp. 30, 34—36.

not fulfil any public functions. This is why; the only practical solution was to make an alliance with the Senate, that is, with the Senate's strongest faction of the *optimates*. In the late spring and summer of 58, a cooperation with the Senate became indispensable, even though the triumvirs did not change their attitude towards that institution. They could not, however, choose any other course of action. To begin an efficient fight against P. Clodius, who was then the most dangerous enemy, they had to compromise, and to align them- selves with the other enemy, who was decisively weaker than Clodius and the *populares*.

Similar reasons and motives were influencing the politicians who were at the head of the Senate, especially because, in comparison with the triumvirs, the situation of that institution was clearly worse.[49] One of the aspects of that inferiority was the fact that all forms of the Senate's activity, such as inau- gurating the sessions, the debates held during them, and the resolutions adopted on that occasion, were, in a very high degree, under the control of the presiding officials, that is the consuls, who were all the time present in Rome. The Senate could not act on its own initiative (and neither could the *optimates* under whose sway the Senate was), it could not then put forward any project, or undertake any action. It was thus completely helpless, especially in the face of P. Clodius's, and his supporters', domination in public life, thus the state- ments of the officials well disposed towards the Senate were in advance doo- med to failure.[50]

The said alliance was then for both sides an exclusively tactical and tem- porary solution. Neither the *optimates*, nor the triumvirs, however, had any other choice. In the situation, as it developed, this was the only solution of the difficulties they faced. From the *optimates*' point of view, the alliance with the triumvirs meant a chance to end their isolation, and to return to active par- ticipation in public life, and, subsequently, to resume their efforts to regain the position in the Republic which they lost in 59.[51]

The fact that both sides, hostile as they used to be to each other, realised the necessity of reaching an agreement was not enough, of course, to forge an alliance. Both parties expected specific benefits from it. This is why the agreement had to satisfy suitable conditions, and had to be based on some

---

[49] Cic., Ad Att. III, 12, 1; 13, 1; 15, 6; 17, 1; 19, 1; 23, 1; Or. sen. gr. eg. 2, 3; Sest. 11, 25—26; 12, 28—29; 14, 32; 15, 34; 35; 19, 42; Plut., Cic. 31, 1; Cass. Dio XXXVIII, 16, 2—6; 30, 4; P. S t e i n: *Die Sentssitzungen...*, pp. 29—30; M. B o n n e f o n d - C o u d r y: *Le Sénat de la Republique romaine de la guerre d'Hannibal à Auguste.* Rome 1989, pp. 207, 433—435.

[50] Cf. e.g.: Cic., Ad Att. III, 19, 1; 23, 1; Or. sen. gr. eg. 2, 3—4; Sest. 31, 67—32, 69; P. S t e i n: *Die Senatssitzungen...*, pp. 29—30; M. B o n n e f o n d - C o u d r y: *Le Sénat...*, pp. 207, 433—435; L. de L i b e r o: *Obstruktion...*, pp. 30, 34, 42, 70—71.

[51] See in this context: Cic., Ad Att. III, 9, 2; 10, 1; 14, 1; 15, 1; 3; 18, 1; fam. XIV, 2, 2; Att. III, 22, 2; fam. XIV, 1, 2; Or. pop. gr. eg. 7, 16—17; Plut., Pomp. 49, 3; Cic. 33, 2; App., BC II, 16, 59; Cass. Dio XXXVIII, 30, 3—4.

kind of shared platform. The triumvirs, for example, could not expect the *optimates* to support them, if they persisted in their intention to dominate the political arena, and to take control of Rome. But also the *optimates* had to reckon with the fact that the triumvirs would not support them in their efforts to take again the helm. Both sides had then to put off, for a while, the achievement of those, most important for them, purposes. Consequently, they had to think of a new purpose, which would be a compromise between them, and would be equally important for both, but also acceptable for both. Since P. Clodius, and the movement of the *populares* he was the head of, were the principal, and common, enemies of both the *optimates*, dominant in the Senate, and the triumvirs, the new alliance had to be constructed in such a way as to found it on the common purpose of fighting against that tribune of the people, and against those who supported him.[52]

In the situation that arose in Rome in 58, the question that both the triumvirs, and the conservative *optimates*, dominant in the Senate, could support, was the recall of Cicero from exile. Many motives determined the position of each side with regard to this matter. But the position of Cicero, and the role he played before his banishment from the city[53] were not the decisive factors, more important considerations were at play.

The *optimates*, insisting on the recall of the great orator from exile, could attack P. Clodius and the policy he stood for. In this way, they could also undermine one of his most important bills, directed principally against Cicero, and indirectly also against the *optimates*, that is also against the Senate. The latter has thus a chance to recover one of its most outstanding members, who belonged the Senate's ruling elite.[54] There was high likelihood that it would be possible to consolidate the whole Senate around Cicero's case, to make it into a coherent, and monolithic political force, vigorously supporting its leaders, and boldly engaging in decisive actions. By recalling the great orator to the capital, the *optimates* could increase the number of P. Clodius's enemies by another, no mean opponent of his. Moreover, since that tribune, in bringing about the orator's exile and the confiscation of his possessions, infringed on the letter of the law, as Cicero and the politicians who supported him claim-

---

[52] Some ancient historians emphasise this point: Plut., Pomp. 49, 3; Cic. 33, 2; App., BC II, 16, 59; Cass. Dio XXXVIII, 30, 3—4.

[53] Cicero emphasises the importance of his own person: Or. sen. gr. eg. 11, 29; Or. pop. gr. eg. 5, 13; Dom. 2, 4; 6, 14; 7, 15—16; 28, 73; 37, 99; Sest. 60, 128—61, 129. Other ancient authors look differently at the role of that orator in the Republic: Plut., Pomp. 49, 2—3; Cic. 33, 2; App., BC II, 16, 59; Cass. Dio XXXVIII, 30, 1—3.

[54] Cicero was considered a member of the senatorial elite since the time of foiling Catiline's plot. In this context, see: Vell. Pat. II, 34, 3; 35, 4; 45, 2; Plut., Cic. 23, 3—24, 1; App., BC II, 6, 24—25; Cass. Dio XXXVIII, 12, 4; M. G e l z e r: *Cicero. Ein biographischer Versuch*. Wiesbaden 1969, pp. 97—104; K. K u m a n i e c k i: *Cyceron...*, pp. 213—220.

ed,[55] his recall from exile could be, for the leaders of the Senate, a very convenient starting point for a campaign against Clodius.

The triumvirs had similar, but also other motives for backing the idea of recalling Cicero from exile. From their point of view, his presence in Rome could, for example, bring about a better balance of political forces in the Senate, it could weaken the position of the conservative *optimates*, since the senators of a similar to his, that is moderate, political persuasion would be given a chance to gather around him.[56] It seemed likely that, as a result of bringing back Cicero to the city, the Senate would be more favourably disposed towards the triumvirs, for they remembered that, in the past, each of them, in spite of the political differences between them and Cicero, could reach some, even in delicate matters, some understanding with him.[57] It seemed that everything would be like that again. Cicero, after all, was at odds with P. Clodius much more than with the triumvirs. This is why, the triumvirs could expect that, having come back to Rome, he would be engaged, together with the other *optimates*, in combating Clodius. By supporting Cicero against P. Clodius, they had a chance to make the orator depend on them, and to make use of him in the future political games.[58]

For the triumvirs, and also for the Senate, dominated by the *optimates*, becoming involved in the efforts to bring Cicero back to Rome was desirable also for other reasons. Cicero was known for his close links with the *equites*.[59] Also Crassus had similar relations with them.[60] To make use of these contacts could then secure, for Clodius's opponents, the support of a small, but in-

---

[55] Cic., Or. sen. gr. eg. 14, 34; Dom. 8, 20; 10, 26; 14, 38; 16, 42; 26, 68—27, 70; Sest. 13, 29; 34, 73.

[56] This was plausible since the most dynamic conservative, and pro-senate, politician, that is M. Porcius Cato, was then in Cyprus, and to Rome he may have returned as late as at the end of the year 56: Plut., Cat. Min. 39, 1—4; Cass. Dio XXXIX, 23, 1; A. A f z e l i u s: *Die politische Bedeutung des jüngeren Cato*. CM, 4, 1941, p. 162; R. F e h r l e: *Cato Uticensis...*, pp. 158—162.

[57] Caesar, e.g., opposed Cicero during the session at which the fate of Catiline's supporters was decided (Sall., Cat. 50—51; 55; Suet., Iul. 14; Plut., Caes. 7, 4—8, 3), Crassus the time of the lawsuit against Clodius in 61 (Cic., Ad Att. I, 16, 5), and Pompey in 60, during the attempts to force through the agrarian bill, made by the tribune of the people, L. Flavius, much devoted to Pompey, with Cicero being strongly against the bill (Cic., Ad Att. I, 18, 6; 19, 4).

[58] This was visible immediately after Cicero's return to Rome, when he had to "work" for Pompey (Cic., Dom.-passim), and also in the years 56—53, when he was obliged to support all three of the triumvirs. See: K. K u m a n i e c k i: *Literatura rzymska. Okres cyceroński*. Warszawa 1977, pp. 249—268; I d e m: *Cyceron...*, pp. 284, 301—339.

[59] Cic., Ad Att. I, 17, 8—10; II, 1, 7—8; Q. fr. I, 1, 1; 11—12; Plut., Cic. 31, 1; Cass. Dio XXXVIII, 16, 4; 6. More on Cicero's relations with the equites in: J. B l e i c k e n: *Cicero und die Ritter*. Göttingen 1995 (AAWG, Phil.-hist. Kl., Dr. Floge, Nr. 213).

[60] See, in this context: Cic., Ad Att. I, 16, 5; 17, 8—9; Suet., Iul. 18; Plut., Caes. 11, 1; F.E. A d c o k: *Marcus Crassus, Millionaire*. Cambridge 1966, pp. 15—19, 44; B.A. M a r s h a l l: *Crassus...*, pp. 82—83, 92—93, 97—98; A.M. W a r d: *Marcus Crassus...*, pp. 207—212, 220—221.

fluential, social group, and to develop thus the coalition organised against him. Through the equites, the lower class Romans could also be influenced,[61] who were Clodius's main base of support in the capital. Apart from that, Cicero was already famous as the best Roman orator; his talent could be then used against P. Clodius, in the Senate's room, in *concilium* plebis, and in courts of law.[62]

All the above-mentioned circumstances led up to a thoroughgoing political reshuffle that took place in Rome in late spring and summer 58. A new constellation took shape, consisting of a coalition of the triumvirs, and the *optimates*, dominant in the Senate, making common front against P. Clodius and the political forces that stood behind him.[63] Owing to this, the Senate could become again an active player on the political scene. It should be borne in mind in this context that the first initiatives aimed at recalling Cicero to Rome arose exactly among the senators from the above-mentioned circles.[64] For the Senate and all the politicians supporting it, a new chapter of their functioning on the Roman political arena, for the said actions meant that the Senate started to fight to regain the position lost in 59. Such suggestions are legitimate because the banishment, or even weakening, of P. Clodius had to lead to the Senate's recovering — temporarily together with the triumvirs — direct influence on the matters of state. What mattered for the *optimates* was that, owing to such moves, the foundations would be laid for a later action against the triumvirs, and, subsequently, for concentrating power in the hands of their leaders, who played prominent roles in the Senate.

---

[61] Examples of this policy, followed in previous years, can be found in: Cic., Ad Att. II, 1, 7—8.

[62] Having come back to Rome, Cicero, attacked him using every opportunity to do so. See, for example: Or. sen. gr. eg.-passim; Or. pop. gr. eg.-passim; Dom.-passim; Sest.-passim; Vat.-passim; Har. resp.-passim; M. Gelzer: *Cicero...*, pp. 149—166; K. Kumaniecki: *Cyceron...*, pp. 283—296. Cicero's oratorical talent was particularly intensely used by the triumvirs in the years 55—54, during the lawsuits brought against their supporters by the *optimates*: I d e m: *Literatura...*, pp. 262—268; M.C. Alexander: *Trials in the Late Roman Republic, 149 BC to 50 BC*. Toronto—Buffalo—London 1990, pp. 136—149.

[63] Cic., Ad Att. III, 10, 1; 13, 1; 14, 1; Q. fr. I, 4, 2—3; 5; Att. III, 15, 1—6; 17, 2; 18, 1—2; 20, 3; fam. XIV, 2, 2; Att. III, 22, 1; fam. XIV, 1, 2; Plut., Pomp. 49, 3; Cic. 33, 2; App., BC II, 16, 59; Cass. Dio XXXVIII, 30, 1—2; E. Meyer: *Caesars Monarchie...*, pp. 102—107; M. Fuhrmann: *Cicero und die römische Republik*. München—Zürich 1990, p. 135; Ch. Habicht: *Cicero der Politiker*. München 1990, p. 63.

[64] Cic., Ad Att. III, 12, 1; 13, 1; 15, 1; 3; 5—6; 17, 2; 18, 1—2; 20, 3; 23, 1—4; Or. sen. gr. eg. 2, 3—4; 8, 19—9, 22; 10, 25—26; 12, 30—31; 13, 33; Or. pop. gr. eg. 3, 8; 4, 10; 5, 11; Dom. 26, 70; Sest. 11, 25—26; 16, 36; 18, 41; 31, 67—68; P. Stein: *Die Senatssitzungen...*, pp. 29—30; G. Nicolini: *I fasti...*, pp. 293, 296—298; M. Bonnefond-Coudry: *Le Sénat...*, pp. 207, 433—435; L. Thommen: *Das Volkstribunat der späten römischen Republik*. Stuttgart 1989 ("Historia Einzelschriften", H. 59), pp. 125—126.

The first stage of the confrontation between the *optimates*, dominant in the Senate, and P. Clodius, continued until the end of 58, and did not bring any effects, apart from the cementing of the coalition against him.[65] The actions undertaken against Clodius and his supporters in early 57 has, similarly, little effect. Only a subsequent clash ended in defeating Clodius and his allies. It was prepared very carefully, especially owing to T. Annius Milo, the tribune of the people, who organised an armed force, as experience showed that it was impossible to undermine Clodius's position by means of purely political measures staying within the law.[66]

The defeat of P. Clodius's supporters by Milo's armed units paved the way for political actions aimed at recalling Cicero. They were, however, prolonged and complicated because there were still strong pro-Clodius sympathies in the capital. Owing, nevertheless, to the support of the Romans living outside the capital,[67] the Senate, in summer 57, passed a bill recalling Cicero from exile. A similar decision was later taken by the *concilium plebis*.[68] As a result, in early September, the great orator finally returned to the capital.[69]

The campaign for recalling Cicero from exile ended in a great success. P. Clodius's domination in the political arena was eliminated, and the pro-Senate coalition took control of the Republic, while the Senate regained its privileged position in it. Since both consuls at that time, since July of that year, fully cooperated with the Senate,[70] it started again to play a key role in public life. In view of this situation, in the second half of 57, particularly after the return of Cicero, P. Clodius could cause only temporary troubles to the Sena-

---

[65] Cic., Ad Att. III, 12, 1; 13, 1; 15, 3; 6; 17, 1—2; 18, 1; 19, 1; 20, 1; 21; 23, 1; Or. sen. gr. eg. 2, 3—4; 4, 8; 10; 7, 16; 11, 29; Or. pop. gr. eg. 6, 14; Dom. 4, 8; Plut., Cic. 33, 2; P. S t e i n: *Die Senatssitzungen...*, pp. 29—31.

[66] Cic., Or. sen. gr. eg. 8, 19; Or. pop. gr. eg. 5, 13; Sest. 41, 88—89; Har. resp. 4, 6; Plut., Cic. 33, 3; App., BC II, 16, 59; Cass. Dio XXXIX, 6, 2; 7, 4—8, 1.

[67] Cic., Or. sen. gr. eg. 11, 27—29; 12, 31; Or. pop. gr. eg. 4, 10; 7, 16—17; Dom. 12, 30; Plut., Pomp. 49, 3; Cic. 33, 3; J. van O o t e g h e m: *Pompée...*, p. 356; R. S e a g e r: *Pompey...*, pp. 109—110.

[68] Cic., Ad Att. IV, 1, 4; Or. sen. gr. eg. 3, 5; 10, 25—11, 27; 12, 31; 15, 39; Or. pop. gr. eg. 8, 18; Dom. 6, 14; Sest. 50, 107; 61, 129; Plut., Cic. 33, 3—4; App., BC II, 16, 59—60; Cass. Dio XXXIX, 7, 1—8, 3; P. S t e i n: *Die Senatssitzungen...*, pp. 33—34; M. B o n n e f o n d - C o u d r y: *Le Sénat...*, pp. 63, 66, 74—75, 360, 374, 434; por.: G. R o t o n d i: *Leges...*, p. 403.

[69] Cic., Ad Att. IV, 1, 5—6; Or. sen. gr. eg. 11, 28; Dom. 3, 5; Plut., Pomp. 49, 4; Cic. 33, 5; App., BC II, 16, 60; Cass. Dio XXXVIII, 30, 1; XXXIX, 5, 1; 9, 1; M. G e l z e r: *Cicero...*, pp. 149—150; M. F u h r m a n n: *Cicero...*, pp. 136—138.

[70] Cass. Dio XXXIX, 8, 2; Cn. Cornelius Lentulus Spinther cooperated with the Senate, particularly in the matter of recalling Cicero from exile, from the beginning of his consulship. Q. Caecilius Metellus Nepos, after much wavering and friction, only since the beginning of July: Cic., Ad Att. III, 26; fam. V, 4, 1—2; Or. sen. gr. eg. 3, 5; 4, 8; 8, 18; 10, 26; Or. pop. gr. eg. 4, 10; 6, 15; Dom. 3, 7; 12, 30; 27, 70; Sest. 33, 72; 62, 130; Cass. Dio XXXIX, 6, 2—3; cf.: Cic., Ad Att. III, 12, 1; 22, 2; 24, 2; P. S t e i n: *Die Senatssitzungen...*, pp. 31—34.

te.[71] The only obstacle in the way of the Senate's taking full control of the state was the triumvirs.

The success of the victorious coalition in its conflict with P. Clodius created, however, new problems, as, with Cicero's return, the main purposes of the *optimates*, and the triumvirs, as they had been formulated at the beginning of their cooperation, were achieved. Further cooperation was pointless, bearing in mind that the said coalition was created against P. Clodius, and its most important task — the elimination of P. Clodius from the political arena — was accomplished. Given the circumstances, both the *optimates*, dominant in the Senate, and the triumvirs started to pursue their other purposed, which, however, were at odds with their partner's intentions. This was because both parties strove to assume control of the situation in the Republic. This led to the subsequent stage of the struggle for power — this time between the former coalition partners. It started almost the moment Cicero arrived in Rome.[72]

The *optimates*, acting in defence of the Senate, set out then on their confrontation with the triumvirs, and they in a clearly better situation than their new antagonists. The *optimates* could draw benefits from the fact that their most important purpose — to concentrate power in the hands of the senatorial elite — was fully compatible with the Republic's *raison d'état*. They had, therefore, an excellent chance to make use, while implementing their plans, of the state apparatus, and to act, as it were, in the name of the Republic. First of all, they could, without let or hindrance, appear in the Senate room and operate under the Senate's aegis, and, additionally, in the context of the tasks which this institution was supposed to fulfil.[73] They could also, owing to the consuls and other officials, make use of various offices and of the *concilium plebis*. The *optimates* could then pursue their anti-triumvir policy quite freely and with good prospects of success.

The Senate, and to the *optimates*, dominant in it, benefited also from the rather complicated, in many respects, situation of their antagonists. There were several aspects of that situation. The triumvirs' chief purpose, i.e. to regain

---

[71] Cic., Ad Att. IV, 1, 6; 2, 2—5; 3, 2—5; Q. fr. II, 1, 2—3; 3, 2—4; Or. sen. gr. eg. 4, 10; Dom. 3, 6; Cass. Dio XXXIX, 11, 1—3; T. Ł o p o s z k o: *Mouvements sociaux à Rome dans les années 57—52 av. J.C.* Lublin 1980, pp. 58—74; W. W i l l: *Der römische Mob...*, pp. 85—90; W.J. T a t u m: *The Patrician Tribune...*, pp. 185—213.

[72] The rivalry took place, first of all, in the Senate, and its most important aspect was the conflict between the *optimates* and Pompey: Cic., Ad Att. IV, 1, 6—7; fam. I, 1, 1—4; 2, 1—4; 4, 1—3; Q. fr. II, 2, 3; fam. I, 5a, 3—4; Q. fr. II, 3, 1; fam. I, 5b, 1—2; see also: Q. fr. II, 1, 1—2; P. S t e i n: *Die Senatssitzungen...*, pp. 34—37; M. B o n n e f o n d - C o u d r y: *Le Sénat...*, passim; R. S e a g e r: *Pompey...*, pp. 110—121; P. G e r e e n h a l g h: *Pompey... (Prince)...*, pp. 21—38.

[73] That was because the matters the conflict centered around, that is *cura annonae*, as well as working out the Republic's position on the so-called Egyptian question (see sources and literature cited in the notes 77—78. Cf. also: Liv., per. CV; Plut., Pomp. 49, 4—7; App., BC II, 18, 67; Cass. Dio XXXIX, 9, 3; 12—14) lay within the competence of Senate.

control of the state, could not be pursued officially. In public, the triumvirs could emphasise only such intentions that the public opinion, and especially its elitist part, could accept. They were not in a position to awake the hostility of various political forces, or to mobilize their enemies against them. Moreover, in order to carry out their actual intentions, Pompey and Crassus had to strengthen their positions, that is, to be given some public functions and, if necessary, some special powers concomitant with them. Bearing in mind that, in early October 57, most officials had already been elected,[74] they had no other choice but to reach for long-term extraordinary functions, which would give them a possibility to act in the public arena for at least several years. This, however, collided with the Roman political tradition, with the interests of the senatorial elite, and, particularly, with the Republic's *raison d'état*. The obvious shortcoming in these intentions was their incompatibility with the public interest. They were about to be realized to protect the interests of a few individuals wishing to extend their influences at the cost of the whole of the senatorial aristocracy, and various institutions, particularly the Senate.[75] The above-mentioned intentions of Pompey and Crassus were also in direct contradiction to the policy they had followed, together with the *optimates*, in favour of the Senate and against P. Clodius, barely several months earlier. They made thus the triumvirs' task more difficult, as they were bound to call into question their integrity. Consequently, the triumvirs had to act prudently and circumspectly. When the political rivalry with their senatorial antagonists started, Pompey and Crassus — as private persons — were also unable to put forward any initiatives in public. To settle their affairs they had to use third parties, which, as the experience of the previous years showed — sometimes failed to bring the desired effect.[76] Moreover, they could not use all their possibilities, as Caesar, allied to them, together with some politicians connected with him, continued his stay in Gaul.

Beginning with Cicero's return to Rome, the conflict between the *optimates* and the triumvirs focused on Pompey's attempts to consolidate his position in

---

[74] A. N e u e n d o r f f: *Die römischen Konsulwahlen von 78—49 v. Chr.* Breslau 1913, p. 49; J. L i n d e r s k i: *Rzymskie zgromadzenie wyborcze od Sulli do Cezara.* Wrocław—Warszawa—Kraków 1966, p. 137.

[75] Concerning the attitude of the Romans, particularly of the senatorial aristocracy, to such plans, see: J. K o r p a n t y: *Rozwój politycznej roli jednostki w republice rzymskiej i jego odbicie w literaturze.* Wrocław—Warszawa—Kraków—Gdańsk 1971, pp. 9—15.

[76] In the years 61—60, Pompey, using the Piso and Afranius, could not achieve the realization of some, very important for him, plans, while, in 58, together with the other triumvirs, and with the help of the consuls L. Calpurnius Piso and A. Gabinius, he could not put under his control the situation in the capital: Vell. Pat. II, 40, 5; Plut., Pomp. 46, 3—4; 48, 5—49, 3; Cat. Min. 31, 1—2; Cic., 33, 1—2; App., BC II, 9, 31—32; 14, 58; Cass. Dio XXXVIII, 30, 1—2; 49—50; M. G e l z e r: *Pompeius...*, pp. 127—139, 152—155; J. L e a c h: *Pompey...*, pp. 114—122, 130—132.

the Republic by obtaining *cura annonae*, and being entrusted with the task of conducting Ptolemy XII Auletes to Egypt and putting him on the throne in Alexandria.[77] The *optimates'* policy, in this respect, consisting in discouraging Pompey from those missions, in protracting the Senate's work on them, and in limiting the extent of special powers connected with them, particularly such powers that could strengthen Ptolemy's position with regard to the Senate dominated by the *optimates*.[78]

Until the end of 57, the attitude of the Senate towards the triumvirs was fairly mild and moderate.[79] After January 1, 56, when the conservative *optimates*, and avowed enemies of the triumvirs, Cn. Cornelius Lentulus Marcellinus and L. Marcius Philippus, who had no links with and no obligations to the triumvirs, took office as new consuls, this attitude became much more hostile.[80] Moreover, the *optimates*, with the passage of time, extended considerably the range of their activities. No longer being satisfied with merely distorting and limiting the attempts to strengthen Pompeys position, they embarked on actions meant to weaken all of the triumvirs, and to shake the foundations of their alliance.[81]

In the early months of 56, there was still another circumstance that favoured the *optimates*, and the Senate dominated by them. M. Tullius Cicero, even though immediately after his return he was a spokesman of Pompey's interests, started gradually to distance himself from the triumvirs, and to cooperate more and more closely with the Senate's ruling elite. These tendencies culminated, in early April, in his motion for the Senate to have, on May 15, a debate in the affair of the lands of Campania.[82] As the anti-triumvirs policy became increasingly intense, which manifested itself in the Senate room, the

---

[77] Cic., Ad Att. IV, 1, 6—7; fam. I, 1, 1—4; 2, 1—4; 4, 1—3; Q. fr. II, 2, 3; fam. I, 5b, 1—2; cf.: Plut., Pomp. 49, 4—5; Cass. Dio XXXIX, 9, 12—14.

[78] Cic., Ad Att. IV, 1, 7; fam. I, 1, 1—4; 2, 1—4; 4, 1—3; Q. fr. II, 2, 3; fam. I, 5a, 3—4; Q. fr. II, 3, 1; fam. I, 5b, 1—2; P. S t e i n: *Die Senatssitzungen...*, pp. 34—40; M. B o n n e f o n d - C o u d r y: *Le Sénat...*, passim; L. de L i b e r o: *Obstruktion...*, pp. 23—25, 34, 76—77.

[79] Cic., Ad Att. IV, 1, 6—7; Q. fr. II, 1, 1—2; Dom. 4, 9—5, 10; 7, 16; 8, 18; 10, 25—27; 12, 31—32; Plut., Pomp. 49, 4—5; Cass. Dio XXXIX, 9, 2—3; cf.: Liv., per. CIV; App., BC II, 18, 67; P. S t e i n: *Die Senatssitzungen...*, pp. 34—37; M. B o n n e f o n d - C o u d r y: *Le Sénat...*, passim; L. de L i b e r o: *Obstruktion...*, pp. 23, 76—77.

[80] Cic., Ad fam. I, 1, 1—4; 2, 1—4; 4, 1—3; Q. fr. II, 2, 3; fam. I, 5a, 3—4; Q. fr. II, 3, 1—4; fam. I, 5b, 1—2; Q. fr. II, 6, 1; 5, 2—3; Cass. Dio XXXIX, 12—14; P. S t e i n: *Die Senatssitzungen...*, pp. 37—40; M. B o n n e f o n d - C o u d r y: *Le Sénat...*, passim; L. de L i b e r o: *Obstruktion...*, pp. 23—25.

[81] Their attacks against Caesar's agrarian bills served exactly this purpose: Cic., Ad Q. fr. II, 1, 1—2; 6, 1; fam. I, 9, 8; P. S t e i n: *Die Senatssitzungen...*, pp. 36, 40; M. B o n n e f o n d - C o u d r y: *Le Sénat...*, pp. 470—471, 509—510.

[82] Cic., Ad fam. I, 9, 8; Q. fr. II, 6, 1; M. G e l z e r: *Cicero...*, p. 164; D. S t o c k t o n: *Cicero. A Political Biography*. Oxford 1971, p. 206; K. K u m a n i e c k i: *Cyceron...*, p. 297; M. F u h r m a n n: *Cicero...*, p. 145.

Senate assumed a great importance — the greatest since the early months of 59.
It was clear enough, that the *optimates* were becoming increasingly self-
confident on the political scene, and that, since the moment they had approved
Cicero's above-mentioned motion, they were pursuing the aim of eliminating
the triumvirs completely from the power game, and, further on, of securing the
Senate's dominance over the Republic, with the Senate's leading politicians
taking the helm.[83] In these circumstances, the Senate's regaining of the
position it had enjoyed until Caesar forced through, during his consulship, the
lex Iulia agraria, seemed only a matter of time.

Such suggestions can be put forward considering that the Senate's improved situation was largely due to the successes scored by the *optimates.* Since
the defeat of P. Clodius and the rout of his supporters, the frequency of the
Senate's sessions significantly increased, just as its activity and involvement in
public affairs. More and more important matters, often of key importance for
the Republic, were the object of its debates. It was also the Senate that increasingly often decided on how these matters should be dealt with.[84] This was
possible owing to the cooperation that, in the second half of 57 and in the early
months of 56, developed between the Senate and various officials, particularly
the consuls of that time.[85] Their collaboration enabled the Senate to exert a lot
of influence on the activity of the magistrates and of the *concilium plebis.* The
Senate became then, and particularly in the above-mentioned period in 56, an
institution that occupied a central place on the political arena, especially
because its enemies were then suffering a series setbacks, which is true of
Clodius, and later also of the triumvirs, particularly of Pompey.[86] In April 56,
the triumvirs were even put on the defensive, and were forced to retreat into
the background.[87] Assuming that the *optimates* continued the policy they had
been pursuing, and managed to successfully press ahead with their plans, there
was a fair chance that they could introduce radical, and favourable for them,
changes in the Republic, particularly in the then existing balance of power. As
a result, they could even achieve a durable weakening the triumvirs' position,

---

[83] This was unambiguously confirmed by Cicero: Ad fam. I, 9, 8.

[84] See: P. S t e i n: *Die Senatssitzungen...,* pp. 32—40; M. B o n n e f o n d - C o u d r y: *Le
Sénat...,* passim; L. de L i b e r o: *Obstruktion...,* pp. 17—18, 23—25, 27, 34, 42, 44.

[85] Cic., Ad Q. fr. II, 5, 2—3; cf.: Att. IV, 1, 6—7; 2, 4—5; 3, 1; 3; Q. fr. II, 1, 1—3; fam. I,
1, 2; 2, 1—2; 4, 1; Q. fr. II, 3, 2; fam. I, 5b, 2; Or. sen. gr. eg. 8, 19—9, 22; 12, 30; 14, 35; Or. pop.
gr. eg. 6, 15—16; 8, 18; Sest. 6, 14—15; 13, 31; 32, 69—33, 72.

[86] See: Cic., Ad Att. IV, 1, 7; 2, 1—5; 3, 2—5; Q. fr. II, 1, 1—3; fam. I, 1, 1—4; 2, 1—2; 4,
1—3; Q. fr. II, 2, 3; 3, 1—4; fam. I, 5b, 1—2; Q. fr. II, 6, 1; 5, 3; Dom. 3, 6; J. van O o t e g h e m:
Pompée..., pp. 360—382; W. W i l l: *Der römische Mob...,* pp. 84—92; W.J. T a t u m: *The Patrician
Tribune...,* pp. 185—213.

[87] The evidence for this is the fact that the Senate resumed its debate on Caesar's agrarian
bills: Ad Q. fr. II, 6, 1; fam. I, 9, 8; P. S t e i n: *Die Senatssitzungen...,* p. 40; M. B o n n e f o n d -
- C o u d r y: *Le Sénat...,* pp. 359—360, 510.

and a reversal of the, unfavourable for them, tendencies in the internal politics, which Caesar initiated, as a consul, in 59. This would, naturally, further strengthen the Senate's hand.

If then the *optimates* put their plans into practice, a major political transformation could ensue, comparable to the one in the late sixties and early fifties, which could put an end to the alliance of Caesar, Pompey, and Crassus, and lead to the Senate's elite taking control of the state. This was very serious threat to the triumvirs, they had to reckon with disastrous consequences, with their careers being destroyed, their importance in public life being reduced, or even with being made to whithdraw from politics altogether.

Therefore, none of the three could afford to allow their antagonists to carry out their designs. The triumvir's response to the *optimates*' actions was the meeting of those potentates at Luca, and the decisions and measures taken there to cement their alliance, to regain power, and to weaken their enemies.[88]

In connection with such plans, the triumvirs started, with much greater intensity than before, to "buy" and recruit new allies, particularly among the politicians sitting in the Senate. As a result, they managed to win over many senators, for, since the conference at Luca, around two hundred of them, that is one third of the members of the Senate, owed their allegiance to the triumvirs.[89] All this had far reaching consequences, the triumvirs emerged as much stronger than before, and new possibilities opened up for them — particularly in the Senate. In particular, the ascendancy of the *optimates* among the senators was diminished, and they could no longer manipulate the sessions so easily. The members of the Senate emerged as divided into two groups that clearly had dominance over the other senators. After the triumvirs' conference at Luca, the *optimates* could no longer use the Senate for their purposes so easily, to pass a bill became much more difficult and complicated.

The decisions taken by the triumvirs at Luca not only secured their current interests, they were tantamount to an attempt to protect themselves, in a more efficient way, against the antagonists' attacks by implementing a new division of influences in the whole of the Roman empire.[90]

---

[88] Suet., Iul. 24, 1; Plut., Caes. 21, 2—3; Crass. 14, 5—6; Pomp. 51, 3—4; Cat. Min. 41, 1; App., BC II, 17, 61—63; C. Luibheid: *The Luca Conference*. CPh, 65 (1970), pp. 88—94; L. Hayne: *Who Went to Luca*. CPh, 69 (1974), pp. 217—220; J.S. Ruebel: *When did Cicero Learn about the Conference at Luca?* "Historia", Bd. 24 (1975), pp. 622—624; A.M. Ward: *The Conference of Luca: Did it Happen?* AJAH, 51 (1980), pp. 48—63.

[89] This fact is emphasised by Plutarch (Caes. 21, 2; Pomp. 51, 3) and Appian (BC II, 17, 62).

[90] The measures aimed at achieving this purpose included the decisions to make Pompey and Crassus consuls in the year 55, to make them, subsequently, governors of provinces, and to prolong Caesar's governorship in the Gallic provinces: Suet., Iul. 24, 1; Plut., Caes. 21, 3; Crass. 14, 5—6; Pomp. 51, 4; Cat. Min. 41, 1; App., BC II, 17, 63; A. Garzetti: *M. Licinio Crasso*. "Athenaeum", Vol. 22 (1944), pp. 21—22; R. Seager: *Pompey...*, pp. 122—123; Ch. Meier: *Caesar...*, p. 331.

The conference at Luca marked then the beginning of the subsequent, the last in the first half of the fifties, stage in the rivalry between the triumvirs and *optimates* for the control of the state. Immediately after that conference, the object of that rivalry was the election of the consuls for the year 55.[91] The politicians defending the cause of the Senate had to do everything to prevent Pompey and Crassus from taking up the posts of the consuls for that year. Had they succeeded in this, they could expect that neither would the triumvirs accomplish their other objectives as defined in Luca, and this would mean that the dominance of the Senate in the Republic, and of the senatorial elite could not only continue, but, in the future, would even be consolidated, for it would be still possible, in such a situation, to eliminate Caesar, Pompey, and Crassus.

After the *optimates'* defeat, the said rivalry continued during the consulship of Cn. Pompeius and M. Licinius Crassus. It focused on the election of other curial officials for the year 55[92], and then on the implementation of other decisions taken at Luca.[93] Also in this case, the efforts of the *optimates* and the senate ended in failure.

As a result, in 55, came another turning point in the political life in Rome — the triumvirs took over, and, in consequence, Caesar's governorship in Gallic provinces was prolonged for another five years,[94] while Pompey and Crassus were entrusted with the governorship of the Spanish provinces, and Syria[95] — and the triumvirs dominance in the Republic was sealed, as these events meant that all of them would enjoy, during the next few years, the status of public persons, so to attack them formally would be, in that period, impossible. Also their position and extended influences made such an attack very unlikely, especially because Pompey and Crassus, having served their term as consuls, and having taken up the governorship of the above-mentioned provinces, had at their disposal, just as Caesar in Gaul, the income from the provin-

---

[91] Vell. Pat. II, 46, 2; Plut., Crass. 15, 1—5; Pomp. 51, 5—52, 2; Cat. Min. 41, 2—42, 1; App., BC II, 17, 64—18, 65; Cass. Dio XXXIX, 27—31; A. Neuendorff: *Die römischen Konsulwahlen...*, pp. 50—54; J. Linderski: *Rzymskie zgromadzenie...*, pp. 139—140; A. Yakobson: *Elections and Electioneering in Rome. A Study in the Political System of the Late Republic.* Stuttgart 1999 ("Historia Einzelschriften", H. 128), p. 169.

[92] Cic., Ad Q. fr. II, 8, 3; Plut., Pomp. 52, 2; Cat. Min. 42, 1—5; Cass. Dio XXXIX, 32; J. Linderski: *Rzymskie zgromadzenie...*, pp. 140—141; A. Yakobson: *Elections...*, pp. 169—170.

[93] Plut., Crass. 15, 5; Pomp. 52, 3; Cat. Min. 43; App., BC II, 18, 65; Cass. Dio XXXIX, 33—37, 1; M. Gelzer: *Pompeius...*, pp. 168—171; A.M. Ward: *Marcus Crassus...*, pp. 273—277; L. Canfora: *Giulio Cesare...*, p. 109.

[94] G. Rotondi: *Leges...*, pp. 404—405; cf.: T. Rice Holmes: *The Roman Republic and the Founder of the Empire.* Vol. 2: *58—50 BC.* Oxford 1923, pp. 299—310; T.R.S. Broughton: *The Magistrates of the Roman Republic.* Vol. 2: *99 BC—31 BC.* New York 1952, p. 215.

[95] G. Rotondi: *Leges...*, p. 408; cf.: G. Niccolini: *I fasti...*, p. 309; T.R.S. Broughton: *The Magistrates...*, pp. 215, 217.

ces, and had command of the armies stationing there. Owing to all this, they were, all three of them, guaranteed, until the year 50, to have a lot of influence on many questions connected with foreign policy. The triumvirs antagonists, particularly the *optimates*, still numerically dominant in the Senate, were practically helpless before them.

Thus, the situation of the Senate in 55 decisively worsened, for it was no longer possible for it to pursue an active, and first of all independent, policy. The Senate lost also its influence on the political situation in the Republic, as it was made dependent on the consuls, Pompey and Crassus, who reduced it to the role of an institution assessing the bills that they decided to introduce. Pompey and Crassus ultimately dealt with important matters even such that were "constitutionally" reserved for the Senate, as, for example, the assignment of provinces to the politicians about to govern them at the *concilium plebis*.[96] As a result, their bills quickly became laws, and were for the *optimates*, prevalent in the Senate, much more difficult to kill than the Senate's decisions, whereas the position of the *concilium plebis* improved, at the cost of the Senate of course, though not so much as in the years 58—57. The activity of the Senate also decreased, as well as the frequency of its sessions.[97] Consequently, the influence of this institution on the state affairs was severely curtailed, first of all, because the *optimates*, who still theoretically were in the majority in the Senate, were deprived of any possibility to attain their aims. This grouping was put on the defensive, and, after the election of all officials for 55, it was even pushed aside and made to retreat from its central place on the political scene. The result was that the senatorial elite, which, until the conference at Luca, played a key role in public life, lost power again.

These tendencies, just as the strong position of the triumvirs, seemed permanent enough. Several other factors, apart from the already mentioned, were at play. First of all, the great number, the greatest since the early fifties, of the triumvirs' allies among the senators, the allies who unanimously and consistently worked for the benefit of their patrons. It was to be expected that, with the passage of time, the number of the senators dependent on the triumvirs would increase, rather than diminish.[98] Of great importance was also that, in 55, among the allies of Caesar, Pompey, and Crassus, there were far more,

---

[96] See in this context: Vell. Pat. II, 46, 2; Plut., Crass. 15, 5; Pomp. 52, 3; Cat. Min. 43, 1; 5; App., BC II, 18, 65; Cass. Dio XXXIX, 33, 2—37, 1.

[97] P. S t e i n: *Die Senatssitzungen...*, pp. 44—46; M. B o n n e f o n d - C o u d r y: *Le Sénat...*, p. 808.

[98] Their further increase in number could have been caused by Caesar's successes in Gaul, and the resultant continuous growth of his army. Similar results must have been brought about taking provinces by the Pompey and Crassus. All these factors must have cause an increased demand for the politicians ready to take up the posts which those potentates, in these circumstances, could offer.

than in the early fifties, senators belonging to the senatorial elite, that is former consuls.[99] Even the politicians counted among the most outstanding members of the Senate, whose personal qualities far exceeded those of their colleagues.[100] Moreover, the triumvirs' allies from a well organised group that was dynamic, active, had good leaders, and was deeply committed to the defence of their patrons' and protectors' interest, for, as is witnessed by many ancient authors, such actions were not usually undertaken for free and most of those senators had a vested interest in supporting the triumvirs.[101]

The triumvirs won some senators over with money, others with important posts or with quick and brilliant careers, and even with other advantages.[102] All three of them had such possibilities of corrupting the politicians connected with them only as long as they had the positions, influences, and the financial means, that is as long as they controlled their provinces, which provided them with income, and had command of the armies stationing there. Thus, it appears that the politicians acting in Caesar's, Pompey's, and Crassus's interests had very close and long-standing links with them.

In 55, the triumvirs took much better precautions against their antagonists, who were now in opposition, than in the times of Caesar's consulship. This is why, any attempt to oust them, or even to undermine their position, or, at least, to weaken their influence, was out of the question. The Senate was powerless against them, for the politicians identifying with it, particularly the most prominent *optimates*, were devoid of any means that would make such moves possible. Another reason why it was so was that — apart from several posts in the college of the tribunes of the people — the *optimates* did not manage to secure any offices that could be used in such activity.[103] Consequently, they had no chance to engage in any offensive actions in public, as they lost the initiative, in this respect, in favour of their opponents. The *optimates* had even to reckon with the possibility that the influence of the three would continue even after the consulship of Pompey and Crassus, that even when this office, and other offices, are taken by politicians inimical to the triumvirs.[104]

---

[99] A large group of them was among the triumvirs' allies already at the time of the conference at Luca: Plut., Caes. 21, 2; Pomp. 51, 3; App., BC II, 17, 62. Cf.: Plut., Crass. 14, 5.

[100] Cicero was the best example of it, but he did so under duress, against his will, Ad fam. I, 9—10; D. Stockton: *Cicero...*, pp. 207—217; K. Kumaniecki: *Cyceron...*, pp. 299—339; T.N. Mitchell: *Cicero. The Senior Statesman.* New Haven—London 1991, pp. 172—194.

[101] Plut., Caes. 21, 1—2; Pomp. 51, 1—4; 52, 2; Cat. Min. 42, 2; 4; App., B.C. II, 17, 62; Cass. Dio XXXIX, 32, 1.

[102] Plut., Caes, 21, 1—2; Pomp. 51, 2; App., BC II, 17, 62.

[103] See in this context: G. Niccolini: *I fasti...*, pp. 309—310; T.R.S. Broughton: *The Magistrates...*, pp. 216—217; P.J.J. Vanderbroeck: *Popular Leadership...*, p. 210.

[104] See, for example, L. Piotrowicz's opinions related to this matter (*Dzieje...*, pp. 421—422).

The dominance of the triumvirs, and the downfall of the Senate were also explicable by the latter's crisis, which had already continued for a considerable period of time.[105] The crisis was deepened owing to various harmful tendencies that appeared in the senators' activity both during the sessions and outside the Senate's room. Its main symptom, however, was the improper way of the Senate's functioning, its inability to fulfil a number of "constitutional" tasks and duties, to deal with many problems and challenges that the Republic had to face.[106]

The triumvirs' opponents still cherished some hope for the improvement of the situation and of the Senate's position, but the only thing they could pin such hopes on was the expected departure of Pompey and Crassus from Rome in connection with their taking office as governors of the provinces they had been entrusted with.[107] What the *optimates* counted on was that, after 55, only the allies of those potentates would be left in the city, but they would be deprived of the guidance and support of their patrons. This created an excellent opportunity to attack their collaborators and allies, and to weaken this anti-senate grouping.

The reality came up to those expectations only up to a point. In 54, several factors conditioned the situation of the Senate. First of all, it was influenced by the results of the election held at the end of Pompey's and Crassus's consulship, which ended in a considerable success for the pro-senate *optimates*.[108] Decisively unfavourable, however, was Pompey's presence in Italy. He delegated the governorship of his province to his envoys, while he himself stayed in the vicinity of Rome and watched the development of the situation so as to protect his and his partners' interests.[109] By creating a state of anarchy, and by

---

[105] Some Romans living at that time also saw this problem, e.g. M. Tullius Cicero, or C. Sallustius Crispus: Cic., Ad Att. I, 18, 6; Leg. III, 8, 19; 9, 22; 12, 29—14, 32; 15, 34; Rep. II, 34, 59; V. 1, 2; Sall., Ep. Ad Caes. 2, 8, 6—11, 2. For more on this see: L.T. B ł a s z c z y k: *Krytyka i projekty reformy senatu w pismach Cicerona i Sallustiusa.* W: I d e m: *Ze studiów nad senatem rzymskim w okresie Republiki.* Łódź 1965, pp. 18—21, 36—39.

[106] In connection with this, both Cicero and Sallust suggested appropriate, in their opinion, measures to reform this institution: Cic., Leg. III, 4, 11; 10, 23; 12, 28—13, 29; Rep. I, 27, 43; Sall., Ep. ad Caes. 2, 11, 2—7; L.T. B ł a s z c z y k: *Krytyka...*, pp. 21—28, 39—43, see also: pp. 43—45.

[107] Plut., Crass. 15, 5—16, 3; Pomp. 52, 3—4; Cat. Min. 43, 1; 5; App., BC II, 18, 65; Cass. Dio XXXIX, 33, 2—3.

[108] Cic., Ad Q. fr. II, 5, 4; Plut., Cat. Min. 44, 1; Cass. Dio XXXIX, 60, 2—3. See also: A. N e u e n d o r f f: *Die römischen Konsulwahlen...*, pp. 54—56; J. L i n d e r s k i: *Rzymskie zgromadzenie...*, p. 142; T.C. B r e n n a n: *The Praetorship in the Roman Republic.* Vols. 1—2. Oxford 2000, pp. 417, 755. Concerning the information on the political orientation of the tribunes of the people elected for 54, see: G. N i c c o l i n i: *I fasti...*, s. 310—313; T.R.S. B r o u g h t o n: *The Magistrates...*, p. 223; and: W.J. T a t u m: *The Marriage of Pompey's Son to the Daughter of Appius Claudius Pulcher.* "Klio", Bd. 73 (1991), pp. 122—129; F.X. R y a n: *The Birth Dates of Domitius and Scipio.* AHB, 11 (1997), pp. 89—93.

[109] Vell. Pat. II, 48, 1; Plut., Pomp. 53, 1; Cat. Min. 45, 1; 46, 1; J. van O o t e g h e m: *Pompée...*, pp. 416—430; P. G r e e n h a l g h: *Pompey... (Prince)...*, pp. 61—70.

spreading rumours about the necessity to appoint a dictator, he successfully paralysed the moves of the *optimates*, and of the Senate, dominated by them, showing, in this way, that they could not rise to the occasion, and govern efficiently.[110] The *optimates*' situation slightly improved only in the second half of that year. This was connected with the death of Julia, Caesar's daughter and Pompey's wife, which led to the loosening of the ties between the two.[111] The same happened to the triumvirs' control of the situation in the capital. Consequently, the *optimates* could intensify their attacks against the triumvirs' allies, the best example of which was the campaign organised against A. Gabrinius, who was connected with Pompey.[112] In response to this, Pompey tried to cause an even greater anarchy, for example, by, among other things, preventing the organisation of the election of the officials for the next year.[113]

In the year 53 the situation of the Senate and the *optimates* did not get any better even after the death of Crassus, and the consequent break-up of the triumvirate,[114] for Pompey's dominance in Rome continued.[115] The situation got slightly better after the election, held in July or August, of the officials for the rest of the year.[116] Since, however, Pompey prevented the election of the officials for 52, that year also started with an interregnum, i.e. with an even greater anarchy, which was also the effect of the growing rivalry between the candidates for the posts of consuls and pretors.[117] The situation of the Senate was so bad that the *optimates*, dominant in it, having acknowledged that the situation had slipped out of control, decided to reorientate their policy. This

---

[110] Plut., Pomp. 54, 2; Cat. Min. 44—46, 1; App., BC II, 19, 69—71; M. Gelzer: *Pompeius...*, pp. 174—178; R. Seager: *Pompey...*, pp. 132—139.

[111] Liv., per. CVI; Vell. Pat. II, 47, 2; Suet., Iul. 26, 1; Plut., Caes. 23, 4; Pomp. 53, 3—5; App., BC II, 19, 68; Cass. Dio XXXIX, 64; XL, 44, 2.

[112] Cass. Dio XXXIX, 60; 62—63. More extensively on the same wrote: T.R.S. Broughton: *The Magistrates...*, p. 218; M.C. Alexander: *Trials...*, pp. 145, 148; cf.: E. Matthews Sanford: *The Career...*, pp. 88—92; E. Fantham: *The Trials of Gabinius in 54 BC.* "Historia", Bd. 24 (1975), pp. 425—443; R.S. Williams: *"Rei publicae causa": Gabinius Defense of His Restoration of Ptolemy Auletes.* CJ, 81 (1985), pp. 25—28.

[113] Plut., Pomp. 53, 3; 5; 54, 2; Cat. Min. 44; 45, 1; 46, 1; App., BC II, 19, 68—69; M. Gelzer: *Pompeius...*, pp. 176—177; J. Leach: *Pompey...*, pp. 150—153. See also: G.V. Sumner: *The Coitio of 54 B.C., or Waiting for Caesar.* HSCPh, 86 (1982), pp. 133—139.

[114] Liv., per. CVI; Vell. Pat. II, 46, 4; Plut., Caes, 28, 1; Crass. 31; Pomp. 53, 6—7; App., BC 18, 66; Cass. Dio XL, 27; 44, 2.

[115] Plut., Pomp. 54, 1—3; App., BC II, 19, 71; Cass. Dio XL, 45—46, 3.

[116] Plut., Pomp. 54, 3; Cass. Dio XL, 46, 1; A. Neuendorff: *Die römischen Konsulwahlen...*, pp. 56—65; J. Linderski: *Rzymskie zgromadzenie...*, pp. 147—148.

[117] Another cause was the fighting in the city provoked by T. Annius Milo, and P. Clodius: Liv., per. CVII; Vell. Pat. II, 47, 3—4; Suet., Iul. 26, 1; Plut., Pomp. 54, 3; Cat. Min. 47, 1—2; App., BC II, 20, 72—22, 83; Cass. Dio XL, 46, 3—50, 3; A. Yakobson: *Elections...*, pp. 171—172.

is why, they agreed to give special powers to Pompey and to enter into an alliance with him. This alliance was founded on the *optimates'* hope to win him over to the Senate's cause, to use him for their own ends, that is, to turn him against C. Julius Caesar, so as to bring about an open conflict between them.[118]

Those hopes, however, just as other calculations of the *optimates*, were dashed. The reason was that the cooperation of the *optimates*, and of the Senate controlled by their leaders, with Pompey did not, from the very beginning, go as the initiators of this alliance had intended.[119] Apart from that, neither the *optimates*, nor the Senate were really a match for Pompey, so they played a subordinate role in this alliance. Such relations continued, in spite of the, apparently favourable for the Senate, moves of Pompey at the beginning of his third consulship, and they even became more permanent, especially when Pompey, having forced through some, advantageous for him, bills, consolidated his position in the Republic, also in relation to his new allies.[120]

The above described situation did not change even when the conflict between Pompey and Caesar broke out.[121] As that conflict developed, the Senate became an object of various manipulations by Ceasar, Pompey, and their closest allies.[122] Such tendencies were particularly visible in 51, when the *optimates'* attempts to pursue a policy that would be independent from Pompey failed,[123] and also in 50, when the trusted confidants of both potentates became particularly active in the Senate's sessions-chamber.[124] As a result, the

---

[118] Cass. Dio XL, 50, 3—5; cf.: Liv., per. CVII; Vell. Pat. II, 47, 3; Suet.., Iul. 26, 1; Plut., Caes. 28, 5; Pomp. 54, 3—5; Cat. Min. 47—48, 1; App., BC II, 20, 72—23, 84.

[119] See, in this context, the assessment of the *optimates'* policy in relation to Pompey, in the first months of 52, by Cassius Dio (XL, 50, 5).

[120] This was his most important purpose at that time: Plut., Pomp. 55, 4—7; App., BC II, 23, 84—25, 95; Cass. Dio XL, 51—58, 1; cf.: Liv., per. CVII; Vell. Pat. II, 47, 3—4; Plut., Caes. 28, 5; Cat. Min. 48; E. M e y e r: *Caesars Monarchie...*, pp. 229—241; M. G e l z e r: *Pompeius...*, pp. 181—192; R. S e a g e r: *Pompey...*, pp. 144—151.

[121] Actions against Caesar were initiated by the consul M. Claudius Marcellus in 51. See: N. R o g o s z: *Senat a konflikt Pompejusza z Cezarem. Wniosek konsula Marcellusa z 51 r. p.n.e. w sprawie odwołania Cezara z prowincji.* W: *Antiquitas.* T. 13. Red. E. K o n i k. Wrocław 1987, pp. 208—211.

[122] At first, the aim of these practices was to derail M. Claudius Marcellus's plans: ibidem: pp. 211, 214—223; I d e m: *Funkcjonowanie senatu w Republice Rzymskiej w 51 r. p.n.e.* W: "Res Historica". Z. 5. Red. L. M o r a w i e c k i. Lublin 1998, pp. 134—136, 140—149.

[123] Its initiator was M. Claudius Marcellus, see: N. R o g o s z: *Senat...*, pp. 210—211, 223—229. On the evolution of the rememberances tendencies in the year 51 see: I d e m: *Funkcjonowanie...*, pp. 140—149.

[124] I d e m: *Stanowisko senatu wobec konfliktu Pompejusza z Cezarem (1 marca — 1 grudnia 50 r. p.n.e.).* AUMC-S, Sect. F. Vol. 49 (Lublin 1994), pp. 53—69; I d e m: *Stanowisko senatu wobec rywalizacji Pompejusza z Cezarem (1 XII 50 r. — 11 I 49 p.n.e.).* W: *Rzym antyczny. Polityka i pieniądz II.* Red. A. K u n i s z. Katowice 1997, pp. 9—37.

4*

role of this institution in the Republic was even more diminished, as the political profile of the Senate, its stance on the topical problems, and its participation in the public life were determined by the senators connected with Caesar and Pompey.[125]

When the civil war broke out and most of the senators left Rome, the Senate lost even more of its importance as it was Pompey and Caesar that exerted the greatest influence on the situation in the empire.[126] This state of affairs continued also in the following years. For a short time, the Senate regained the position proper to it after the murder of Caesar in 44.[127] Already in the following year, however, when the second triumvirate was formed, the Senate lost that position, this time irreversibly.

It should be stated, in the context of the above remarks, that the beginning of those negative phenomena took place in 59, during C. Julius Caesar's consulship, as it was then that — for the first time in the period discussed in the present article — the Senate was made to relinquish its leadership, and its position in the Republic was challenged. After an over year-long crisis, in spite of the initial setbacks, and as a result of the efforts initiated by the *optimates* defending the Senate, the latter — in summer 57 — regained its proper position in the state system. This was, at the same time, a signal for the *optimates* to intensify their efforts and to turn against the triumvirs, who had been cooperating with them for some time. After some initial successes, in the last months of 57 and the early months of 56, however, those actions ended in a failure. In this context, and particularly in the light of the tendencies, signalled above, in the political life of Rome in the late fifties, we may conclude that the downfall

---

[125] The influence of the senators dependent on Caesar and Pompey on the function and attitude of the Senate during the key debates (on March 1, and December 1, 50) related to the conflicts between those potentates. See: N. R o g o s z: *Debata senatu nad wyznaczeniem Cezarowi następcy w prowincjach galijskich (1 marca 50 r. p.n.e.).* W: *W 2500-lecie powstania Republiki Rzymskiej.* Red. A. K u n i s z. Katowice 1995, pp. 65—96; I d e m: *Debata senatu z 1 grudnia 50 r. przed narodzeniem Chrystusa w świetle konfliktu Pompejusza z Cezarem.* W: *Wieki stare i nowe.* T. 2. Red. I. P a n i c, M.W. W a n a t o w i c z. Katowice 2001, pp. 19—42.

[126] What greatly contributed to this effect was the Senate's division beacause after Caesar's enter to the Italy the majority of the senators followed Pompey and moved to the East, losing thus contact with the political centre. Caesar's allies, on the other hand, stayed in Rome: E. M e y e r: *Caesars Monarchie...*, pp. 299—302; R. K a m i e n i k: *Klęska obozu republikańskiego w wojnie domowej 49—48 r. przed n.e. a odpowiedzialność Pompejusza.* AUMC-S, Sect. F, 18 (1963), pp. 24—27; I d e m: *Kwestia naczelnego dowództwa Pompejusza i ewakuacja Italii przez wojska republikańskie w wojnie domowej 49 r. p.n.e.* AUMC-S, Sect. F, 19 (1964), pp. 58—59, 74-84. Cf. in this context: B. F u c h s: *Die Parteigruppierung im Bürgerkrieg zwischen Caesar und Pompeius.* Bonn 1920; D.R. S h a c k l e t o n - B a i l e y: *The Roman Nobility in the Second Civil War.* CQ, 10, (1960), pp. 253—267; H. B r u h n s: *Caesar und die römische Oberschicht in den Jahren 49-44 v. Chr.* Göttingen 1978.

[127] H. B e n g t s o n: *Die letzen Monate der römischen Senatsherrschaft.* In: ANRW. Bd. 1. Berlin—New York 1972, pp. 967—981.

of the Senate's position, in 55, as a result of the implementing, by Pompey and Crassus, of the decisions taken by all the triumvirs at Luca, was permanent. It was also part and parcel of the general crisis of the Republic and its political system.

Norbert Rogosz

OCENA POLITYCZNEJ ROLI SENATU W REPUBLICE RZYMSKIEJ W LATACH 59—55

Streszczenie

W latach 59—55 przed Chrystusem w starożytnym Rzymie doszło do osłabienia pozycji i znaczenia senatu — jednej z najważniejszych instytucji w Republice. Uwidoczniło się to w odebraniu mu steru rządów, odsunięciu na dalszy plan sceny politycznej i zmniejszeniu jego wpływu na sprawy państwa. Nie było to wynikiem ograniczenia uprawnień senatu, lecz efektem rozgrywek między utożsamiającymi się z nim, przewodzącymi mu i broniącymi go senatorami o optymackiej orientacji a ich przeciwnikami.

Niniejszy artykuł jest poświęcony ocenie roli odegranej przez senat w życiu politycznym Republiki Rzymskiej w tym okresie, a przedmiotem zainteresowania autora jest w tym kontekście aktywność senatu, jego funkcjonowanie, udział we wspomnianych rozgrywkach, a przede wszystkim w walkach politycznych toczonych przez dominujących w nim optymatów z jego przeciwnikami o należną mu pozycję w państwie. Znaczenie senatu w Republice ocenia więc, śledząc ich przebieg, eksponując czynniki, które przyczyniły się do zasygnalizowanych już zmian w jego położeniu oraz akcentując przetasowania w układzie sił wśród rzymskich ugrupowań politycznych i polityków w gronie senatorów oraz poza nim. Ponieważ rola senatu w Republice Rzymskiej w latach 59—55 zależała od przebiegu rozgrywek między jego obrońcami a ich przeciwnikami, nie była ona stabilna. W związku z tym autor artykułu wskazuje także wszelkie zmiany jego pozycji na forum publicznym oraz okresy, w których one nastąpiły.

Norbert Rogosz

LE JUGEMENT SUR LE RÔLE DU SÉNAT DANS LA RÉPUBLIQUE ROMAINE DANS LES ANNÉES 59—55

Résumé

Dans les années 59—55 avant Jésus Christ dans la Rome antique on observait un affaiblissement de la position et de la signification du sénat — une des institutions les plus importantes de la République. Le processus était visible dans l'enlèvement des effectifs, la remise au fond de la scène politique et la diminution de son influence sur l'état. Cela n'était pas l'effet d'une limitation du pouvoir du sénat mais le résultat des conflits entre les sénateurs, qui s'identifiaient à l'institution, qui la dirigeaient et défendaient, et leurs opposants.

Cette étude est destinée à une évaluation du rôle joué par le sénat dans la vie politique de la République Romaine dans cette période; l'objet de recherches reste dans ce contexte l'activité du sénat, son fonctionnement, la participation dans les conflits mentionnés et avant tout dans les luttes politiques menées entre les optimates, qui dominaient dans le sénat, et leurs opposants combattant pour sa forte position au sein de l'état. L'auteur estime la signification du sénat dans la République en suivant les événements, en exposant les facteurs qui intensifiaient des changements signalisés et en accentuant les modifications dans les groupements politiques et entre les politiciens. Puisque le rôle du sénat dans la République Romaine dans les années 59—55 dépendait des conflits entre ses défendeurs et ses ennemis, il n'était pas stable. Par conséquent l'auteur de l'article démontre aussi tous les changements de sa position sur le forum publique et les périodes où ils avaient lieu.

RAFAŁ BUTOR

Decimus Clodius Albinus
in the Civil War of 193—197

The civil war of 193—197, when Lucius Septimius Severus was laying the foundations for the future of his dynasty, was a significant event in the history of the *Imperium Romanum*. After the death of Commodus and the brief reign of Helvius Pertinax in Rome the imperial power was seized by Marcus Didius Iulianus, who promised, after a disgraceful "auction", 25,000 sesterces to each one of the praetorians in exchange for their support.

However, the support of the Guard had been, at that time, an asset already too weak in the struggle for power in the Empire. The commanders of the provincial armies had joined in the struggle for the throne. Almost simultaneously, the governor of *Pannonia Superior* Lucius Septimius Severus and the governor of Syria Caius Pescennius Niger had been proclaimed emperors, and it was between those two that the struggle for power had taken place. No less significant role was played by the governor of Britain Decimus Clodius Albinus, who initially, in result of an agreement with Septimius Severus, had received the title of *Caesar* in exchange for an alliance. After defeating Niger, as he had been no longer necessary for Severus, he himself had become an object of attack. After his victory in the battle of Lugdunum in 197 and the death of Albinus, Septimius Severus became a sovereign ruler of the Empire and the civil war had come to an end.

Despite the fact that the governor of Britain had not played a paramount role in the war between Severus and Niger, considering the complexity of his relations with Severus and his popularity, especially among the senatorial aristocracy, he appears to be, from the scholar's point of view, an interesting participant of the conflict of 193—197.

Decimus Clodius Albinus[1] belonged to the same generation as Pescennius Niger and Septimius Severus. He was born on 25 November ca. 140.[2] Unfortunately, very little may be said of the life and career of Albinus, as the only relevant source description, contained in the *Historia Augusta*, arouses a great deal of controversy. It is even not quite certain whether he descended, as according to his biography, from Hadrumetum in Africa, although most historians take this information to be true.[3]

From the *Life of Albinus*, contained in *Historia Augusta*, we know that he devoted himself to the military craft.[4] It is difficult, however, to determine the posts and ranks which he had held. According to the account in the above-mentioned source, as a tribune he had commanded the Dalmatian cavalry and the legions *IV* and I.[5] He began his senatorial career in a traditional manner, from the quaestors' office, after which he had assumed the post of *aedile*. He had not held that position for very long, as he was entrusted with military tasks. During the rebellion of Avidius Cassius he had maintained

---

[1] Not much space has been devoted to this figure; there are just a few items concerning the subject: J. H a s e b r o e k: *Die Fälschung der Vita Nigri und Vita Albini in den Scriptores Historiae Augustae*. Berlin 1916; C.E. van S i c k l e: *The Legal Status of Clodius Albinus in the Years 193—96*. "Classical Philology", Vol. 23 (1928), pp. 123—127; G. A l f ö l d y: *Herkunft und Laufbahn des Clodius Albinus in der Historia Augusta*. Bonn 1968 ("Bonner Historia Augusta Colloquium 1966/1967"), pp. 19—38; A.J. G r a h a m: *The Numbers at Lugdunum*. "Historia", Bd. 27 (1978), Wiesbaden, pp. 625—630; J. B a l t y: *Essai d'iconographie de l'empereur Clodius Albinus*. Bruxelles 1966, L. S c h u m a c h e r: *Die politische Stellung des D. Clodius Albinus (193—197 n. Chr.)*. "Jahrbuch des Römisch-Germanischen Zentralmuseums Mainz", Bd. 50 (2003), pp. 355—369.

[2] HA, *Clod. Alb*. 4, 6 gives the day (the seventh day before the December Calendae = 25 November) and mentions that Albinus' father had informed the proconsul of Africa at that time, Aelius Bassianus, about the birth of his son; G. A l f ö l d y: *Herkunft...*, p. 23, refrains from a more precise determination of the date of birth, pointing to the fact that since he was a consul in 187, and it must be considered that the required and customarily accepted age had been 40, the year of his birth should be dated around 147.

[3] J. H a s e b r o e k: *Die Fälschung...*, p. 13 ff., has completely renounced the credibility of the account in the *Historia Augusta*, regarding as authentic only the fact that Albinus had come from Hadrumetum; the African origin is also supported by A.R. B i r l e y: *The Coups d'Etat of the Year 193*. "Bonner Jahrbücher", Bd. 169 (1969), pp. 265—266; cf. G. A l f ö l d y: *Herkunft...*, pp. 20—22.

[4] HA, *Clod. Alb*. 6, 1—3.

[5] Which does not give us sufficient information, as this could be: *leg. I Minerva* from *Germania Inferior, I Adiutrix from Pannonia Superior; I Italica* from *Moesia Inferior* and *IV Flavia* from *Moesia Superior, IV Scythica* from Syria — perhaps, the information is wrong.

some undetermined troops in Bithynia loyal to him, which could suggest that he had been governor of that province, but the same source mentions that it was during Commodus' reign that Albinus held the praetorship,[6] and therefore he could not have held the governorship at some earlier time. It is more probable that he had performed some sort of military function in Bithynia, commanding the auxiliary troops stationed there.[7] After his praetorship he had probably commanded, as *legatus legionis*, the legion *V Macedonica* in Dacia and participated in military actions against the barbarians inhabiting that region.[8] As regards the consulship, Albinus must have held that office in the second half of the 80s, to proceed later to the rank of governor of *Germania Inferior*, most likely at the end of the 80s and the beginning of the 90s. He had succeeded there in his fight against the Germanic tribes, which is corroborated by a number of mentions in the account of his life.[9] Most probably, he had led the expeditions beyond the Rhine in order to keep the barbarians living there in order and discourage them from thinking about attacking the frontiers of the Empire.

The last office held by Clodius Albinus until his death had been his governorship of Britain, which he had taken over no later than in 192.[10] He had commanded there as many as three legions and a great number of auxiliary troops.[11] It is probable that Albinus had taken part in an extensive conspiracy to assassinate the emperor Commodus; his task was probably to maintain order among the troops in Britain and enforce obedience to a new ruler. We have some circumstantial evidence which may indicate to the fact that Clodius Albinus had belonged among the people close to Pertinax. First, most probably he had come from Hadrumetum, which is mentioned in the *Historia Augusta*, and therefore he was an "African", just as Laetus and Severus.[12] Another circumstantial evidence may be the fact that Pertinax' father-in-law, Flavius Sulpitianus, had been condemned to death by Severus as a follower of Clodius Albinus, after the civil war had been finished. It may be some proof of

---

[6] HA, *Clod. Alb.* 6, 2—7.

[7] Cf. G. Alföldy: *Herkunft...*, pp. 25—26.

[8] Dio, LXXII, 8, 1; G. Alföldy: *Herkunft...*, pp. 26, 37.

[9] HA, *Clod. Alb.* 6, 3—4; G. Alföldy: *Herkunft...*, pp. 28—30, 38 on the basis of a reconstruction of the inscription CIL XIII 8598.

[10] A.R. Birley: *The Roman Governors of Britain*. "Epigraphische Studien", Bd. 4 (1967), pp. 77—78; G. Alföldy: *Herkunft...*, pp. 30—31, 38.

[11] Legions: *II Augusta, VI Victrix, XX Valeria Victrix*; the number of the auxiliary troops may have reached even about 50,000 — according to A.J. Graham: *The Numbers...*, p. 629.

[12] HA, *Clod. Alb.* 1, 4; 4, 1; HA, Sev. 11, 3 — the place of birth is of significance here, if we accept the thesis propagated by A.R. Birley: *The Coups...* that the conspiracy to assassinate Commodus was plotted by a party of African origin. The evidence of his descent from Hadrumetum may be the coins relating to the godhead *Saeculum Frugiferum* (RIC IV/I, *Clod. Alb.*, Nos. 8—10 and 12), which are similar to its representations on the coins from Hadrumetum, issued in the reign of Augustus.

the contacts between those two men and the trust that the followers of Pertinax had put in Albinus. The situation had changed only with the death of Pertinax. In view of the unresolved question of succession and the seizure of power by Iulianus, who did not have a broader base of support, the governors of Upper Pannonia and Syria — who had at their disposal considerable numbers of loyal troops — had come forth to fight for the throne. What was the role of Clodius Albinus in those events?

The only account in the sources — which is unambiguous in stating that Albinus' proclaiming himself emperor had taken place almost at the same time as the armies of Severus and Niger proclaimed them emperors — is the *Life of Albinus*.[13] In addition, it gives the wrong information that the fact had taken place in Gaul. Neither Dio nor Herodian mentions that the proclamation of Albinus occurred at the same time as the proclamations of Severus and Niger. Moreover, no single inscription or coin, according to which Albinus would have been presented as emperor in 193, has been found. Besides, if Albinus had indeed been proclaimed emperor in 193, an agreement between him and Severus would have been more difficult, as the proposal to be a *Caesar* to Severus would not have to be attractive for the person who had already become an emperor. All the above-mentioned premises thus indicate that the version included in the *Life of Albinus* (according to which he had been proclaimed emperor by the legions in Britain as early as 193) may arouse doubts and perhaps may have been created by interpolating the events of 196 on to the situation in 193, which was performed by the author of the *Life of Albinus*.[14]

Considering the questions presented above, it may be assumed that in 193 Albinus continued to remain the governor of Britain and controlled the three legions stationed there and a large number of auxiliary troops. Septimius Severus, aware of the fact that in the west of the Empire there is a man with such a great military force at his disposal, had sent to Albinus — before the Imperatorial proclamation or shortly afterwards[15] — an entrusted man,

---

[13] HA, *Clod. Alb.* 1, 1.

[14] For another opinion to this effect, see also J. B a l t y: *Essai...*, pp. 9—10.

[15] Regarding this particular question, the sources do not offer unequivocal explanation. H e r o d i a n (II 15, 1—5) claims that Severus had made the proposal to Albinus only upon his arriving at Rome (after 1 June 193), but this is contradicted by Cassius D i o (LXXXIV 15, 1—2), who is generally a better informed writer; he claims that Severus made the proposal of assuming the position of *Caesar* to Albinus even before the march on Rome. This version is also preferred by historiography, see: M. P l a t n a u e r: *The Life and Reign of the Emperor Lucius Septimius Severus*. London—Edinburgh—Glasgow—New York—Toronto—Melbourne—Cape Town—Bombay 1918, p. 61; J. H a s e b r o e k: *Untersuchungen zur Geschichte des Kaisers Septimius Severus*. Heidelberg 1921, pp. 25—29; A.R. B i r l e y: *The African Emperor Septimius Severus*. London 1988, p. 98; T. K o t u l a: *Septymiusz Sewerus. Cesarz z Lepcis Magna*. Wrocław—Warszawa—Kraków—Gdańsk—Łódź 1987, p. 16.

Aurelius Heraclit,[16] and made a proposal to the governor of Britain that he assume the rank of *Caesar*. Albinus had accepted the proposal and therefore the governor of Upper Pannonia had secured his rears and could march on Rome and then against his most important rival, Pescennius Niger.

But what was the role and scope of authority of Caesar Clodius Albinus in the period when Severus had been fighting in the eastern part of the *Imperium Romanum*. Did he maintain control over the western part of the empire, or was he just a figurehead whose extent of power had been limited to his own province, Britain? In order to resolve this question, an analysis of Albinus' coins with his *Caesar* titulature may prove very helpful.

The Albinus' "caesar" issues had been coined at the Rome mint. However, we know that Rome was captured by Septimius Severus' legions, whereas Albinus had not taken control of the capital. To what extent, then, did Clodius Albinus' coins with the title of *Caesar* reflect his own political programme? We may attempt to solve this problem upon the basis of Herodian's mention, according to which it was Severus who had ordered to have the "caesar" coins minted. On the other hand, however, at the time when Severus had set out on a campaign against Niger, Albinus could have been able, through his followers at Rome, to exert at least some partial influence on the coinage of the mint at the capital.[17]

The best method which may be helpful in attempting to resolve that question will be to analyze the numismatic material and compare the ideological contents represented on the reverse of Albinus' coins issued in 193—195, with those which appear in the Imperatorial coinage of this ruler. Secondly, we ought to find out if there are any correlations with the policy, also a monetary one, conducted by Septimius Severus during the period of the war with Pescennius Niger, because if we assume that it was *Augustus* who decided on the content propagated by his *Caesar*, those relations would be apparently evident.

Among the coins of Clodius Albinus issued in the years 193—195, there are several types of issues which refer directly to *Augustus*. We should list here those with the following inscriptions on the reverse:

a) PROVID. AVG. COS. (and the ases with the inscriptions PROVID. AVG. COS. S.C.)[18]

---

[16] PIR² H, 88—90; A. Birley: *Septimius Severus. The African Emperor*. London 1971, p. 338 (Appendix III).

[17] Such a supposition has been made by V. Zedelius: *Untersuchungen zur Münzprägung von Pertinax bis Clodius Albinus*. Leipzig 1975, p. 75; cf. Herod., II 15, 5; on the basis of the inscription (CIL VIII 26498), C.E. van Sickle: *The Legal...*, p. 125, is of the opinion that Albinus did not possess the tribunal authority, and his position as *Caesar* was very limited.

[18] RIC IV/I, *Clodius Albinus*, p. 44, No. 1 a, b, c; RIC IV/I, *Clodius Albinus*, p. 51, No. 50; further on in the article, with the identical inscriptions on bronze coins, which differ only in the added S.C., the text shall give the version of the inscription from golden or silver coins, whereas the bronze ones will be enumerated only as footnotes.

b) FORTVNAE AVG. COS. II[19]

c) ANNONA AVG. COS. II S.C.[20]

There is no reason to doubt that this *Augustus* is Severus, whose foresight had made him to grant the title of *Caesar* to Albinus (a). The goddess of fortune, Fortuna (b), was to assure him success in his war against Pescennius Niger. In the case of the inscription ANNONA AVG. (c), the characteristic thing is the propagation of *Augustus*' (Severus) good cultivation skills, through invoking the favour of the Roman goddess Annona, personification of good crops, supply of grain to Rome, or provisions for the Army. Interestingly, the coins with the inscriptions ANNONA AVG. do not appear any more in Clodius Albinus' Imperatorial coinage, but they are minted by Septimius Severus.

With a great degree of certainty we may assume that the above-mentioned types of coins had carried out the ideological agenda enforced by Severus, because otherwise there would not have been direct references to his person in the inscriptions.

A different group of coins is that whose inscriptions no longer relate directly to Septimius Severus, yet their propaganda content refers to him. They are as follows:

FORT. REDVCI COS. II[21]

They represent the goddess of fortune holding the helm and the cornucopia (horn of plenty). H. Mattingly and E.A. Sydenham[22] express the opinion that they aroused the hope of Albinus' return from his province *Britannia* to Rome. It is hard, however, to agree with this statement due to the following two reasons: firstly, those issues date back to the year 194 or 195, i.e. to the period when *Augustus* (Severus) had waged his campaign against Pescennius Niger, who ruled the eastern provinces. It is very likely, then, that this does not concern Albinus, but the Emperor's safe return from his expedition to the east; secondly, this particular inscription appears often in the coinage of Septimius Severus exactly in the periods when he had led his campaigns — first against Niger,[23] and then against Albinus.[24] In the Imperatorial coinage of the latter it appears only once, on a bronze coin (*As*).[25]

There is a similar question with the following inscription:

CONCORDIA S.C.[26]

---

[19] RIC IV/I, *Clodius Albinus*, p. 45, No. 6; much less probable is the anticipation of succession, cf. ibidem, p. 41.

[20] Ibidem, p. 52, No. 51.

[21] Ibidem, p. 44, No. 5 a, b; p. 53, Nos. 59, 64.

[22] Ibidem, p. 41.

[23] RIC IV/I, *Septimius Severus*, p. 135, No. 350; p. 138, Nos. 1—5; p. 142, Nos. 376B—383A; p. 143, Nos. 383B—388; p. 150, Nos. 437A, 439; p. 151, No. 440; p. 152, Nos. 448 a, b—453.

[24] Ibidem, p. 155, Nos. 469, 477—479; p. 156, Nos. 479A—479B.

[25] RIC IV/I, *Clodius Albinus*, p. 53, No. 64.

[26] Ibidem, p. 53, Nos. 62—63.

We have no reason to doubt that the coins bearing that inscription on the reverse propagated the idea of concerted co-operation between *Augustus* and *Caesar*.

The above-mentioned examples prove that the actual control over Albinus' actions in the area of political propaganda on coins, was held by Severus, perhaps not directly, but through his entrusted men, who had controlled — on his behalf — the activity of the Rome mint.[27]

However, there are coinages which may indicate the existence of an independent coinage policy of Albinus in the period when he had held the title of Caesar. These are the coins with the following inscriptions on the reverse:

a) SAECVLO FRVGIFERO,[28] SAEC. FRVGIF. COS. II,[29] SAECVLO FRVGIFERO COS. II[30]

b) MINER. PACIF. COS. II,[31] MIN. PAC. COS. II[32]

In the case of the former group (a), we must ascertain that the coins of this type — which represent the youthful figure of a god with an aureole and a caduceus in his right hand and a prong in his left hand — had appeared first with Severus,[33] and therefore their appearing under Albinus had been a re-enactment of this pattern. Interestingly, that motif is no longer present on the Imperatorial coins of the ruler from Lugdunum, which makes us to reflect even more that the authority inspiring the coinage with the inscription SAECVLO FRVGIFERO was, after all, Severus.

We have, however, one peculiar example in this group, on the reverse of which a figure of a godhead can be seen, wearing a head-gear similar to the tiara and a long robe, and sitting on the throne with some ears of corn in his hand. Two sphinxes can be seen on either side of that deity.[34] Possibly, this pattern may be linked to Hadrumetum, the home town of Clodius Albinus,[35] as the similar one can be found on a coin from that town.[36]

---

[27] At Rome, the interests of Severus were taken care of by: C. Domitius Dexter as *praefectus urbi* and Flavius Iuvenalis and Veturius Macrinus as Prefects of the Guard, see A. B i r l e y: *Septimius Severus. The African Emperor*. London 1971, pp. 164, 169—170; L.L. H o w e: *The Pretorian Prefect from Commodus to Diocletian*. Chicago 1942, pp. 68—69; J. F i t z: *The Policy of Septimius Severus in the Military Direction of the Civil War between 193 and 197*. In: *Acta of the Fifth International Congress of Greek and Latin Epigraphy*. Oxford 1971, p. 426; G. V i t u c c i: *Ricerche sulla Praefectura Urbi in età imperiale*. Roma 1956, p. 119.

[28] RIC IV/I, *Clodius Albinus*, p. 45, No. 12.

[29] RIC IV/I, *Clodius Albinus*, p. 45, No. 8.

[30] Ibidem, p. 45, No. 9 (a, b); p. 52, No. 56 (a, b, c); p. 53, No. 61 (a, b).

[31] Ibidem, p. 45, No. 7; p. 52, No. 54 (a, b, c).

[32] Ibidem, p. 48, No. 30; p. 53, No. 60.

[33] RIC IV/I, *Septimius Severus*, p. 93, No. 19; see also: Z. K á d á r: *"Saeculum frugiferum" a Katonacsászárok penzein*. "Numizmatikai Közlöny", 60/71 (1961/1962), p. 23 ff. (Resume 102).

[34] RIC IV/I, *Clodius Albinus*, p. 45, No. 10.

[35] V. Z e d e l i u s: *Untersuchungen...*, p. 76.

[36] W. F r o e h n e r: *Les médaillons de l'empire Romain*. Paris 1878, p. 150.

This does not mean, of course, that the above-mentioned specimen had not been minted at the inspiration of Severus, who may have had a special coinage issued in order to commemorate the town where Albinus was born.

The latter group (b), which represents an image of the goddess Minerva with the helmet on, the shield, spear, and an olive branch in her hand, may refer to the province *Hispania* (Spain), where she was venerated as the deity guarding olive groves.

There is a similar case with the coins with the inscription COS II,[37] representing Asklepios, who may be identified with Apollo Grannus, venerated in Gaul.[38]

The coins bearing the images of Minerva and Asklepios (Apollo Grannus) could actually be an attempt made by Clodius Albinus to gain support among the inhabitants of Spain and Gaul. If that had been done with Severus' consent, we do not know.

We should also bear in mind that whereas the coins referring to the "Minerva bringing peace" appear later on in Albinus' emperor's coinage, the Asklepios (Apollo Grannus) motif was no longer used by him.

Could it be, then, that Albinus — when he had finally stood up openly against Severus — did not care any more about referring to the religious sentiments of the inhabitants of Gaul?[39] Perhaps, that purpose had been fulfilled with the coinage issued at Lugdunum, which had borne the inscription GEN. LVG. COS. II.[40]

Therefore, who may have had an influence on the coinage representing the images of Minerva and Asklepios? It seems likely that it might have been issued at the inspiration of Albinus or his followers at Rome, but that must have been accepted by Severus himself, or by the people he had left at Rome in order to watch over his interests.[41]

There also remains one enigmatic coin with an inscription on the reverse P.M. TR. P. COS. III FEL. P. R., but most probably this specimen is a counterfeit dating back to antiquity.[42]

---

[37] RIC IV/I, *Clodius Albinus*, p. 44, No. 2.

[38] RIC IV/I, p. 41; V. Z e d e l i u s: *Untersuchungen...*, p. 75.

[39] At that time he should have been more considerate in this respect, as Gaul, Britain and Spain constituted Albinus' back-up territories in his war against Severus. In the period when he had been *Caesar*, the provinces of Gaul and Spain had not been probably controlled by him, as indicated by: C.E. van S i c k l e: *The Legal...*, pp. 126—127.

[40] RIC IV/I, *Clodius Albinus*, p. 47, No. 23 (a, b, c, d); p. 48, No. 24.

[41] See at footnote 153.

[42] RIC IV/I, *Clodius Albinus*, p. 46, no. 12A; Mattingly and Sydenham suppose that this is an ancient forgery, for which a stamp with the Hadrian reverse had been used; the possession of tribunal power by Albinus was already excluded by C.E. van S i c k l e: *The Legal...*, p. 125, drawing on the inscription dated 195, in which the titulature of *Augustus* and *Caesar* reads as follows: "Pro salute Imp. Caes. L. Septimi Severi Pertinacis Aug. Parthici — Arabici, Paethici

In view of the analysis presented above, we shall argue that the relevant facts indicate that despite the coinages bearing the image of *Caesar* Decimus Clodius Albinus, the Rome mint had remained in full control of *Augustus* Lucius Septimius Severus. This is confirmed by the already cited Herodian's mention[43] as well as the instances of coincidence of the inscriptions and iconography of Albinus' coins, from the mint at Rome, with those of Severus; on the other hand, there is no continuity in some of the characteristic patterns in the Imperatorial coinage of the emperor from Hadrumetum.

Therefore, we can assume that only the coinage from Lugdunum had been effected under unrestricted control of Clodius Albinus and fully reflected his political programme; consequently, they may be taken into consideration for the purpose of describing the methods he had used to disseminate his propaganda.

It does not seem plausible, then, that at the time when Severus had been leading his campaign against Niger, Albinus had played, as *Caesar*, a more significant role in the western provinces of the Roman Empire. As the analysis presented above shows, he had not been able to control his own coinages issued at Rome.

In spite of the fact that neither Clodius Albinus nor his troops participated directly in the confrontation between Septimius Severus and Pescennius Niger, it is still interesting whether his accord with the governor of Upper Pannonia had caused any Niger's reaction.

We do not have any information in the sources which would allow us to determine if Niger had known of the fact that governor of Britain had become an ally of Severus and assumed the position of *Caesar* to the emperor. We can notice, however, a characteristic strategic decision, taken by Niger during his brief campaign in Europe. It consisted in governor of Syria's crossing over into the continent of Europe and leaving proconsul of Asia Asellius Aemilianus in the territory of Asia Minor,[44] with the task of defending its coasts against a landing by Severus' troops. Keeping in mind that Aemilianus was a kinsman of Clodius Albinus,[45] it could have attested to the fact that either Niger did not know anything about governor of Britain's role in the struggle for imperial power or he had so much trust in Aemilianus' loyalty that he had left him in Asia Minor without any anxiety. In the event of proconsul's betrayal, Niger's

---

— Adiabenici, pont. Max., trib. Potest. III, cos. II, p.p., et D. Clodi Septimi Albini Caes..." (CIL VIII 26498). As it appears, in 195 Albinus did not hold tribunal authority. If we assume that the coin had been struck at Lugdunum at the time when Albinus, already a self-appointed emperor, must have possessed tribunal power, then why the titulature on the obverse presents him as a *Caesar* only?

[43] Herod., II, 15, 5.
[44] Herod., III, 2, 2.
[45] Dio, LXXV, 6, 2.

strategic situation would have been enormously difficult, as he would have to face the overwhelming forces of Severus without the possibility of relying on reinforcements from the east, which would have been stopped by Aemilianus. What is more, in the case of his failure in Europe, Niger would have no way to retreat back to the east.

The argument presented above leads us to the conclusion that at the time of taking the decision on leaving Aemilianus on guard in Asia Minor, Niger probably had not known yet of the role Albinus played in the Septimian camp. Otherwise, considering Aemilianus' family ties, he would have taken him to Europe, because with Aemilianus at his side and being able to control his actions, he could be more confident of the Asian proconsul's loyalty.[46]

After the victory over Pescennius Niger, Severus no longer needed the alliance with Clodius Albinus, who — as Caesar — could be treated as his successor, which evidently stood in the way of Septimius Severus' dynastic plans.

Despite the position of Caesar, Severus had not left for Albinus many official capacities and influences in the western part of the Empire. The arrangement with the governor of Britain was only a tactical move for him, calculated to ensure peace in the west of the Empire at the time when he was himself waging a war against a much more dangerous rival, Pescennius Niger.[47]

Undoubtedly, the initiator of a new war had been Septimius Severus, who had sent assassins to kill Albinus. They had been disclosed and the Caesar could no longer delude himself that he was not standing in the way of Severus' dynastic aspirations. Obviously, it is very likely that a number of senators would favour the governor of Britain on the Roman throne, as Albinus was a representative of a respectable aristocratic family. Perhaps, they had even tried to convince him to take advantage of Severus' engagement in the east and take over the power at Rome. The fact that Albinus had not done such a thing can testify best to his loyalty as Caesar and places the responsibility for starting the war upon Severus' shoulders.

After his return from the east, and claiming the Caesar's disloyalty and intrigues, Severus had led to proclaiming Albinus public enemy. In the aftermath, Severus' elder son, Caracalla, had been acclaimed Caesar at Viminacium.[48]

---

[46] Let us remember that probably Severus had hoped as well that Asellius Aemilianus would come forth to support him; he must have counted on his family ties to Albinus. Severus' bitter disappointment is confirmed by a peculiar hatred which he had, according to the *Historia Augusta account* (Sev. 8, 15), felt for Aemilianus. Doubts as to Asian proconsul's commitment to Niger's cause are also raised by H e r o d i a n (III, 2, 3). The older literature claimed that it was Aemilianus, not Niger, who had led operations over the area between Byzantium and Perinthus (M. P l a t n a u e r: *The Life...*, p. 83), which is contradicted by Dio's account (LXXV, 6, 3), clearly stating that it was Niger who had directed the attack on Perinthus.

[47] H e r o d i a n ' s opinion on Severus' motives was critical (III, 5, 2—8).

[48] As confirmed by the coins (RIC IV/I, *Caracalla*, p. 212, Nos. 1—6; p. 213, Nos. 7—16) and inscriptions (IGRR IV, 566).

The outcome of the war was easy to predict. Despite the fact that Clodius Albinus had at his disposal probably the largest provincial army in the entire Roman Empire,[49] he could not even think of defeating the forces of the whole of the Empire. He must have been aware of that situation, yet he had nothing to lose in the face of Severus' openly hostile stance. He had led, therefore, to proclaiming him *Augustus* by the legions of Britain, and had entered into Gaul after crossing the *Fretum Gallicum* channel. He may have had his chance in convincing the German legions,[50] nevertheless both *Germania Superior* and *Inferior* remained loyal to Septimius Severus. Albinus had only received support from the governor of Spain, Lucius Novius Rufus[51] along with the legion *VII Gemina*, stationed in that province. Besides, the governor of Britain had at his disposal a naval fleet which had made it possible for him to transport the troops from the island to the continent.[52]

Unfortunately, not much can be said about the military operations during that warfare due to scarcity of recorded material, but we know that after Albinus had been declared enemy, he was not waiting idle in Britain, but crossed over to the continent and captured *Gallia Lugdunensis*, whence a governor supporting Severus, Titus Flavius Secundus Filipianus, had fled.[53] From then on, Albinus' headquarters had been at Lugdunum, where the mint started striking off his coins, this time bearing the inscriptions IMP. and AVG. in the titulature.[54]

---

[49] It comprised three legions of Britain (*leg. II Augusta, leg. VI Victrix* and *leg. XX Valeria*) as well as 35,000 soldiers of auxiliary troops — A.R. Birley: *The African...*, p. 124; A.J. Graham: *The Numbers...*, p. 629 mentions that the number of *auxilia* in Britain may have been even up to 50,000; none of the three-legion provinces had such a high number of auxiliary troops.

[50] Because Albinus had been governor of *Germania Inferior* in the period ca. 189—191 — G. Alföldy: *Herkunft...*, pp. 19—38.

[51] PIR2 N, 189 — at that time he was governor of the province *Hispania Citerior*, also known as *Hispania Tarraconensis* since Augustus' reign; his participation among the supporters of Albinus is not certain, but it is somehow indicated by not mentioning the *leg. VII Gemina* in Severus' coinage and the fact that Novius Rufus had fallen victim during the persecution of Albinus' followers after the end of the Civil War (HA, *Sev.* 13, 7).

[52] It was *Classis Britannica*, used to transport soldiers and provisions on to the island, defended the coasts against attacks from the sea, and also enabled the trade between the island and the continent; this question has been discussed in detail by W. Kaczanowicz: *Classis Britannica*. "Annales Universitatis Marie Curie-Skłodowska. Sectio F — Historia. Terra, mare et homines", 49 (1994), pp. 199—207.

[53] PIR2 F, No. 362; ILS 1152; G. Alföldy: *Septimius Severus und der Senat*. "Bonner Jahrbücher", 168 (1968), p. 139.

[54] Along with the change in Albinus' status, the contents of the propaganda displayed on his coins had changed as well. While his Roman coinages were, as we know, under overwhelming influence of Severus, the propaganda displayed on the coins issued at Lugdunum had corresponded in full to Albinus' own political programme.

By analyzing the coinage of Albinus at Lugdunum, we can shed a great deal of light upon the political programme of the Gaulian emperor. Three categories of contents are displayed on his coins. The inscriptions appearing on the reverse of the first one of the three groups refer to the provinces supporting Albinus in his confrontation with Severus.[55]

The second group of the coins propagated the virtues which the emperor wished to emanate among his subjects. Their inscriptions and titulature referred to the deities being personifications of those virtues.[56]

The propaganda content propagated by the third group of the coins was connected directly with the military operations during his war against Severus. Albinus had cared in particular about ensuring loyalty of his troops[57] and presenting himself as invincible and fortunate commander,[58] favoured by the gods traditionally associated at Rome with warfare and the military.[59]

---

[55] The coins displaying the inscriptions MIN. PAC. COS. II (RIC IV/I, *Clodius Albinus*, p. 48, No. 30) and GN. LVG. COS. II (RIC IV/I, *Clodius Albinus*, p. 47, No. 23 (a, b, c, d), p. 48, No. 24). Goddess Minerva, the peace-bringer, was worshipped in Spain, while the reference to Lugdunum, through its personification, as to a deity, had reflected a significance of *Gallia Lugdunensis* and its capital in Albinus' policy. It had been also an expression of complimenting the inhabitants of the province, which had supported Albinus in his struggle for the throne. Interestingly, we do not find any coins that would refer to Britain. Possibly, Albinus' position in that territory may have been secure enough, so that he had not needed any additional actions in terms of propaganda.

[56] The invocations to the deities: Aequitas, Felicitas, Fortuna, Moneta, Pax, Providentia, Salus, Spes, are also found in the reign of other emperors and this is the cannon repeated frequently by a number of rulers throughout the history of the Roman Empire. It is worth mentioning the coins with the inscription CLEMENTIA AVG. COS. II (RIC IV/I, *Clodius Albinus*, p. 46, No. 14); they are not found among the coins minted for any of the pretenders to the imperial throne in the years 193—197, except for Albinus. The personification of clemency (Clementia) or concord (Concordia) is displayed on the coin of Iulia Domna, Severus' wife, (RIC IV/I, *Julia Domna*, p. 173, No. 600), but this is not surprising as those characteristics were traditionally attributed to women. Therefore, why did Albinus refer to such "unmanly" features of character? Perhaps, that was a propaganda move aimed at Severus, who was regarded as vengeful and cruel. Portraying Albinus as a gentle and benevolent man may have resulted in a greater number of adherents among the people tired of the atrocities of the civil war or afraid of Severus' violent retaliation. The receivers of such content may have been, in particular, senators and representatives of the richest classes of society, concerned by Severus' proclivity to confiscate property.

[57] FIDES AVG. COS. II (RIC IV/I, *Clodius Albinus*, p. 47, Nos. 17—18); FIDES LEGION. COS. II (RIC IV/I, *Clodius Albinus*, p. 47, Nos. 19—20 a, b, c).

[58] FORTITVDO AVG. INVICTA (RIC IV/I, *Clodius Albinus*, p. 47, No. 21); VIRTVTI AVG. COS. II and VIRTVTI AVGVSTI (RIC IV/I, *Clodius Albinus*, p. 51, No. 48(a, b)—49).

[59] IOVI VICTORI COS. II and IOVIS VICTORIAE COS. II (RIC IV/I, *Clodius Albinus*, p. 48, Nos. 25—27; see also: P.V. Hill: *Aspects of Jupiter on Coins of the Rome Mint, A.D. 65—318*. "Numismatic Chronicle" ser. VI, Vol. 20 (1960), pp. 113—128; MAR. VLT. COS. II and MARS PTER COS. II (RIC IV/I, *Clodius Albinus*, p. 48, Nos. 28—29); VICT. AVG. COS. II (RIC IV/I, *Clodius Albinus*, p. 50, Nos. 43 (a, b, c, d)—46; p. 51, No. 47).

The main recipients of the coins issued at Lugdunum were probably legionaries, as indicated by an overwhelming majority of *denarii* (only two types are *aurei*,[60] while ases are exceptionally rare coins[61]). It was in *denarii* that the soldiers received their pay and that was why those coins were so prevalent. The *aurei* would have been, in that case, a currency with too much of a buying power, as for soldiers' daily needs, while bronze coins would be bound to pose too much inconvenience due to their considerable weight.[62]

This proves the importance of a problem that the candidates to the imperial throne had to deal with, namely concern for the favour of soldiers; they were practically the only social class upon whom success in the struggle for the imperial purple had come to depend.[63]

Clodius Albinus did not have, however, any actual chance to win in the war against Severus, who had at his disposal an overwhelming advantage in the number of the legions supporting him. He had to stand up and fight, because, after Severus' troops had considered him enemy, he had nothing to lose. He could, of course, rely on the support of many senators, but in the reality of the late-second-century Empire, such support did not have any practical significance.

Persuading the four German legions may have offered a certain chance, but they had remained loyal to Severus.[64] It was exactly the direction that the offensive of Albinus' troops after seizing *Gallia Lugdunensis*, had taken. Albinus had forgone marching on Rome,[65] as he would not gain anything by seizing the capital. Instead, he had turned east, towards *Gallia Belgica*, *Germania Superior* and *Inferior*. Most probably, he wanted to capture as vast a territory as possible in the west of the Empire, which could have persuaded the governors of *Germania Superior* and *Inferior* to support his cause. A growing number of military successes would strengthen the prestige of a victorious Albinus, as well as the support among his troops.

We do not have more detailed accounts regarding the actions undertaken by Albinus after the capture of Lugdunum. However, we know from Cassius Dio's account that he had defeated the governor of Lower Germania, Virius

---

[60] RIC IV/I, *Clodius Albinus*, p. 48, Nos. 24—25.

[61] RIC IV/I, *Clodius Albinus*, p. 53, No. 64.

[62] This question, along with the relevant current state of research, has been discussed by A. Kunisz: *Wojny a pieniądz. Z badań nad obiegiem srebrnej monety na wschodnim pograniczu Imperium Rzymskiego w epoce Sewerów (193—235)*. Katowice 1998, pp. 16—17.

[63] The role of soldiers in the attaining of imperial power has been discussed in detail by J.B. Campbell: *The Emperor and the Roman Army 31BC — AD235*. Oxford 1984.

[64] Even with the four German legions on Albinus side, Severus would still have had the advantage over his adversary.

[65] Severus had ordered to man the Alpine passes to secure Italy (Herod., III, 6, 10). This task had been entrusted to the commander of one of the newly formed Parthian legions, Caius Iulius Pacatianus (CIL XII 1865).

Lupus and killed a great number of soldiers.[66] At the same time, one of the legions of *Germania Inferior*, the *XXX Ulpia*, which did not possess the cognomen *pia fidelis*, had already borne it in 207,[67] and therefore it must have received that cognomen during the war against Albinus. This proves that the first target of the army of the governor of Britain after the capture of Lugdunum was *Germania Inferior*. The next step taken by Albinus was an attack on *Gallia Belgica*, where his troops had laid a siege of Treverorum, defended by divisions of the *XXII Primigenia*.[68] He had not managed, however, to capture the city, which was Albinus' first major setback during that war. The above-mentioned facts attest that Albinus' plans to persuade the legions of *Germania* to support him, had come to nothing. The armies from both Germanias had continued to remain loyal to Severus and had taken on the burden of fighting against the army of Albinus, before the troops led by Severus had entered Gaul.

Returning from the east, the emperor had arrived at Rome for a short time, which may attest that he was troubled by the senators' support for Albinus and probably that visit was intended to remind the members of the *curia* who the real emperor is.[69]

Severus had not stayed at Rome for too long[70] and moved through Pannonia,[71] Noricum and Raetia to *Germania Superior*. From there he had marched together with his army towards Albinus' headquarters at Lugdunum.

In the vicinity of this city the crucial battle between the armies of *Augustus* and his erstwhile *Caesar*, had taken place. According to Cassius Dio, 150,000 soldiers on each side took part in the battle,[72] which would add up to the total number of 300,000 fighting soldiers. It appears that this number is definitely

---

[66] Dio, LXXVI, 6, 2.

[67] ILS 9493; G.J. M u r p h y: *The Reign of the Emperor L. Septimius Severus from the Evidence of the Inscriptions.* Philadelphia 1945, p. 19.

[68] CIL XII 6800; G.J. M u r p h y: *The Reign of the Emperor L. Septimius Severus from the Evidence of the Inscriptions.* Philadelphia 1945, p. 19. The town Treverorum may be, most likely, identified with Augusta Trevirorum in *Gallia Belgica*.

[69] In this expedition to Rome Severus was accompanied with the *vexillationes* under the command of Lucius Fabius Cilo (CIL VI 1408).

[70] According to A.R. B i r l e y's findings (*The African...*, pp. 123—124), who had analyzed the Code of Iustinian, there are some extant rescripts to be considered: one from 195, one dated 1 January, 196, one dated 30 June, 196, and as many as ten from the period 1 October — 29 December, 196; this may attest to the fact that Severus had been staying at Rome in the autumn of 196 and moved to Gaul in late autumn or early winter.

[71] Allegedly, the augures there had presented to him a prophecy of his victory in that war, and that his enemy would die near water (HA, Sev. 10, 7); see also: G. A l f ö l d y: *Pannoniciani augures.* "Acta Antiqua Academiae Scientiarum Hungaricae", 8 (1960), pp. 145—164 = *Die Krise des Römischen Reiches. Geschichte, Geschichtsschreibung und Geschichtsbetrachtung.* Stuttgart 1989, pp. 139—163.

[72] Dio, LXXVI, 6, 1.

too high[73] and thus Cassius Dio's mention should rather be understood as a joint number of 150,000 soldiers on both sides.[74]

The troops of Albinus consisted of the three legions from Britannia and, most probably, one legion from *Hispania Tarraconensis*,[75] along with a great number of *auxilia*.[76] Also, the soldiers of urban cohorts, stationed at Lugdunum as protection of the mint located in the city, may have constituted some reinforcement.[77] Even though we know from Herodians' account that Albinus had sent off letters with requests for assistance to the governors of all the western provinces, we do not have any clues, except in the case of Novius Rufus, to presume that any of the western governors had come to aid Albinus with his military assistance.[78]

The troops from the entire Empire had come to square up to the army of the governor of Britain, though of course not all of them could have taken active part in the combat. The eastern legions had remained at their positions, safeguarding the imperial frontier against attacks of Parthians and their allies. The troops from both Germanias also must have remained in place. They formed a sort of cordon around the provinces supporting Albinus.[79] However, Severus had at his disposal a formidable force of the two newly formed *Parthica* legions,[80] four legions from Moesia, which had already taken part in the siege of Byzantium, five legions from Pannonia, two from Dacia, and two from Raetia and Noricum. This would present a powerful force of fifteen legions, along with a certain, difficult to determine, number of auxiliary troops. We also ought to add the newly established Praetorian Guard that accompanied the emperor. Obviously, it would be hard to assume that Severus

---

[73] Cf. A.J. Graham: *The Numbers...*, pp. 625—630.

[74] The distortion as to the number of troops must have occurred during Xyphilinos' compiling of Dio's work, as noticed by A.J. Graham: *The Numbers...*, p. 625.

[75] The participation of the *Legio VII Gemina* in the battle is not sure, but the support of the governor of *Hispania Tarraconensis* for Albinus may suggest just that, even though the fact that he had been granted the title *pia* attests to the contrary (A.R. Birley: *The African...*, p. 126).

[76] Cf. footnote 49, also from Spain, as well as the *Legio VII Gemina* (if we assume that the troops of that province had supported Albinus), an indefinite number of auxiliary troops may have arrived.

[77] G.W. Webster: *The Roman Imperial Army of the First and Second Centuries A.D.* Norman 1998, p. 99.

[78] Even though we have an inscription of Tiberius Claudius Candidus, which says that he was "[...] *adversus rebelles h(omines) h(ostes) p(opuli) R(omani) item Asiae, item Noricae*[...]", and which may suggest that there were Albinus' followers in Noricum as well, this is not sufficient evidence to consider the *Legio II Italica* as part of Albinus' army, as seemingly suggested by A.J. Graham: *The Numbers...*, p. 628, note 24. Noricum was separated from Gallia Lugdunensis, by Raetia and Germania Superior, and therefore it would be difficult to connect the *Legio II Italica* with Albinus' troops.

[79] A.R. Birley: *The African...*, p. 125.

[80] One of them had guarded, as we know, the passes in the *Alpes Cottiae* under the command of Caius Iulius Pacatianus (CIL XII 1865).

had stripped half of the empire of the troops stationed there in order to lead them against Albinus. Some detachments from those 15 legions must have remained in the provinces, but at any rate we should assume that at Lugdunum Severus commanded an overwhelming military force. Besides, he could rely on the reinforcement in the form of legions from *Germania*, which had moved towards Lugdunum as soon as the danger of Albinus' offensive subsided.

The first clash between the troops of Albinus and Severus had taken place at Tinurtium, where the soldiers of Severus had won their first victory, forcing the enemy to retreat towards near Lugdunum. That was where a crucial battle was bound to take place, a battle which was to decide the fate of Clodius Albinus.

The course of the battle is difficult to re-create, due to insufficient and contradictory information in the sources.[81] Herodian and Cassius Dio, whose accounts are our main source of information, both emphasize an unusual fury with which Albinus' troops had faced up to the army of Septimius Severus. On the flank where Severus himself had been, the units of his adversary had attacked with such vehemence that Severus' troops had started to flee, together with their commander-in-chief. Cassius Dio mentions that the emperor himself had persuaded his soldiers to return to the battle-field. This is the official pro-Severus version of the events. On the contrary, Herodian presents a pro-Albinus version,[82] according to which Severus himself had started to flee, throwing off his imperial cloak to avoid being recognized. He had fallen off his horse so that it seemed he had been killed. At that moment, new reinforcements commended by Laetus had appeared on the battle-field.[83] According to Herodian's and Dio's accounts, he had been waiting with his troops near the battle-ground and joined the fight only when it seemed that Severus had been killed. Perhaps, Laetus had wanted to win the imperial throne for himself, coming to rescue the army of Severus after its leader's alleged death. It seems probable in view of the fact that during the second Parthian campaign Laetus had been sentenced to death,[84] which could have been due to the fact that he had fallen into disfavour with Severus.

---

[81] Dio, LXXVI, 6, 1—8; H e r o d., III, 7, 2—6; HA, *Sev.* 11, 1—9; although the latter source does not mention Lugdunum directly.

[82] Z. R u b i n (*Civil War. Propaganda and Historiography*. Bruxelles 1980, pp. 125—126) is of the opinion that this may have been a version propagated by a group of senators hostile to Severus and favourable to Albinus.

[83] PIR² L 69; at Lugdunum, Laetus commanded a contingent of cavalry. Most probably, he is the Iulius Laetus who had previously led the avant-garde of Severus' troops crossing into Italy against Didius Iulianus, and then in Mesopotamia, in 195, he commanded one of the columns of the army penetrating the territories of Adiabena and Osrhoene.

[84] H e r o d., III, 7, 4; Severus tended to hold grudges — he rewarded favours done to him and took revenge for betrayals; therefore, it is hard to presume that he would cause the death of a person who had saved him, from an inevitable defeat. Most likely, therefore, Herodians thesis explaining the strange procrastination in Laetus actions at Lugdunum, is true.

It is an extremely interesting question, as it would mean that nearly four years after his imperial proclamation, Severus' authority among his own soldiers and commanders had not been solid enough to be sure of absolute loyalty of his soldiers. This throws a completely different light upon the cruelty with which he quelled any opposition to his power. It did not stem, perhaps, from his character, as the sources try to convince us,[85] but from the necessity of maintaining authority among his subordinates. Any kind of weakness on his part could have been used by them in order to oust him from power.

Regardless of the motives guiding Laetus, his appearance at the battle-field had tipped the scales of victory in favour of the Septimians. Albinus' army, surprised by the appearance of fresh units of the adversary, had started to retreat rapidly, chased by Severus' victorious soldiers. Lugdunum had been seized and burned; during those events Albinus had died.[86]

The death of his rival to the throne did not mean for Severus that the civil war was coming to an end. He had to crush the resistance of the last remaining troops supporting Albinus in the provinces of *Germania* and *Hispania*.[87]

It was only after the last resistance had ceased that Severus commenced a ruthless purge among the followers of his rivals. It is significant as it was only then that final purge of Pescennius Niger's supporters had been carried out.

As we know, perhaps out of care for public opinion, Severus had, after the defeat of Niger, treated his followers fairly leniently. He spared the lives of the eastern pretender's wife and sons, who had been condemned to exile. The senators supporting him were only punished with confiscation of their property (except for Aemilianus), while the legionaries from the east had received amnesty.

It was only after defeating Albinus, when he faced no more real danger to his power, the emperor had begun to carry out widespread repressions against the followers of all his rivals in the civil war. Niger's wife and sons, still living on exile, had not been spared, and those senators who had any connection with Albinus or Niger had been condemned to death. The *Historia Augusta* mentions the names of many members of the *Curia* who had fallen victim to

---

[85] For instance: H e r o d., III, 8, 6—8; HA, *Sev.* 13, 9.

[86] Dio, LXXVI, 7, 3 writes that Albinus had hidden himself in his house at Lugdunum, but when he had, seen that he had been surrounded, he committed suicide; on the other hand, H e r o d i a n claims (III, 7, 7) that Severus men had captured Albinus and beheaded him; the *Historia Augusta* gives the date of this event — 19 February, 197.

[87] HA, *Sev.* 12, 5; the evidence of the fighting in *Germania* is a dedication for the emperor made by the inhabitants of Magnesia (IGRR IV 1337), where it appears in the titulature of Severus as Γερμανικός; G.J. M u r p h y: *The Reign...*, p. 6; Tiberius Claudius Candidus had become a new governor of *Hispania Tarraconensis*; in the *Historia Augusta* (*Sev.* 12) we have a mention (which is hard to verify) that the mutiny against Severus was also raised by the legion *III Cyrenaica* from Arabia.

proscriptions.[88] As it appears, it was only with the total defeat of his last rival that the process of pacification of the Niger camp had been terminated. We cannot, therefore, divide the period of the Civil War 193—197 into phases of confrontation with Niger and then Albinus.[89] The roles played by both of these figures in the events in question are inseparably connected. At the time when Severus had been fighting his war against Niger's armies, Albinus had been holding the rank of *Caesar*, and without his good will and loyalty it would have been hard for the Septimians to defeat the legions from the east of the Empire.

Conversely, preparing for his final confrontation with Albinus, Severus must have postponed his revenge on the supporters of Pescennius Niger, so that with this deceiving benevolence he could "buy" peace in the eastern provinces during the time when his armies had been fighting in Gaul.

As regards the final stand-off with all the followers of the defeated rivals, Severus had deferred action until the time when, after Albinus' defeat at Lugdunum, there had been nobody who could pose a real threat to his power.

---

[88] HA, *Sev.* 13, 1—9.

[89] Due to low intensity of fighting, it is hard to call the conflict with Didius Iulian a warfare.

Translated by Marcin Fijak

Rafał Butor

DECYMUS KLODIUSZ ALBIN W WOJNIE DOMOWEJ Z LAT 193—197

Streszczenie

Decymus Klodiusz Albin, namiestnik Brytanii z racji złożoności relacji, jakie wiązały go z Sewerem, i popularności, zwłaszcza wśród arystokracji senatorskiej, wydaje się interesującym badawczo uczestnikiem zmagań o tron cesarski w wojnie domowej z lat 193—197.

Należał on do tego samego pokolenia rzymskich wodzów i polityków co jego dwaj konkurenci: Septymiusz Sewer i Pescenniusz Niger. Podobnie jak oni przechodził różne szczeble kariery wojskowej oraz senatorskiej, m.in. był dowódcą legionu *V Macedonica* w Dacji, namiestnikiem Dolnej Germanii i wreszcie namiestnikiem Brytanii.

Istnieją poszlaki, które mogą wskazywać, że Albin należał do szerokiego grona ludzi powiązanych ze spiskiem na życie cesarza Kommodusa, trudno jednakże rozstrzygnąć tę kwestię ostatecznie z racji braku jednoznacznych wzmianek w źródłach.

Można natomiast z dużą dozą pewności przyjąć, że Albin nie został obwołany cesarzem przez swoje wojska w 193 roku równocześnie z Sewerem i Nigrem. To Septymiusz Sewer, ruszając do walki z Pescenniuszem Nigrem, złożył Albinowi propozycję objęcia funkcji cezara i tym samym zabezpieczył sobie tyły, mając świadomość dużego potencjału militarnego, jakim rozporządzał namiestnik Brytanii. Obwołanie Albina cesarzem nastąpiło dopiero po rozstrzygnięciu wojny Sewera z Nigrem i było wynikiem jawnej wrogości, jaką Sewer zaczął okazywać swemu dotychczasowemu sojusznikowi.

W okresie, w którym namiestnik Brytanii zadowalał się funkcją cezara przy Sewerze, nie odgrywał faktycznie żadnej poważniejszej roli w zachodniej części imperium opanowanej przez Sewera, o czym najlepiej świadczy fakt, że nie kontrolował nawet swych „cezariańskich" emisji monetarnych wybijanych w Rzymie. Po analizie materiału numizmatycznego ustalono, że mennica rzymska, w tym jej emisje dla Albina, znajdowały się pod kontrolą Septymiusza Sewera. Poza wzmianką Herodiana przemawiają za tym wnioskiem zarówno korelacja pomiędzy treściami propagandowymi tych emisji oraz działaniami samego Sewera, jak przykłady zbieżności legend oraz ikonografii monet Klodiusza Albina z tego okresu z monetami Sewera. Z drugiej strony brak jest kontynuacji niektórych wzorów na monetach Albina z Lugdunum, co do których nie ma wątpliwości, że powstały już pod jego wyłącznym nadzorem. Dopiero więc emisje z Lugdunum, wybijane po obwołaniu Albina cesarzem, odzwierciedlały jego program polityczny.

W czasie konfliktu Sewera z Nigrem Albin nie odgrywał żadnej militarnej roli, ale mógł mieć wpływ na sytuację swojego krewnego prokonsula Azji Aselliusza Emiliana odgrywającego pierwszoplanową rolę wśród stronników Pescenniusza Nigra. Wydaje się, że wschodni pretendent do tronu albo nie wiedział o porozumieniu Albina z Sewerem, albo dalece ufał Emilianowi, ponieważ przeprawiając się z wojskiem do Europy, pozostawił go na straży Azji Mniejszej. W razie zdrady prokonsula Azji sytuacja Nigra byłaby tragiczna gdyż musiałby stawić czoło przeważającym siłom Sewera, a na posiłki ze wschodu nie mógłby liczyć, gdyż zatrzymałby je Emilian. Co więcej, w razie niepowodzenia w Europie Niger miałby odciętą drogę odwrotu na wschód.

Rozważając z kolei kwestię konfliktu Sewera z Albinem, można zauważyć, że rezultat zmagań był łatwy do przewidzenia. Mimo że namiestnik Brytanii dysponował prawdopodobnie największą armią prowincjonalną w całym imperium, to jednak nie mógł myśleć o zwycięstwie nad siłami całego prawie Cesarstwa Rzymskiego, którymi rozporządzał Sewer. Cesarza z Lugdunum poparł jedynie namiestnik Hiszpanii Tarrakońskiej Nowiusz Rufus wraz ze stacjonującym tam legionem *VII Gemina*. Fiaskiem natomiast zakończyła się próba pozyskania dla sprawy Albina czterech legionów germańskich, a to właśnie one przyjęły na siebie ciężar zmagań z armią Albina, zanim do Galii wkroczyły wojska, które prowadził ze sobą Sewer.

Decydująca bitwa pod Lugdunum zakończyła się klęską i śmiercią Albina, tym samym Sewer pozostał jedynym panem Imperium Romanum. Krótko po tym cesarz rozpoczął rozprawę ze stronnikami swych konkurentów do tronu, wśród których było wielu zwolenników Decymusa Klodiusza Albina.

Rafał Butor

DECIMUS CLODIUS ALBINUS ET LA GUERRE CIVILE EN 193—197

Résumé

Decimus Clodius Albinus, le proconsul de la Bretagne, semble être un participant particulièrement intéressant des luttes pour le titre impérial pendant la guerre civile en 193—197 à cause de la complexité des relations qui le liaient à Sévère et la popularité dans le milieu du sénat.

Il appartenait à la même génération des chefs militaires et politiques que ses deux concurrents : Septime Sévère et Pescennius Niger. Comme eux, Albinus passait par tous les rangs de la carrière militaire et politique, entre autres il a été le commandant de la légion *V Macedonica* en Dacie, proconsul en Germanie et enfin proconsul en Bretagne.

Certains indices suggèrent qu'Albinus appartienne à un large groupe des comploteurs qui ont organisé un coup d'état contre l'empereur Commode, cependant il est difficile de juger l'équité de cette théorie manque de données dans les sources.

Nous pouvons cependant admettre qu'Albin n'étaient pas proclamé empereur par ses troupes en 193 parallèlement avec Sévère et Nigre. C'est Septime Sévère qui, en voulant se débarrasser de Pescennius Niger, a proposé à Albin le titre de César et ainsi consolidait sa position en bénéficiant de l'effectif puissant de l'armée dirigée par le proconsul de la Bretagne. L'intronisation d'Albin a lieu après la guerre de Sévère contre Niger et était le résultat d'une malveillance déclarée que Sévère commençait à manifester envers son ancien allié.

Durant la période où le proconsul de la Bretagne se contentait de la fonction de César, il ne jouait aucun rôle important auprès de Sévère et dans les provinces d'ouest, gouvernées par lui. La preuve en est qu'il ne contrôlait même pas ses monnayages césariens à Rome. Après une analyse numismatique nous constatons que la Monnaie romaine, y compris l'émission pour Albin, se trouvait sous le contrôle de Septime Sévère. Outre une remarque chez Herodianus, une corrélation entre les agissements de Sévère et sa propagande soutient cette thèse, en plus on observe une convergence des légendes et de l'iconographie de la monnaie de Clodius Albinus et celle de Sévère. Mais il n'y a pas de continuation de certains modèles de la monnaie d'Albinus, fabriquée à Lugdunum, qui sûrement étaient battues sous sa surveillance personnelle. Alors seulement l'émission de Lugdunum, battue après l'intronisation d'Albin, reflétait son programme politique.

Pendant le conflit entre Sévère et Niger, Albin ne jouait aucun rôle militaire, mais il pouvait influencer la situation de son parent, le proconsul de l'Asie, Asellius Emilianus, qui était un des premiers alliés de Perscennius Niger. Il nous semble que le prétendent oriental au trône soit ne savait rien sur l'alliance entre Albin et Sévère, soit il avait une confiance aveugle en Emilianus, car il a décidé de traverser avec l'armée en Europe, en le laissant en garde de L'Asie Mineure. Au cas de la trahison de la part du proconsul de l'Asie, la situation de Niger serait tragique car il devrait affronter les légions de Sévère et il ne pourrait compter sur le secours de l'est, arrêtés par Emilianus. En plus, en situation de défaite, le chemin de retour à l'est serait découpé.

En examinant la question du conflit entre Sévère et Albin, on peut constater que son résultat était facile à prévoir. Bien que le proconsul de la Bretagne ait disposé d'une armée la plus puissante dans tout l'empire, il ne pouvait pas rêver d'un triomphe sur des légions de tout l'Empire Romain, dirigés par Sévère. Seul le proconsul de l'Espagne à Tarracone, Novius Rufus avec la légion y stationnant *VII Gemina*, soutenait le césar de Lugdunum. La tentative de gagner l'assistance de quatre légions germaniques n'a pas réussi, même au contraire, ces soldats luttaient contre l'armée d'Albin avant l'arrivée des légions de Sévère.

La bataille décisive de Lugdunum termine par la faillite et la mort d'Albin, ainsi Sévère demeure le seul gouverneur de l'Empire Romain et commence le combat contre les partisans de ses concurrents parmi lesquels on trouvait de nombreux alliés de Decimus Clodius Albinus.

PRZEMYSŁAW DYRLAGA

The Emperor Macrinus and the Senate

with an Appendix:
Macrinus — Caracalla's Murderer
Truth or Forgery of Elagabalus
and Severus Alexander Propaganda?

In the period from Augustus to the Severi (27 BC — AD 235) the composition and status of the Roman Senate and the *ordo senatorius* had undergone a substantial evolution.[1] The proportions between the number of the Italic-born and the provincial senators had changed. The latter had been growing in number due to an advantageous policy of some of the emperors. Also, the proce-

---

[1] On the role of the Senate in the imperial period, relations between the Senate and the emperors, and transformations within the senatorial estate, extensively in: M. Hammond: *The Composition of the Senate, A.D. 68—235.* "Journal of Roman Studies", Vol. 47 (1957), pp. 74—81; F. Millar: *The Emperor in the Roman World (31 BC—AD 337).* London 1977, p. 290 ff., esp. pp. 341—355; R.J.A. Talbert: *The Senate of Imperial Rome.* Princeton 1984, in particular pp. 163—174; D. Kienast: *Der "heilige" Senat. Senatskult und "kaiserlicher" Senat.* "Chiron", Bd. 15 (1985), pp. 253—282; A. Chastagnol: *Le sénat romain á l'époque impériale. Recherches sur la composition de l'Assembleé et le statut de ses members.* Paris 1992; G. Alföldy: *Historia społeczna starożytnego Rzymu.* Poznań 1998, pp. 158—166, 216—220 (earlier literature in these items). Cf. also interesting comments on the position and role of the Senate by E. Dąbrowa in the study: *"Victoriae senatus romani". Senat a cesarze w latach 235—260.* W: "Historia i Współczesność". T. 3: *Problemy schyłku świata antycznego.* Red. A. Kunisz. Katowice 1978, pp. 28—51.

dure known as *adlectio* had appeared, by which the successive rulers had introduced their own entrusted men into the ranks of the senators. They formed the group of *homines novi*, whose position was owed solely to the emperor's grace, their own abilities and ambitions as well as long-standing and loyal service in the administration or the army, but not to their origin.[2] It is also obvious that this had an effect on the relations of those *nouveaux riches* with the representatives of the old senatorial families (who did not like the class of those "new rich"). Those changes were accompanied by a division of the highest social class into a number of circles with diverse views as to their own role in the state. Whereas some of them nurtured old-time, and already anachronistic, traditions of republican provenance, others believed that they had been called to rule jointly with the emperor. There were also those who were content with the role of obedient tools in the hands of the ruler, primarily focused on their own interest in taking advantage of the privileges bestowed on their estate and looking out for the benefits in accepting a new reality. All of this, however, had not changed one thing — the Senate continued, at least formally, to remain one of the primary institutions of the Roman state, whose favours were often sought by the rulers, and which, though only nominally (but in exceptional cases also in actual fact), decided on the most significant matters of the Empire. The Senate also continued to remain an institution which had to confirm the legitimacy of each emperor's power.

Even though the significance of the *ordo equester* was increasing, the emperors were trying to gain favour with the senators as it was from among them that top-ranking military commanders and state officials were recruited; their loyalty constituted a guarantee of the endurance of the imperial power as well as an undisturbed reign. However, some of the rulers were not hindered in their endeavours to "purge" the Senate — as the Severi did — and eliminate the opposition within, especially when it had gained too many followers.[3]

---

[2] On *adlectio and homines novi*, see: F. Millar: *The Emperor in the Roman World...*, pp. 293—297; R.J.A. Talbert: *The Senate...*, pp. 15—16, 20, 133—134, 245—246; J.-P. Coriat: *Les homes nouveaux à l'epoque des Sévères.* "Revue historique du droit française et étranger", Vol. 56 (1978), pp. 5—27; A. Chastagnol: *"Latus clavus" et "Adlectio". L'accès des hommes nouveaux au Sénat romain sous le Haut-Empire.* Dons: *Des ordres à Rome.* Ed. C. Nicolet. Paris 1984, pp. 199—216.

[3] Concerning the relations between the Severi and the Senate, see: G. Alföldy: *Septimius Severus und der Senat.* "Bonner Jahrbücher", Bd. 168 (1968), pp. 112—160; Idem: *Der Sturz des Kaisers Geta und die Antike Geschichtsschreibung.* In: Idem: *Die Krise des Römischen Reiches. Geschichte, Geschichtsschreibung und Geschichtsbetrachtung. Ausgewählte Beiträge.* Stuttgart 1989, pp. 203—208; Idem: *Historia społeczna...*, p. 218 ff.; T. Kotula: *Septymiusz Sewerus. Cesarz z Lepcis Magna.* Wrocław 1987, pp. 89—99; A. Birley: *The African Emperor: Septimius Severus.* London 1988, passim; S. Sillar: *Caracalla and the Senate: the aftermath of Geta's Assassination.* "Athenaeum", Vol. 89 (2001), pp. 407—423.

In spite of all those changes, and the loss of the position of the real deci-sion-maker in the state to the emperor's advantage, the Senate in the imperial era was still regarded as an extraordinarily splendid, timeless symbol of the permanence and power of the state as well as a significant opinion-forming factor. It should be added here, however, that most of the extant historiogra-phical works from the period of Imperial Rome are of the senatorial prove-nance and as such they represent the viewpoint of those circles (e.g. the accounts of Tacitus, Suetonius, Cassius Dio), while the rest of them are more or less dependant on that tradition (e.g. the work of Herodianus and *Historia Augusta*). Thus the senatorial circles had, and frequently continue to have, a tremendous influence on the shaping of the image of the successive rulers of the Empire. In other words, we look at the Roman emperors and their actions through the eyes of the representatives of the Senate, with their own political options, world-view, and attitudes to particular rulers. In late antiquity it was particularly reflected in the division into the "bad" and "good" emperors.[4] It should be emphasized, however, that a designation into either group was decided by the attitude of an author of an ancient account, and through that author by certain circles of the senatorial estate, to the emperor and the actions he had undertaken. Consequently, that division basically reflects the division of the emperors into those who co-operated with the Senate and those whose attitude to this institution was at least not too favourable, although in some cases it is not consistent — primarily due to the *damnatio memoriae* of the rulers.

The procedure of *damnatio memoriae*, and often also hostile propaganda actions by the successors, compelled those who used it to ascribe, often with no regard to the actual merits of the emperor, all the characteristics of the bad ruler, cruel tyrant, to him, leading to a distortion of his image in the eyes of the posteriority. Among the rulers of the Roman Empire who have suffered such a fate, is Marcus Opellius Severus Macrinus (April 11, 217 — past June 8, 218). We shall devote this monographic article to the issue of his relations with the Senate, hitherto insufficiently covered or even overlooked in the relevant literature.[5]

---

[4] See: T. Kotula: *"Dobrzy i źli cesarze" w opiniach późnych autorów łacińskich*. W: *Terra, mare et homines. Volumen in honorem Thaddei Łoposzko*. Lublin 1994 ("Annales Universitatis Mariae Curie-Skłodowska". Sectio F., Vol. 49), pp. 127—137.

[5] On Macrinus and his reign, see: H.J. Bassett: *Macrinus and Diadumenianus*. Menesha (Wisconsin) 1920; H. v. Petrikovits: *Die Chronologie der Regierung Macrins*. "Klio", Bd. 31 (1938), pp. 103—107; Idem: *M. Opellius Macrinus*. In: *Realencyclopädie der klassischen Alter-tumswissenschaft* [further on as RE]. Bd. XVIII/1. Stuttgart 1939, col. 540—558; H. Mattingly: *The Reign of Macrinus*. In: *Studies Presented to David Moore Robinson*. Vol. 2. Eds. G.E. My-lonas, D. Raymond. Saint Louis 1953, pp. 962—969; P. Salama: *L'empereur Macrin Part-hicus Maximus*. "Revue de Études Anciennes", Vol. 66 (1964), pp. 334—352; P. Cavuoto: *Mac-

Before Macrinus had donned the purple in a situation difficult for the state after Caracallas death on April 8, 217 — he had been a praetorian prefect.[6] In the circles of power Opellius belonged to the class of *homines novi*,[7] and he owed his career to his legal education, abilities, as well as reliability and diligence in discharging duties entrusted to him. Marching up the ladder of the equestrian career, starting from procurator up to praetorian prefect, he had also taken advantage of the patronage by such influential figures as the prefects C. Fulvius Plautianus and L. Fabius Cilo, and even the emperors of the Severan house.[8]

Macrinus had achieved the peak of his administrative career in the first months of 217, when Caracalla conferred on him the senatorial title *clarissimus vir* along with *ornamenta consularia*.[9] The clarissimate which he had received was probably a hereditary one, because Diadumenianus, Macrinus' son, had

---

rino. Napoli 1983; *Prosopographia Imperii Romani saeculi I. II. III*. Ed. altera [further on as PIR[2]]. Berolini-Lipsiae 1987, O 108 (pp. 445—450); D. B a h a r a l: *The Emperor Marcus Opellius Macrinus and the Gens Aurelia*. In: *Classical Studies in Honor of David Sohlberg*. Ramat Gan 1996, pp. 415—432; E a d e m: *Victory of Propaganda. The Dynastic Aspect of the Imperial Propaganda of the Severi: The Literary and Archaeological Evidence AD 193—235*. Oxford 1996, pp. 43—51, 96—98; T. F r a n k e: *Macrinus*. In: *Der Neue Pauly. Enzyklopädie der Antike. Altertum*. Bd. 7. Hrsg. v. H. C a n c i k, H. S c h n e i d e r. Stuttgart—Weimar 1999, col. 626—627.

[6] On the circumstances of Caracalla's death, see: H.J. B a s s e t t: *Macrinus...*, pp. 19—21; E. H o h l: *Das Ende Caracallas. Eine quellenkritische Studie*. "Miscellanea Academica Berolinensia", Vol. II/1 (1950), pp. 276—293; F. K o l b: *Literarische Beziehungen zwischen Cassius Dio, Herodianus und der Historia Augusta*. Bonn 1972, pp. 118—135; P. C a v u o t o: *Macrino...*, pp. 17—20; see also the appendix: *Macrinus — Caracalla's Murderer. Truth or Forgery of Elagabalus and Severus Alexander Propaganda?*

[7] Macrinus was counted among the members of this group by the author of HA *Macrinus* 7, 1.

[8] See: Cass. D i o, 79(78), 11, 2; cf. HA *Macrinus* 4, 4. On the significance of patronage and protection in the equestrian career, see first of all R.P. S a l l e r: *Promotion and Patronage in Equestrian Careers*. "Journal of Roman Studies", Vol. 70 (1980), pp. 44—63. On the career of Macrinus, see also: H.J. B a s s e t t: *Macrinus...*, pp. 15—18; H. v. P e t r i k o v i t s: *M. Opellius Macrinus...*, pp. 542—543; H.-G. P f l a u m: *Carriéres procuratoriennes équestres sous le Haut-Empire Romain*. Vol. 2. Paris 1960, pp. 667—672; P. C a v u o t o: *Macrino...*, pp. 7—20; PIR[2] O 108 (pp. 447—448).

[9] *Ornamenta consularia* are mentioned by Cass. Dio 79(78), 13, 1—2, while the title *clarissimus vir* is confirmed independently in: *Codex Iustinianus* 9, 51, 1 and *Corpus Inscriptionum Latinarum* [further on as CIL] XV 7505 (= Inscriptiones Latinae Selectae. Ed. H. D e s s a u [further on as ILS], 461). The similar rank had also been conferred on the other of the two prefects — M. Oclatinius Adventus (on him: H.-G. P f l a u m: *Carriéres procuratoriennes...*, pp. 662—667; PIR[2] O 9). Of the previous prefects, those official ranks were only bestowed on Plautianus (PIR[2] F 554; T. K o t u l a: *Septymiusz Sewerus...*, pp. 79—84) and Q. Mecius Letus (PIR[2] M 54) during the reign of Septimius Severus. On the consular ornaments cf. also: O. H i r s c h f e l d: *Rangtitel der römischen Kaiserzeit*. München 1901, p. 582; R.J.A. T a l b e r t: *The Senate...*, pp. 366—370; B. S a l w a y: *A Fragment of Severan History: The Unusual Career of...atus, Praetorian Prefect of Elagabalus*. "Chiron", Bd. 27 (1997), p. 135.

become *clarissimus puer*.[10] It is very difficult to specify the social and political status of a person who held such high-ranking titles — as Opellius continued to remain one of the praetorian prefects, the highest equestrian officials. Dio and Herodianus claim that at the time of election to the imperial throne, Macrinus was still an *eques*.[11] Therefore, he would be the first emperor who had not been a member of the senatorial estate beforehand.[12] It is possible, however, that such an opinion is prejudiced and not entirely correct. In the case of Dio, it could have been based on the personal dislike of a member of an old-time senatorial family towards the promotion of Opellius, who had owed his higher status — and it should once again be stressed here — to his own abilities and the patronage by some influential figures, and not to his birth.[13]

The achievements of Macrinus — the highest of the prefectures joined with the senatorial office ranks, *ornamenta consularia* and the title *clarissimus vir* — have made his status into something intermediary between the membership in the *ordo equester* and the *ordo senatorius*. The reception of the senatorial official titles did not have to be equivalent with the *adlectio inter senatores*,[14] even though it elevated the status of the holder, in this case — of Opellius, so high that from that moment on he could have been regarded as a "honorary

---

[10] CIL XV 7505 (ILS 461). On Diadumenianus, see: H. v. Petrikovits: *M. Opellius Diadumenianus*. RE XVIII/1, col. 539—540; PIR² O 107 (pp. 442—445); R. Syme: *The Son of the Emperor Macrinus*. In: Idem: *Historia Augusta Papers*. Oxford 1983, pp. 46—62; P. Dyrlaga: *Los Diadumeniana. Przyczynek do badań nad polityką wewnętrzną cesarza Makryna*. W: *Studia z dziejów antyku. Pamięci Profesora Andrzeja Kunisza*. Red. W. Kaczanowicz. Katowice 2004, pp. 173—191. On the titles of Diadumenianus see also P. Cavuoto: *Nome e titoli di Macrino e Diadumeniano*. In: *Ottava Miscellanea greca e romana*. Roma 1982, pp. 345—350.

[11] See: Cass. Dio 79(78), 14, 3—4 and 41,4. Cf. Herod. 5, 1, 5.

[12] Concerning this question, cf. the comments by K.-P. Johne: *"Imperator et nondum senator". Senat, Ritterstand und die ersten Kaiser nichtsenatorischer Herkunft*. In: *Krise — Krisenbewußtsein — Krisenbewältigung. Ideologie und geistige Kultur im Imperium Romanum während des 3. Jahrhunderts*. Halle 1988, pp. 43—47. On holding the office of praetorian prefect by persons with senatorial titles, see also: M.T.W. Arnheim: *Third Century Praetorian Prefects' Senatorial Origin. Fact or Fiction?* "Athenaeum", Vol. 49 (1971), pp. 74—88.

[13] Cf. the personal characteristics mentioned by Herodianus (5, 1, 1—8) in a fictitious letter by Macrinus to the Senate, which had helped him in his career crowned with the putting-on of the purple.

[14] Thus in P. Cavuoto: *Macrino...*, pp. 12—13, especially note 33. L.L. Howe (*The Pretorian Prefect from Commodus to Diolectian (AD 180—305)*. Chicago 1942, p. 48, note 28) is of the opinion that Macrinus and Adventus "were honorary senators, with the title of *clarissimus* gained as a result of consular *ornamenta* granted them as prefects". Cf. C.L. Clay: *The Roman Coinage of Macrinus and Diadumenian*. "Numismatische Zeitschrift", Bd. 93 (1979), p. 27, note 30; R. Turcan: *Histoire Auguste*. T. 3. 1ère partie: *Vies de Macrin, Diadumènien, Héliogabale*. Paris 1993 [further HA Ed. R. Turcan], pp. 125—126, note 23. According to Cassius Dio (79(78), 14, 3—4), Adventus, as holding the *ornamenta consularia* and being a *clarissimus vir*, should not take on the senatorial office of the prefect of the City, and he had received the right to do so only through *adlectio inter senatores*.

senator" and he was considered as such in society. The offices which he held and the received honours allowed him also to make proper acquaintances and contacts with many influential personages close to the ruler. At the time of announcing him as *Augustus*, Opellius must have been therefore well known in the senatorial circles — first as one of the imperial procurators, later as a praetorian prefect, the first person after the emperor in the Roman system of power, endowed with the highest ranks available to a man of his estate and status.

Upon receiving the purple, Macrinus inherited from his predecessor a number of unresolved problems troubling the Empire, such as a crisis in finances, steadily aggravating from some time and determining the whole of the internal politics, as well as a threat — over the eastern frontiers of the Empire — of a retaliatory assault by the Parthians, provoked by an earlier expedition into their lands. The threat of an invasion by the Iranian neighbour, and later the war waged with them and the usurpation by Elagabalus, had all caused that Macrinus had been staying in the East throughout the time of his reign. As an emperor, he had never come to Rome and never appeared in the Curia in person. He maintained contact with the Senate by means of numerous letters, whose contents had been luckily communicated in many items of information by Cassius Dio, the senator present at that time in Rome and at the Curia when the letters were read out. The information passed on by him — although the account has been saved only in a summary of the Byzantine chronicler Johannes Xiphilinos (11th century) — is all the more valuable as it is a first-hand account from a person who had direct contact with imperial-senatorial correspondence.[15] Moreover, some indications regarding the relation between the emperor and the Senate can also be found in other sources — in Herodianus[16] and in the lives of Macrinus and Diadumenus (i.e. Diadumenianus), part of the collection *Historia Augusta*, whose anonymous author probably had drawn the information mainly from the emperors' biographies written by Marius Maximus.[17]

---

[15] See: F. M i l l a r: *A Study of Cassius Dio*. Oxford 1964, pp. 22, 160—168.

[16] Most of all, see W. W i d m e r: *Kaisertum, Rom und Welt in Herodians META MARKON BASILEIAS ISTORIA*. Zürich 1967; G. A l f ö l d y: *Herodians Person*. "Ancient Society", Vol. 2 (1971), pp. 204—233; H. S i d e b o t t o m: *Herodianus's Historical Methods and Understanding of History*. In: *Aufstieg und Niedergang der römischen Welt. Geschichte und Kultur Roms im Spiegel der neueren Forschung*. Teil II: *Prinzipat*. Hrsg. v. H. T e m p o r i n i, W. H a a s e [further ANRW II]. Bd. 34/3. Berlin—New York 1997, pp. 2775—2836; M. Z i m m e r m a n n: *Kaiser und Ereignis. Studien zum Geschichtswerk Herodians*. München 1999.

[17] *Historia Augusta* has always aroused a great deal of controversy. Of the newer works first of all see the introductions to the latest editions: HA Ed. R. T u r c a n and A. C h a s t a g n o l: *Histoire Auguste. Les empereurs romains des IIe et IIIe siècles*. Paris 1994 [further HA. Ed. A. C h a s t a g n o l]. See also: *Vademecum historyka starożytnej Grecji i Rzymu*. T. 3: *Źródłoznawstwo czasów późnego antyku*. Red. E. W i p s z y c k a. Warszawa 1999, pp. 140—148 (therein

It should be noted, however, that all the above-mentioned accounts from ancient times may have been somewhat influenced by the propaganda disseminated by the successors of Macrinus, i.e. Elagabalus and Severus Alexander, marked by their dislike of Opellius. Being usurpers themselves, his successors were compelled to discredit the predecessor in order to emphasize the "legitimacy" of the coup and acquisition of power over the Empire.[18] Therefore the description of events and the relations between the emperor and the Senate, though in some regards similar and convergent in the accounts, may be distorted and partial in some points.[19]

The sources have devoted the most attention to the first Macrinus' letter to the Senate, after the imperial acclamation. In this letter Opellius informed the Senate of the events that had happened in Syria in April 217. Most of all, he notified the *patres* of the death of Caracalla and justified himself, assuring them that he had not known anything of the conspiracy.[20] He also informed them of the fact that he had been elected by the army as a new *Augustus*. It is worth stressing here that in relation to this latter information Macrinus had used in his letter all the titles due to the emperor: *Imperator, Caesar, Severus, Pius, Felix, Augustus, Proconsul*, even though formally his acclamation had not yet gained sanction by the Senate. It is worth noting that he was reproached for that by Cassius Dio.[21] It is also characteristic that

a broad collection of relevant literature). On Marius Maximus, generally identified with L. Marius Maximus Perpetuus Aurelianus, *praefectus Urbi* during the reign of Macrinus (PIR² M 308), an excellent study lately written by A.R. B i r l e y (*Marius Maximus: The Consular Biographer*. In: ANRW II, Bd. 34/3. Berlin—New York 1997, pp. 2678—2757). He believes that the work of Maximus had been the main source for all of the biographies in *Historia Augusta* up to Elagabalus.

[18] Cf. HA *Heliogabalus* 8, 4—5. See also HA. Ed. A. C h a s t a g n o l, pp. 179—181, note 45.

[19] The correlations between the above-mentioned sources are discussed in detail by F. K o l b: *Literarische Beziehungen...* In his opinion (pp. 134—135), the account of Cassius Dio was a source of information for Herodianus and *Historia Augusta*. However, it should be noted here that one cannot exclude the possibility of Dio's quoting only the official version of the events, propagated by the courts of Elagabalus and Severus Alexander, with which he was associated.

[20] HA *Macrinus* 5, 9. Considering a high opinion of the emperor's reliability and probity held by the ancient historians chronologically closest to him (cf. Cass. Dio 79(78), 11, 2; H e r o d. 5, 2, 1—2), it may be supposed that in the letter to the Senate discussed above he did not depart from the truth. The historiography of ancient times, influenced by the propaganda of Macrinus successors, depicted a distorted vision of the conspiracy, in which he had been assigned the role of the chief *provocateur* as well as the conspirators' leader. A more thorough analysis indicates that Macrinus had probably not taken part in the conspiracy, and his leadership was forced on him *in silentio*. His successors had to discredit him in some way. Anyhow, an appraisal of the credibility of that justification depends to a large extent on whether or not Macrinus' conspiracy against Caracalla was predominantly or completely an invention by the propaganda of post-Macrinus times. See also the appendix.

[21] Cass. Dio 79(78), 16, 2—4; 37, 5; HA *Macrinus* 6, 5 (inauthentic letter to the Senate), cf. 7, 1—4.

purely for reasons of propaganda right after the imperial acclamation Opellius had accepted the *cognomen Severus* as an honorary title, and a bit later he conferred the title of *cognomen Antoninus*[22] on his son, who had been appointed *Ceasar*. Thus the new *Augustus* had emphasized his connection with the previous dynasty, the house of Antonines-Severi in particular with Septimius Severus, and set himself up as a continuator of their tradition and political agenda.[23]

Moreover, according to Herodianus, who quotes an inauthentic, though not without certain facts, content of that letter to the Senate, Macrinus declared, which was particularly important to the senators but not necessarily obliging for the ruler, that he would not undertake to do anything without consulting the Curia and the *patres* would live in peace and liberty.[24]

The Senate heard the news of Caracalla's death with unconcealed joy. The deceased ruler did not enjoy great popularity among the senatorial circles. At the beginning they were rather reluctant to believe the news from the East, most probably suspecting a guise on the emperor's part, eager to find new sources of money which could come from confiscation of the property held by the rich citizens, i.e. senators. It was only when the news turned out to be true and Caracalla's death was confirmed that the senators had given release to their rancour, condemning him and his decisions. According to Cassius Dio, the death of Caracalla was greeted with joy and joking that his murderer Martialis should be honoured with panegyrics and statues, and Macrinus was generally recognized as a new emperor.[25] *Historia Augusta* suggests that the Senate had willingly recognized Opellius as an emperor on account of his predecessor's crimes (notably, crimes against the senators).[26] However, nobody dared to level the *damnatio memoriae* against Caracalla, which could have resulted from the attitude of the army, associated with the Severi, as well as the new ruler's lack of approval for such an action. On the contrary, he seemed to

---

[22] On the meaning of the title of *Antoninus*, see an interesting study by R. S y m e: *Nomen Antoninorum*. In: I d e m: *Emperors and Biography. Studies in the Historia Augusta*. Oxford 1971, pp. 78—88. Several inscriptions also ascribe to Diadumenianus the *cognomen Severus*, see e.g.: CIL XV 7238 (= ILS 462); XV 7331 (= ILS 462a). See also: PIR² O 107 (p. 443). It is hard to tell if that was a mason's mistake, or a deliberate local initiative inspired by the desire to gain favour of the ruler.

[23] See: D. B a h a r a l: *The Emperor Marcus Opellius Macrinus...*, p. 415—432; E a d e m: *Victory of Propaganda...*, pp. 43—51.

[24] Herod. 5, 1, 8. Herodianus's suggestions confirm to a certain extent the words of Macrinus as quoted by Cassius Dio (79(78), 12, 2) that it is not right to condemn a senator to death; the words were spoken during the dispute concerning the senator Aurelianus with the soldiers who hated that senator.

[25] Cass. Dio 79(78), 18, 3—4.

[26] HA *Macrinus* 2, 3—4.

suggest a *consecratio* of his predecessor, yet did not order the measure officially to avoid irritating the senators.[27]

There was nothing that the Senate could have done as regards an emperor elected by the Army. It did not possess the military force; nor could it afford to counter him with an appropriate rival. Therefore the *patres* had accepted the army's decision and the traditional titles taken on by Macrinus; they also provided him with the following ones — *pontifex maximus*, and later *pater patriae*.[28] Thanksgiving offerings had been made at Rome, as confirmed by the issues of coins with the inscriptions VOTA PVBL(ICA) P. M. TR. P. (S.C.), featuring the emperor accompanied by the highest of the Roman gods, Jupiter, or the personifications of such imperial *virtutes* as *Felicitas, Fides, Salus* and *Securitas*.[29] It is also due to note here that probably on account of the emperor's absence in the capital, the Senate had obtained a certain measure of control over the output of the mint at Rome, which was reflected in the selection of content and wording propagated in the iconography and inscriptions of the coins made there.[30]

---

[27] Compare Cass. D i o 79(78), 17, 2—3; HA *Caracalla* 11, 5; *Macrinus* 5, 9; 6, 8—9. Answering the question, whether during the reign of Macrinus a *consecratio* of Caracalla was made has been stirring a controversy (in relation to that question there remains also the problem of deification of his mother, Iulia Domna). According to H.J. B a s s e t t (*Macrinus...*, p. 24) and C.L. C l a y (*Roman Coinage of Macrinus...*, p. 33, note 56), the deification of Caracalla was executed during the time of Macrinus' reign, while H. M a t t i n g l y (*The Reign of Macrinus...*, p. 963, note 1) is of the opinion that it had happened during the reign of Elagabalus. In J.F. G i l l i a m ' s opinion (*On Diui under the Severi*. In: *Hommages à Marcel Renard*. Ed. J. B i b a u w. Vol. 2. Bruxelles 1969, pp. 284—289) Caracalla was consecrated during the time of Macrinus' reign, whilst Iulia Domna probably at that time as well or under Elagabalus. However, J. F e j f e r (*Divus Caracalla and Julia Domna. A Note*. In: T. F i s c h e r - H a n s e n et al.: *Ancient Portraiture*. Copenhagen 1992, pp. 207—219) thinks that we cannot unambiguously determine if Caracalla and Iulia Domna were deified during the reign of Macrinus. D. B a h a r a l (*The Emperor Marcus Opellius Macrinus...*, pp. 419—420, also note 13; *Victory of Propaganda...*, p. 97, notes 17 and 18) asserts that Caracalla had been consecrated no earlier than during the reign of Elagabalus and Iulia Domna probably as late as under Severus Alexander. In view of the above, opinions on the chronology of Caracalla's *consecratio* are divided and an unequivocal solution to this problem may only be brought about by a discovery of sources that would throw some new light on this matter.

[28] Concerning the role of the Senate in granting the titles of imperial power and other *honores*, see: R.J.A. T a l b e r t: *The Senate...*, pp. 354—371.

[29] *The Roman Imperial Coinage*. Vol. IV/2: *Macrinus to Pupienus*. Eds. H. M a t t i n g l y, E.A. S y d e n h a m, C.H.V. S u t h e r l a n d. London 1968 [further RIC IV/2 (Macrinus)], p. 6, Nos. 5—13; p. 16, Nos. 126—133. On the meaning of the motifs used, see also.: P. D y r l a g a: *Motywy religijne w ikonografii i legendach monet cesarza Makryna. I: Jowisz i Wiktoria*. "Magazyn Numizmatyczny" (PTN Oddz. w Częstochowie), nr 32 (2004 — published 2005), pp. 113—121; I d e m: *Motywy religijne w ikonografii i legendach monet cesarza Makryna. II: Virtutes*. "Magazyn Numizmatyczny" (PTN Oddz. w Częstochowie), nr 33 (2005), pp. 77—86.

[30] Cf. P. D y r l a g a: *Á propos doboru haseł propagandowych w mennictwie cesarza Makryna*. "Magazyn Numizmatyczny" (PTN Oddz. w Częstochowie), nr 31 (2003 — published 2004), pp. 84—97.

The emperor's expression of his willingness to co-operate must have been a pleasant surprise to the senators, though some of them could have been afraid that it would not go beyond a mere declaration of intent. As a result, Macrinus had made a clear reference to the best traditions of the Antonines' epoch, to the times of Traianus, Antoninus Pius or Marcus Aurelius, with a definite departure from the line of his predecessor, whose relations with the Senate were far from the best.[31] This is why the sources suggest that the senators uttered, without any resistance, cries of jubilation to the honour of the new emperor and decreed the granting to him of all the official ranks, previously held by his predecessors,[32] additionally accepting his family, *gens Opellia*, to the patrician families.[33] As it appears, the Senate was aware of the fact that a change had taken place and the reign of Macrinus may be less disagreeable than that of the Severi, which was not free from confiscations and deaths of senators.[34] However, as Herodianus had sceptically summed it up, the joy was not so much at Macrinus' accession to the throne as at the death of Caracalla.[35]

The sources are unambiguous in pointing out that Macrinus had enjoyed a certain degree of support by the Senate from the beginning of his reign.[36] It could have been due to the fact that during the time of the Severi reign he had held important procuratorial positions and was also a praetorian prefect. Those official ranks allowed him to be in frequent contact with the members of the elites of power in Roman society, and thus also with the senatorial circles. Perhaps Macrinus had cared about maintaining good relations with the Senate, as it was the most respectable of all the Roman institutions, still enjoying the gravity and prestige in society. It cannot also be excluded that the emperor had seen in the Senate a sort of counterbalance to the army, of which he could be afraid with regard to the undertaking of the reform of the

---

[31] See G. Alföldy: *Der Sturz des Kaisers Geta...*, pp. 203—208. In general, however, Caracalla continued to a great extent his father's policy towards the Senate (cf. G. Alföldy: *Septimius Severus und der Senat...*, pp. 112—160; F. Kolb: *Literarische Beziehungen...*, pp. 89—97; T. Kotula: *Septymiusz Sewerus...*, pp. 89—95), primarily tending to get rid of the opponents. On the causes of conflicts between the Senate and the emperors of the Severan family, see also: G. Alföldy: *Historia społeczna...*, pp. 218, 236.

[32] Herod. 5, 2, 1; HA *Macrinus* 7, 1—4 (he was granted the title of *pontifex maximus*, the appellation *Pius*, and his tribunal and proconsular powers had been confirmed). See also: HA *Macrinus* 11, 2: *Et cum illum senatus Pium ac Felicem nuncupasset, Felicis nomen recepit, Pii habere noluit*. Concerning this mention, compare HA Ed. R. Turcan, p. 131, note 42.

[33] Concerning Macrinus: HA *Macrinus* 7, 1; concerning Diadumenianus: Cass. Dio 79(78), 17, 1.

[34] Cf.: G. Alföldy: *Septimius Severus und der Senat...*, pp. 112—160; J.B. Campbell: *The Emperor and the Roman Army 31 BC—AD 235*. Oxford 1984, pp. 401—404; T. Kotula: *Septymiusz Sewerus...*, pp. 89—95.

[35] Herod. 5, 2, 1.

[36] Cf. Herod. 5, 2, 1; HA *Macrinus* 7, 1—4.

army's finances and the restoring of the discipline within the ranks of the legions.[37]

The social status of Macrinus, who had made a career during the reign of the Severi thanks to his own abilities and patronage by some influential figures, could have been — nevertheless — a stick in the eye for certain groups of senators, especially those from the old senatorial families. Just like Cassius Dio, they could have been irritated by the fact that although Opellius was a *homo novus*, he had been ranked among the patricians, the old traditional Roman aristocracy. Therefore, it was not by coincidence that such a sentiment echoed in the account of Cassius Dio, who respected Macrinus and his capabilities as a state official, but not as an emperor, reproaching him on several occasions, mainly with regard to his appointment policy.[38]

Cassius Dio mentions the first letter of the Senate to Macrinus, as he could have been present at the Curia at the time of its drafting. In the letter the *patres* informed the ruler, among other things, of accepting the election, passing a resolution to organize horse-racing competition in order to celebrate the beginning of his reign, and granting Diadumenianus, the emperor's son and heir apparent, the titles of Patrician, *Princeps Iuventutis* and *Caesar*. The emperor had accepted everything except for the horse-racing, as he asserted that his *dies imperii* had been sufficiently honoured during the celebration of Septimius Severus' birthday, on 11 April.[39] It should be added here that the elevation of Macrinus' son was tantamount to formal acceptance by the Curia of the ruler's dynastic policy along with all of its consequences.

During the time of Macrinus' reign the Senate was not solely an executor of the emperor's orders; it had also undertaken certain steps, which had not however infringed upon the emperor's sovereignty of power. Cassius Dio mentions that even though the Senate had not dared to recognize Caracalla as

---

[37] Macrinus carried out a reduction in the amount of *stipendium* for new recruits, payments of which had been an excessive burden on the budget (Cass. Dio 79(78), 12, 7; 28, 1—4; 36, 1—3) and began to restore order in the Army, cf.: *Epitome de Caesaribus* 22: *quod Macrinus militarem luxuriam stipendiaque profusiora comprimeret*. As it appears, the methods used by the emperor to improve the morale of the army were not very lenient (cf. HA Macr. 12, 1—5; 12, 7) and as a result not all of the soldiers liked him (apparently, some kind of unrest among the soldiers had broken out), see Cass. Dio 79(78), 20, 4; 31, 1; Herod. 5, 2, 5—6; HA Macr. 5, 4—5; 12, 2; 14, 1; cf. also Cass. Dio 79(78), 28, 1—29, 2. On Macrinus' reforms and his relations with the Army see also: P. C a v u o t o: *Macrino...*, p. 40 ff.; J. S ü n s k e s T h o m p s o n: *Aufstände und Protestaktionen im Imperium Romanum. Die severischen Kaiser im Spannungsfeld innenpolitischer Konflikte*. Bonn 1990, p. 68 ff.

[38] See e.g. the charges concerning appointing Adventus *praefectus Urbi* before he had been appointed senator (Cass. Dio 79(78), 14, 1—4), or appointing Ulpius Iulianus and Iulianus Nestor praetorian prefects (Cass. Dio 79(78), 15, 1). Cf. R.J.A. T a l b e r t: *The Senate...*, p. 85.

[39] Cass. Dio 79(78), 17, 1. On *dies natalis* of Septimius Severus, see: P. H e r z: *Kaiserfeste der Prinzipatszeit*. In: ANRW II. Bd. 16/2. Berlin—New York 1978, pp. 1181—1184; D. K i e n a s t: *Römische Kaisertabelle. Grundzüge einer römischen Kaiserchronologie*. Darmstadt 1996, p. 156.

enemy of the people and announce his *damnatio memoriae*, it had drawn up a list of his victims, demanded that the horse-racing festivities in honour of his birthday be discontinued, his statues made of gold and silver recast, and informers active under his reign punished.[40] To gain even more favour with the senators, the emperor had fulfilled the latter demand, especially that as a result he gained more popularity and the question did not harm the interests of his imperial policy. In consequence, it was Macrinus who had carried out a peculiar *census* of the Senate and — according to Cassius Dio's account — disclosed the names of three senators: Manilius,[41] Iulius[42] and Sulpicius Arrenianus,[43] who had been involved previously in informing. Those people were stripped of their offices and banished, as the emperor had forbidden to kill them. Forced to testify and also banished was Lucius Priscillianus,[44] who — under Caracalla's reign — had been personally involved in accusing many *equites* and senators before the Senate, among them Pomponius Bassus,[45] a generally known and respected man, the son of Pomponius Bassus, governor of *Moesia Inferior*. The offices and ranks held by the banished had been granted to those who were wronged by them. Among others, a man named Flaccus was given back the office of *praefectus alimentorum*, which was previously taken away from him and granted to Manilius.[46] It must have been then that Macrinus had effected, by means of *adlectio inter senatores*, the co-opting of new members into the Senate; among those members were Marius Secundus and a former praetorian prefect M. Oclatinius Adventus.[47] Therefore the changes in the composition of the Senate introduced by the emperor

---

[40] Cass. Dio 79(78), 17, 4—18, 2.

[41] Cf. PIR² M 106 and 128. According to P. C a v u o t o (*Macrino...*, p. 40) probably identical with Ti. Manilius Fuscus (PIR² M 106), who was a legate of *Legio II Gemina* in Dacia in 191, legate of the province Syria *Phoenice* in 194, consul in 195 or 196, proconsul of Asia about 210 and, finally, a consul again (*consul ordinarius*) in 225.

[42] PIR² I 102.

[43] *Prosopographia Imperii Romani saeculi I. II. III.* Ed. prima [further on as PIR¹], S 708.

[44] Cf. H.-G. P f l a u m: *Carriéres procuratoriennes...*, p. 672 ff. (therein a discussion on identification of this figure with a senator L. Lucillius Pansa Priscillianus, known from an inscription, or his son, L. Lucillius Priscillianus.

[45] Cf. an interesting hypothesis in relation with the case of Bassus, brought forward by V. K o n d i ć (*Two Recent Acquisitions in Belgrade Museums*. "Journal of Roman Studies", Vol. 63 (1973), pp. 47—48), connecting the ancient episode with the finding of Macrinus' head made of bronze, at the village of Boleč near Belgrade.

[46] Cass. Dio 79(78), 22, 1—2. On this subject, cf. P. C a v u o t o: *Macrino...*, pp. 39—40. In the same piece of text Cassius Dio also mentions that Domitius Florus, who had previously been in charge of the Senate's protocols and was an aedile, later stripped of his office by Plautianus, regained the office and thanks to recruiting the followers (the account is not entirely clear, whether they were his, or Macrinus' followers) had been additionally appointed as tribune.

[47] Cass. Dio 79(78), 14, 1 (cf. 14, 3); 35, 1. See also: R.J.A. T a l b e r t: *The Senate...*, pp. 34—35.

were far from drastic and had been measured, on the one hand, to satisfy the Senate's broader circles, gain their favour and thus strengthen the ruler's position at the Curia and — on the other hand — to avoid unnecessary friction.

In view of Cassius Dio's account, it is also evident that from the beginning of his reign, Macrinus had given up *laesae maiestatis* trials and nullified the verdicts issued earlier by Caracalla.[48] However, it was not an ordinary act of grace by a new emperor, but, as it appears, a deliberate and politically motivated step. The emperor wished to rule in accordance with the law, not false or fabricated accusations, and most of all he did not want to lower himself to the level of the wicked *Vitelli, Nerones et Domitiani*.[49] According to Herodianus, he had ordered to kill the "professional" informers and slaves who denounced their owners, "and so Rome and nearly all of the world subject to Roman rule had been cleansed of those perverse people, as some of them were punished, some banished, and if there remained some who had managed to hide themselves, they were afraid and sitting still. Thus in full peace, with appearances of freedom, the people lived for that one year when Macrinus reigned" — as the ancient historian recounts.[50] Such measures had, obviously, a proper propaganda aspect and had most likely helped Macrinus to gain some popularity with the wealthy circles of society, who were the groups most vulnerable to all sorts of accusations and heavily afflicted by those under the previous ruler. The measures are also evidence of Macrinus' great respect for the law and its enforcement.

In spite of those Senate-friendly gestures, the emperor did not hesitate, if necessary and with silent consent of the *patres*, interfere in the questions of proconsular nominations in the senatorial provinces, of which the particularly significant had been Asia and Africa Proconsularis, both of them among the richest and most affluent provinces of the Empire. The echoes thereof are present in the account of Cassius Dio, who gives us some detailed information on the matters of M. Aufidius Fronto[51] and C. Iulius Asper.[52] The former was son of the famous C. Aufidius Victorinus — praetorian prefect, commander and friend of the emperor Marcus Aurelius, and he had drawn the lot giving him the governorship of Africa Proconsularis. However, under pressure of the protests by the inhabitants of that province, Macrinus had first refused to hand over the authority of Africa Proconsularis to Fronto, and later he did the

---

[48] Cass. Dio 79(78), 12, 1—2.

[49] Cf. HA *Clodius Albinus* 13, 5; cf. also e.g.: HA *Heliogabalus* 1, 1; *Severus Alexander* 9, 4. See also: HA. Ed. R. T u r c a n, p. 156; T. K o t u l a: „*Dobrzy i źli cesarze*"..., p. 133.

[50] Herod. 5, 2, 2. Cf. HA *Macrinus* 12, 11 — he condemned the informers to death, if they were not able to prove their claims; if they could do it, they were rewarded with money.

[51] On him PIR² A 1385.

[52] On him PIR² I 182.

same with Asia, which he had himself previously assigned to him. Instead, the emperor had only given to the would-be governor the appropriate proconsular remuneration — one million sesterces — which he had not accepted.[53] Conversely, in Asia, instead of C. Iulius Asper, in charge of the province under Caracalla, the emperor had appointed Q. Anicius Faustus as proconsul. Initially, Asper had been in Macrinus' good graces, as the emperor thought that he would restore order in the province, possibly disturbed by the actions undertaken by the Pergamenians against the new emperor,[54] and probably as a result he had not accepted his request to be discharged of his duties, which he had previously submitted to Caracalla.[55] His ineptness or inability of countering the crisis spreading over the rich province, coupled with the emperor's suspicions of disloyalty or ill-will, had finally led Macrinus to relieve the governor of his duties.[56] However, those minor differences which had resulted from a clash between the Senate's rights and the current needs of the state represented by the emperor, who could not afford disturbances of peace in such important provinces, did not have a considerable impact on the overall picture of Macrinus' co-operation with the Senate; their mutual relations had been satisfactory.

During the reign of Opellius Macrinus the role of the Senate did not end, however, at passing resolutions corresponding to the actual situation and in conformity with the emperor's wishes, and endorsing his decisions, as the ruler, it appears, had seen in that institution an important ally and guarantor of the legitimacy of his power.[57] Likewise, some of the legislative changes such as repealing Caracalla's tax laws on inheriting property, liberating slaves and restoring the former position of the *iuridici* — senatorial officials, who had been responsible for administering justice in the four judicial circuits of Italy,

---

[53] Cass. Dio 79(78), 22, 3—4. Also note the significance of Asper's words that he had wanted the governorship, not the money (Cass. Dio 79(78), 22, 5).

[54] Cass. Dio 79(78), 20, 4. Admittedly, the reason for them was that Pergamon had been stripped of its privileges, granted by Caracalla after his recuperation at the *asklepeion* there.

[55] Dio must have been fully aware of the situation that had arisen in the province of Asia, because — first of all — he had himself come from Nicomedia, in the neighbouring province of Bitinia, and, secondly, Macrinus had appreciated his skills, knowledge and capacities, and it was not a coincidence that he had entrusted Dio with the supervision of the cities Smyrna and Pergamum (80(79), 7, 4); for the dating of this fact, compare F. M i l l a r: *A Study of Cassius Dio...*, p. 23.

[56] Among other reasons for Asper's recall from the office, Cassius Dio (79(78), 22, 3) also mentions his inappropriate remarks concerning Macrinus, which had reached the emperor.

[57] Cf. an interesting, though chronologically incorrect suggestion in *Historia Augusta* (*Diadumenus* 2, 6) that right after proclaiming Diadumenus as Caesar, his coins had been issued in Antoch, while the coins of Macrinus had not been issued until it had been ordered by the Senate. This mention, even though it contains false information (cf. HA. Ed. R. T u r c a n, pp. 144—145, note 11), underscores once again Macrinus' amicable relations with the Senate and the emperor's respect for that institution.

were measures designed to gain favour with the Senate. Cassius Dio claims that at the emperor's order, the amount of the tax burden, increased by Caracalla from 1/20 up to 1/10 of the value of inherited property or a freed slave, had been returned to the amount existing during the reign of Septimius Severus, and the *iuridici* had ceased to issue verdicts beyond the limits determined by Marcus Aurelius.[58] These steps were meant also to incur popularity for Macrinus and strengthen his position in the Senate, as well as in other political circles.

Not without support from the senatorial circles (*ex senatu consultum*), as early as at the end of 217, Macrinus had also been co-opted into two of the prestigious high-priest collegiate bodies, *sodales Augustales Claudiales*[59] and *sacerdotes in aede Iovis Propugnatoris consistentes*.[60] Those two acts of co-opting — the former on December 28, 217, the latter not far from that date — had, despite the emperors absence in Rome, a tremendous propaganda significance, by raising the prestige status of the *gens imperatoria*, emphasizing the legality of its rule and the divine protection over them. They are also proof of the Senate's full approval of the ruler and his power.

From the very beginning of his reign, Macrinus had thus cared about the formal side of his relations with the Senate, making use of its support and favour, and taking advantage of the social prestige vested in the members of that institution. In his correspondence sent to the *patres*, the emperor had usually informed them of diverse, not always the most important for the state, matters, but the final word always belonged to him. We can find examples of such conduct in the sources. At the beginning of his reign, Macrinus had prohibited the organizing of horse-racing festivities in honour of his taking-over of imperatorial rule,[61] and after the end of the war against the Parthians he had not sent to the Senate a full account of his negotiations with the king Artabanus IV, even though the *patres* had decreed offerings in honour of the emperor's victory and granted him the title *Parthicus*. The emperor, however, had refused to accept it,[62] although for propaganda reasons the coin with the

---

[58] Cass. Dio 79(78), 22, 1. Cf.: H.J. B a s s e t t: *Macrinus...*, p. 55; H. v. P e t r i k o v i t s: M. *Opellius Macrinus...*, col. 551; P. C a v u o t o: *Macrino...*, p. 35.

[59] CIL VI 1984 (2), v. 13—17 (= ILS 5025). On the Roman emperor's role in priestly collegial bodies, see: F. M i l l a r: *The Emperor in the Roman World...*, pp. 355—361.

[60] CIL VI 2009, v. 5—8 (= ILS 466).

[61] Cass. Dio 79(78), 17, 1.

[62] Cass. Dio 79(78), 27, 3. D. B a h a r a l (*The Emperor Marcus Opellius Macrinus...*, p. 420, also note 15) thinks that it may be a reminiscence of Septimius Severus' refusal of accepting such a title after his first Parthian war. In her opinion, it is very probable that in both cases the reason was to be found in the character of the peace treaty with the Parthians, who might have considered accepting such a title as a provocation. In one inscription, however, Macrinus bears the title *Parthicus Maximus* (P. S a l a m a: *L'empereur Macrin Parthicus Maximus...*, p. 334 = *L'Année Épigraphique* [further on as AE] 1964, No. 229), though we cannot be sure that he had accepted it

inscription VICTORIA PART(HICA) and the proper iconography glorifying the success[63] — had been issued.

The situation of Macrinus and his son changed on May 15, 218, when the divisions of the *Legio III Gallica*, camped at Raphanea, near Emesa, had proclaimed a new *augustus* — 14-year-old Varius Avitus, admittedly Caracalla's son, in fact grandson of Iulia Maesa, sister of Iulia Domna, Septimius Severus' wife.[64] The usurper had questioned the rights of the *Opellii* to wear the imperial purple and, by drawing on the tradition of his "father", had taken on his name and represented himself as Marcus Aurelius Antoninus since then.[65] Thus the usurper, as a "legitimate" successor of Caracalla, had become his avenger, acting as if Macrinus and his son were usurpers.

The sources testify to the fact that during his war against Elagabalus, Macrinus had been carrying on quite an extensive correspondence with the Senate. The first letters of the emperor, written probably right after the rebellion had broken out, had reached Rome no sooner than at the end of May, or, which is more likely, only at the beginning of June, when the course of the conflict had been reaching its crucial phase.

In the first of these letters, whose contents have been summarized by Cassius Dio, the emperor did not fail to notify the Senate of the incidents in Syria, he complained to the *patres* that the usurper appointed the governors, as if he had been the legitimate ruler; moreover, he criticized the adolescent age of

---

officially. Cf.: P. K n e i s s l: *Die Siegestitulatur der römischen Kaiser. Untersuchungen zu den Siegerbeinamen des ersten und zweiten Jahrhunderts.* Göttingen 1969, pp. 166—167; C.L. C l a y: *Roman Coinage of Macrinus...*, p. 29 (in his opinion, "the inscription must actually belong to the beginning of 218, before Macrinus' refusal of title Parthicus had been publicized"); P. C a v u o t o: *Nome e titoli...*, pp. 344—345; P. C a v u o t o: *Macrino...*, pp. 29—30.

[63] RIC IV/2 (*Macrinus*), p. 9, Nos. 49—50; p. 12, Nos. 96—98; p. 18, Nos. 164—166; p. 21, No. 209. Those issues are the most controversial in Macrinus' coinage. There is an extensive literature on the subject, in which a propaganda forgery is seen, cf. H. T h i e r f e l d e r: *Die römische Reichspolitik von Septimus Severus bis zum Senatkaisertum (193—238 n. Chr.) im Spiegel der Münzen.* "Wissenschaftliche Zeitschrift der Karl-Marx-Universität Leipzig", 6 Jg, Gesellschafts- und Sprachwissenschaftliche Reihe, Heft 3 (1956/1957), p. 277; K.-H. Z i e g l e r: *Die Beziehungen zwischen Rom und dem Partherreich. Ein Beitrag zur Geschichte des Völkerrechts.* Wiesbaden 1964, p. 135; R. B i l u c a g l i a: *Victoria Parthica Macrini Aug.* "Quaterni Ticinesi. Numismatica e Antichità Classiche", Vol. 4 (1975), pp. 231—238; P. C a v u o t o: *Macrino...*, p. 29; J. W o l s k i: *Imperium Arsacydów.* Poznań 1998, pp. 213—214. However, lately some attention has been paid to the possibility of other motifs in the issues of such coins, see P. D y r l a g a: *"Victoria parthica" cesarza Makryna. Prawda czy propagandowe fałszerstwo?* "Magazyn Numizmatyczny" (Oddz. w Częstochowie), nr 30 (2002), pp. 33—40 (additional literature therein). Regarding the iconographic motifs employed, see also P. D y r l a g a: *Motywy religijne w ikonografii i legendach monet cesarza Makryna. I: Jowisz i Wiktoria...*, pp. 115—117.

[64] Cass. Dio 79(78), 30, 2 ff., in particular 31, 4; Herod. 5, 3, 12; HA Macr. 9, 6. See also: P. C a v u o t o: *Macrino...*, p. 53 ff.

[65] Cass. Dio 79(78), 32, 2; Herod. 5, 3, 12; HA Macr. 7, 6; 9, 6. See also: D. B a h a r a l: *Victory of Propaganda...*, pp. 52—63.

his rival and accused him of insanity.[66] Upon receiving this letter, the Senate
— despite the propaganda action undertaken by Elagabalus' followers,[67] did
not have any doubt as to which one of the pretenders should be supported;
Elagabalus was recognized as enemy of the people, and in consequence thereof,
the provisions against him and his family, traditional in such cases, had been
issued. The *patres* had also carried into effect Macrinus' promise of immunity
to everyone who would have deserted the usurper.[68] The war against the
purported son of Caracalla and his followers had thus been fully legalized by
the Senate and thence, according to the law, they had been considered rebels,
who could not count on any leniency; acting against the majesty of the emperor, they had acted also against the majesty of the Senate and the people of
Rome.

The role of the Senate had not finished, however, at that time with issuing
the provisions relevant to the situation and compliant with Macrinus' wishes.
The emperor, as it seems, had seen in the Senate not only a tool in his struggle
against the usurper, but also an important ally warranting the legitimacy of his
rule. Therefore, he continued to send detailed information to the senators
concerning the events happening in the East, and he expected support from
them. This is confirmed by the fact that probably in a different letter, also
summarized by Dio, he had written to the senators that even though many
would like to see the dead body of the murdered emperor, he did not think that
any of them wished him death.[69] From the emperor's trust in the Senate,
which is evident in the fact that he provided such information, we may assume,
although carefully, that he continued to enjoy full support of the *patres* and
they remained loyal to him.[70]

It is also worth adding that, as Dio mentions, during Elagabalus' rebellion
Macrinus had omitted — in his letter to the Senate — the title *Antoninus*,
which he had previously granted to his son, but he did not omit his own
cognomen Severus.[71] In a certain way, it could suggest a change in the course
of imperial politics — Septimius Severus possessed a neutral position, while his
son, as the alleged father of a usurper, his parent's avenger, did not. His name,
therefore, had become, considering the existing situation, an unwanted addition in an official letter to such a venerable institution. However, it did not

---

[66] Cass. Dio 79(78), 36, 1; Cf. also: Cass. Dio 79(78), 38, 2; 80(79), 1, 4.

[67] Cass. Dio 79(78), 33, 1—2; 34, 6—8; cf. Cass. Dio 80(79), 1, 2; HA *Macrinus* 2, 5; 3, 8; 4,
7—8; 5, 9; 7, 5; HA *Diadumenus* 1, 1; HA *Heliogabalus* 2, 3; HA *Maximini* 4, 4.

[68] Cass. Dio 79(78), 38, 1. Cf: R.J.A. Talbert: *The Senate...*, p. 356.

[69] Cass. Dio 79(78), 36, 4—5.

[70] The case of senator Fulvius Diogenianus, as mentioned by Cassius Dio (79(78), 36, 5—37,
2), who claims that the senator was mentally ill, was rather an unusual and isolated example.

[71] Cass. Dio 79(78), 37, 6.

prevent the emperor from appointing Diadumenianus Antoninus as *augustus* and proclaim him as Elagabalus — pseudo-Antoninus' rival. Macrinus' son was supposed to be a continuator of the good Antonines, whilst the usurper was not.[72] Perhaps that was the reason why Commodus, most likely not without the Senate's approval, had been given his second *damnatio memoriae*.[73] Intending to avoid direct condemnation of Caracalla, which would additionally aggravate the military, Macrinus had condemned his namesake, who did not have a good opinion and had died a long time ago. In that way he attempted to strike a blow against the prestige of Elagabalus, who had exactly the same name as Commodus and Caracalla, while Diadumenianus, alongside his own family name, was only given the title *Antoninus*.

It is also due to be mentioned here that beside the direct correspondence with the Senate, Macrinus had been exchanging official letters with the *praefectus Urbi* L. Marius Maximus Perpetuus Aurelianus. This high-ranking official, a senator, had a tremendous influence on what was going on in the capital, and therefore also on the position of the Senate. In one of the letters addressed to him, also read out at the Curia, the emperor complained about the decline of the discipline in the Army during the rule of his predecessors, and stated that even the newly enlisted recruits demanded that their soldiers' pay and privileges be increased, as previously granted by Caracalla, which could not possibly be paid out due to the lack of funds. At the same time, the emperor conceded however that the soldiers should not be given nothing at all, and he estimated the amount needed to pay out the increased soldiers' pay at 70 million drachms, i.e. 280 million sesterces.[74] The information contained in the letter to Marius Maximus proves that the uproar in the military was on the rise, which the emperor was afraid of and which he could not prevent from happening due to lack of funds. Perhaps by informing the *praefectus Urbi*, and the senators as well, of the actual situation, Macrinus was expecting some help from them in order to solve those difficult problems.[75]

---

[72] See: P. D y r l a g a: *Diadumenianus Augustus w propagandzie cesarza Makryna w okresie walki o władzę z Elagabalem (16 maja — 8 czerwca 218 roku)*. W: *Wieki stare i nowe*. T. 3. Red. I. P a n i c, M.W. W a n a t o w i c z. Katowice 2003, pp. 20—26.

[73] See: D. K i e n a s t: *Römische Kaisertabelle...*, p. 148. Cf. the interesting comments by R.O. F i n k: *'Damnatio memoriae' and the Dating of Papyri*. In: *Synteleia V. Arangio-Ruiz*. Napoli 1964, pp. 232—236.

[74] Cass. Dio 79(78), 36, 1—3. See also: H.J. B a s s e t t: *Macrinus...*, p. 70; J.B. C a m p b e l l: *The Emperor and the Roman Army...*, pp. 175—176, cf. p. 196. On the political role of the City prefect, see: G. V i t u c c i: *Ricerche sulla praefectvra vrbi in età imperiale (sec. I—III)*. Roma 1956, pp. 83—111; R.J.A. T a l b e r t: *The Senate...*, pp. 22, 146.

[75] It should be noted here that interpretation of the intention of this letter is made difficult due to our lack of knowledge concerning the character of the relation between Macrinus and Marius Maximus. We do not know if the letter was an official or private one.

The fate of the war was decided on June 8, 218 near Antioch, when Macrinus' army was defeated and he himself escaped through the lands of Asia Minor to the West.[76] It is not in vain that the ancient historians emphasize that by his escape to Rome, Macrinus had counted on the support from the Senate and the people.[77] According to Dio, the emperor had enjoyed support in those circles and could count on their aid; nevertheless, the chronicler does not explain the character of the expected aid, as the Senate did not have any military force at its disposal, able to change the course of the war.[78] However, Macrinus' calculations failed, the emperor had been captured by the chase and, on the way to Antioch where the victorious usurper had temporarily resided, killed by one of the escorting soldiers.[79]

Right after the victory Elagabalus had sent letters to the Senate. They were taken to Rome by Claudius Pollio.[80] The usurper had pointed to Macrinus' low family background and the fact that he had made 9-year-old Diadumenianus a co-*augustus*; he had also called him Caracalla's murderer.[81] Furthermore, Elagabalus had presented to the Senate and the soldiers Macrinus' letters to the prefect of Rome, whose content was supposed to disgrace the emperor.[82] It should be considered, however, whether they were authentic letters, or forgeries meant to reveal the defeated emperor's indolence and thus gain yet another argument justifying the usurpation.

Herodianus claims that the news of Macrinus' defeat and death was received at Rome, particularly in the Senate, without jubilation, but the overwhelming force of the victor's army prevailed and the defeated emperor was condemned along with his son. Even the emperor's conduct had been condemned, with the accusation that he had himself chosen his own fate.[83] In the face of the emperor's defeat, the Senate, a respectable institution with serious political and opinion-forming influence — as already mentioned, did not possess any real power to counter the usurper. In a situation like this it could only change the course and yield to the victor, considering his claims as justified. The senators could not do anything but proclaim against Macrinus and Diadumenianus everything that they had proclaimed against Elagabalus

---

[76] In more detail on the usurpation of Elagabalus and the civil war between Elagabalus' and Macrinus' followers, see: H.J. B a s s e t t: *Macrinus...*, pp. 65—77; H. v. P e t r i k o v i t s: *M. Opellius Macrinus...*, col. 553—557; P. C a v u o t o: *Macrino...*, pp. 53—62.

[77] Cass. Dio 79(78), 39, 3—4; Herod. 5, 4, 11—12.

[78] Cass. Dio 79(78), 39, 3—4.

[79] On the circumstances of Macrinus' death, see: H. v. P e t r i k o v i t s: *Die Chronologie...*, pp. 106—107; I d e m: *M. Opellius Macrinus...*, col. 556—557; P. C a v u o t o: *Macrino...*, pp. 53—62, especially 59 ff.

[80] Cass. Dio 80(79), 2, 4; cf. Exc. Val. 403.

[81] Cass. Dio 80(79), 1, 2—4.

[82] Cass. Dio 80(79), 2, 1—2.

[83] Herod. 5, 4, 12; 5, 5, 2; cf.: Cass. Dio 80(79), 2, 5—6; HA *Heliogabalus* 3, 3.

and his followers not very long before. The names of *Opelli* had been subjected to *damnatio memoriae* and condemned to oblivion,[84] as confirmed by their *nomina* hammered out of the inscriptions,[85] and deleted or erased from the papyri.[86] In this way the victor, not without the Senate's forced support, wanted to erase the memory of his predecessors and their rule.[87]

In conclusion, we can ascertain to the best of our knowledge that during the reign of Macrinus none of the *patres* had been condemned to death, and the relations between the emperor and the Senate had been correct. The sources do not testify to any traces of rivalry or conflict between them; on the contrary, we may find numerous traces of co-operation and mutual respect. The emperor did not seek confrontation with the *patres*; he saw them as allies in his struggle to heal the situation in the state and consolidate his authority. He cared about the formal aspect of his relations with the Senate, made use of its support and favour, took advantage of the splendour surrounding it and the prestige which it possessed in society.

In the correspondence addressed to the *patres* he formally informed them of various matters, not always the ones most important for the state, expecting them to approve of his actions — yet the final word usually belonged to him. The emperor decided upon the composition of the Senate, incorporating therein the people loyal to him and removing the informers from his predecessor's times; he approved or disapproved of senatorial governorships; finally, he also decided on the necessary legislative and financial reform, considering the Senate as an important ally and a counterbalance to the influence of the military. The compromises in favour of the Senate had not diminished his imperial prerogatives, although they could have significant impact in terms of prestige for the members of the Curia. They strengthened the sense of common responsibility for the Empire, augmented the authority of the institution as the

---

[84] See: Cass. Dio 80(79), 2, 5—6; cf.: Cass. Dio 80(79), 8, 1 — on this mention in the context of other, especially papyrological, sources, see extensively in: E. Van't D a c k: *Encore la damnatio memoriae de Macrin: une innovation παρά τό καθεστηκός (Dion Cassius 79.8.1)*. In: *Romanitas-Christianitas. Untersuchungen zur Geschichte und Literatur der römischen Kaiserzeit. Johannes Straub zum 70. Geburtstag am 18. October 1982 gewidmet*. Berlin 1982, pp. 324—334.

[85] See: P. S a l a m a: *L'empereur Macrin Parthicus Maximus...*, inventory after p. 340; J. Š a š e l: *Pro salute Macrini (Šempeter bei Celeia)*. "Zeitschrift für Papyrologie und Epigraphik", Bd. 62 (1986), pp. 263—266.

[86] See: P.J. S i j p e s t e i j n: *Macrinus' damnatio memoriae und die Papyri*. "Zeitschrift für Papyrologie und Epigraphik", Bd. 13 (1974), pp. 219—227 (see also: L. K o e n e n: *Eine Berechnung der Regierungsjahre der Augustus vom Tode Caesars. Zur Datierung der Gesprächssituation von Tacitus' Dialogus (17, 3)*. "Zeitschrift für Papyrologie und Epigraphik", Bd. 13 (1974), pp. 228, 230); E. Van't D a c k: *Encore la damnatio memoriae...*, pp. 324—334; P. C a v u o t o: *Macrino...*, p. 61; R. P i n t a u d i: *Fragmmento di un documento con la 'damnatio memoriae' di Macrinus e Diadumenianus (P. Cair. J.E. 87697)*. "Aegyptus", Vol. 67 (1987), pp. 95—98.

[87] HA *Heliogabalus* 8, 4—5. See also: HA. Ed. A. C h a s t a g n o l, pp. 179—181, note 45.

second, after the emperor, decision-maker in the state (although a rather nominal one), and restored the order of the Antonines' period, who were treated with general respect and favourable memory among the members of the *ordo senatorius*. In general, then, with regard to the *patres*, the emperor showed a considerable talent for diplomacy, which enabled him both to gain the senator's support and approval, and enforce his own position, without arousing much outrage, not to mention any sentiments leading to opposition.

In conclusion, it must be noted that Macrinus' relations with the Senate should result in a rather positive image in ancient historiography. We have the right to suppose that this would have happened, as in the chronologically earliest accounts by Cassius Dio and Herodianus critical comments are found along with some more favourable opinions referring to him.[88] The posthumous *damnatio memoriae* and the propaganda hostile to the *Opelli*, disseminated by his successors — Elagabalus and Severus Alexander, compelled to discredit the predecessor in order to legitimize their own usurpation, had exerted a certain effect on the image of Macrinus' reign. Most probably, they influenced the late-antiquity authors to label Macrinus and his son as "bad emperors", and, in consequence, portrayed them using the stereotyped features characteristic of cruel tyrants, such as low birth, exceptional cruelty, dissipation, etc.[89] In view of the actual image of the emperor's reign, in particular his relations with the Senate, it seems to be a certain paradox.[90]

Appendix

Macrinus — Caracalla's Murderer
Truth or Forgery of Elagabalus and Severus Alexander Propaganda?

In the history of the Roman Empire conspiracies against rulers and assassinations of rulers were not rare incidents. Both the emperors regarded as tyrants and those considered as benevolent rulers had died at the hands of assassins. None of the successors of Augustus from the Julio-Claudian dynasty died of natural causes. Similarly, the ephemeral emperors of the year 68 and the last emperor of the Flavian dynasty, Domitian, died a violent death. From the year 192 on, i.e. from the murder of Commodus, the last of the Antonines, and especially in the third century A.D. the taking-over of power after the killing of the predecessor, and often also of the other pretenders, had become

---

[88] Cf.: Cass. Dio 79(78), 11, 2; H e r o d. 5, 2, 1—2.

[89] See, for instance: HA *Diadumenianus* 8, 2—9, 6; HA *Macrinus* 2, 1; 6, 1 (*improbus imperator*); 11, 1; 12, 1—10; 13, 3; 14, 1; HA. *Heliogabalus* 2, 3. On the emperor's low birth, cf. B. M o u c h o v à: *Ignobilitas Macrini*. "Listy Filologické", Vol. 106 (1983), pp. 174—177.

[90] Regarding the assessment of Macrinus as emperor, cf. also: H.-G. P f l a u m: *Carriéres procuratoriennes...*, p. 672; P. C a v u o t o: *Macrino...*, pp. 61—62.

a rule.[91] Septimius Severus, who had died a natural death, was the only exception to the rule. However, the portrayal of some conspiracies may raise certain doubts and one should consider, whether the ancient tradition has always rendered a reliable course of the events, and indicated the real murderers and their motives. In some cases we can notice certain distortions in the actual course of events, caused by the purposeful propaganda action of the successors, interested in discrediting the predecessor's portrait. In this contribution we shall attempt to indicate just such shortcomings of the ancient tradition on the example of the emperor Marcus Opellius Severus Macrinus (April 11, 217 — past June 8, 218).

The ancient sources agree in blaming Macrinus for the conspiracy and death of his predecessor, Caracalla. The versions of the events connected with the conspiracy, as transferred by Cassius Dio and Herodianus, are convergent in many regards.[92] According to the sources Caracalla asked the commander of armies in Rome (*praefectus vigilum?*) Flavius Maternianus,[93] to ask the augurs about his end. Maternianus conceived himself, or it was actually prophesied to him (ancient authors also had their own doubts as to the truth of that information), that Macrinus, one of the praetorian prefects at that time,

---

[91] Regarding mechanisms of the transmission of the power in the Roman Empire in the 1st—3rd century AD, there is a considerable amount of literary sources. Scholars have paid particular attention to the undertaken, though basically unsuccessful, attempts at introducing the dynastic power, see e.g.: M. H a m m o n d: *The Transmission of the Power of the Roman Emperor from the Death of Nero in A.D. 68 to That of Alexander Severus in A.D. 235.* "Memoirs of the American Academy at Rome", Vol. 24 (1956), pp. 61—133; B. P a r s i: *Désignation et investiture de l'empereur romain (Ier—IIe siècle après J.C.).* Paris 1963; T. K o t u l a: *Ideologia dynastyczna w pięćdziesięcioleciu 235—284.* W: *Studia z dziejów starożytnego Rzymu.* Red. A. K u n i s z. Katowice 1988, pp. 65—96; A. K l u c z e k: *Polityka dynastyczna w Cesarstwie Rzymskim w latach 235—284.* Katowice 2000 (with an ample bibliography therein).

[92] Cass. Dio 79(78), 4, 1—5, 3; Herod. 4, 12, 3—13, 2. *Historia Augusta*, based in some measure on Herodianus contains only some supplementary information in the biographies of Caracalla (6, 6) and Macrinus (4, 7—8). In more detail, the correlation among these three sources in the matter of Caracalla's death has been discussed by F. K o l b: *Literarische Beziehungen...*, pp. 118—135.

[93] On him PIR² F 319. V. V i t u c c i (*Ricerche sulla praefectvra vrbi...*, pp. 119—120) omits him as the prefect of the City, contrary to G. T u r t o n (*The Syrian Princesses. The Women Who Ruled Rome AD 193—235.* London 1974, p. 128 sqq.) and P. C a v u o t o (*Macrino...*, p. 18), who do not have doubt regarding the office held by Maternianus. Elsewhere in his text, Cassius Dio (79(78), 21, 2) shows that the emperor did not apply capital punishment against senators (cf. also Cass. Dio 79(78), 12, 2; Herod. 5, 1, 8). Therefore, as Maternianus was not a senator, he could not hold the office of *praefectus Urbi*. The other "commander" administering the armed forces in Rome was only the *praefectus vigilum*. His equestrian status does not clash with Dio's information and it is probable that Maternianus held just such an office. Thus, he would have been the predecessor of Valerius Titanianus, *praefectus vigilum* in 217, who is known from inscription, see: CIL XIV 4393 = ILS 465.

was aiming to take over the power.[94] Consequently, Maternianus, who was loyal to Caracalla, wrote to the emperor that he should get rid of Opellius. Cassius Dio adds that the letter has been sent first to Iulia Domna, the emperor's mother residing at Antioch, who did not allow the less important letters to reach her son. Since then, she must have known about everything.[95] However, it was Ulpius Iulianus who informed Macrinus in writing about that letter.[96] Maternianus' letter was delivered to the emperor, but he ordered the prefect to look through all the letters. Having found the potentially incriminating letter, the prefect concealed it, as he was afraid that Maternianus would send another one, which would reach the emperor. Therefore, he decided to act. Herodianus also adds that Macrinus had his own personal reasons, to be afraid for his life and to conspire against Caracalla. The emperor often mocked his laziness and effeminacy, and even threatened him with death.[97] Therefore, the prefect coaxed the tribunes of the praetorian guard, brothers Aurelius Apollinaris and Aurelius Nemesianus,[98] as well as the emperors adjutant officer (*evocatus?*), Iulius Martialis,[99] whose brother had been executed recently and who was refused promotion to the position of centurion by Caracalla, to kill the emperor. *Historia Augusta* also mentions the legate of *legio II Parthica* Aelius Triccianus and the prefect of the fleet, and probably a former procurator *ab epistulis*, Marcius Claudius Agrippa. It also mentions that many lower-rank officials, incited by Martialis, knew about the plot.[100]

---

[94] Characteristic expression of propaganda actions in antiquity was, among others, disseminating information about various omens, both good and bad. They were a very comfortable tool of forming the public opinion of the societies in which there was no clear border between *sacrum* and *profanum*. In the sources describing Macrinus' rule we can also find many examples of using the omens as a political instrument, see cf.: Cass. Dio 79(78), 4, 1—2 and 4—5; HA *Diadumenus* 4, 1—5, 6; cf. HA *Macrinus*, 3, 1—6.

[95] Cass. Dio 79(78), 4, 2—3. It is however surprising why Iulia Domna did not inform her son about the letter in her own correspondence, but she sent back Maternianus' letter by return post.

[96] On him PIR¹ V 555; L.L. H o w e: *The Pretorian Prefect...*, p. 73. After Macrinus' imperial acclamation, he was appointed one of the praetorian prefects by the emperor: Cass. Dio 79(78), 15, 1; he was killed later during Elagabalus' usurpation at Raphanea: Cass. Dio 79(78), 34, 4; Herod. 5, 4, 2—4; HA *Macrinus* 10, 1—2.

[97] Herod. 4, 12, 2.

[98] On them: PIR² A 1452 and A 1561.

[99] On him: PIR² I 412.

[100] HA *Caracalla* 6, 7. On Triccianus: PIR² A 271; on Marcius Agrippa: PIR² M 224, cf. C 775. Triccianus' role in the conspiracy may be confirmed by his *damnatio memoriae* after Macrinus' fall, see: CIL III 3714; 3720; 3724; 3725; 3726; 3276 = 10635; 4636 = 10658; 10618; 10629; 10637; 10644; 10647; S. S o p r o n i: *Kiadatlan Pannóniai mérföldkövek*. "Archaeologiai Ertesitö", No. 1 (1951), p. 45 (= AE 1953, No. 11), No. 2 (= AE 1980, No. 716). However, it may also be the result of Triccianus' loyalty to Macrinus during the power struggle against Elagabalus, who took revenge, after his victory, on the followers of the defeated enemy. There is a similar story regarding Marcius Agrippa, cf. CIL XIII 7800 = ILS 9363.

On 8 April, 217,[101] when Caracalla was on his way from his quarters at Edessa to the temple of the moon god at Carrhae, in order to offer a sacrifice, he stopped halfway to answer a call of nature. Then Martialis, in a moment of inattention and under the pretence of being called by the emperor, approached him and stabbed him in the deck with a dagger. The emperor died and Martialis was trying to get away on horseback, but the Germanic riders from the adjutant's guard closest to the emperor caught up with him and killed him. Meanwhile, Macrinus was the first one to run up to the dying emperor.[102]

For many scholars it is obvious that Macrinus led the conspiracy against Caracalla.[103] Reservations as to whether he really prepared an attempt on his predecessor's life, although careful were advanced only by Harold Mattingly and Alexander Krawczuk, suggesting that it may have been invented by the emperors political enemies.[104]

However, upon analyzing the sources, it is possible to notice some more essential basis for doubt. First, our anxiety may be aroused by the convergence of the information contained in the independent sources. It seems to suggest that they come from a single source, which could be used to promote the only and true official version of the incidents, created by the imperial propaganda of Macrinus' successors — Elagabalus and Severus Alexander, pretending to be Caracalla's sons and intent on discrediting Opellius as the murderer of their

---

[101] The date mentioned by Dio (79(78), 5, 4) is broadly accepted, see: H.J. Bassett: *Macrinus...*, p. 21; E. Hohl: *Das Ende Caracallas...*, p. 276—293; R. Hanslik: *Caracalla*. In: *Der Kleine Pauly. Lexikon der Antike der Grundlage von Pauly's Real-Encyclopädie*. Bd. I. Hrsg. von K. Ziegler, W. Sontheimer. München 1964, col. 1051; C.L. Clay: *The Roman Coinage of Macrinus...*, p. 29; P. Cavuoto: *Macrino...*, p. 19; D. Kienast: *Römische Kaisertabelle...*, p. 163; T. Franke: *Macrinus...*, col. 627. *Historia Augusta (Caracalla 6, 6)* is mistaken in the information that Caracalla had been murdered two days earlier, 6 April, 217, cf. M. Hammond: *The Transmission of the Power...*, p. 117, note 344.

[102] Cass. Dio 79(78), 4, 1—5, 3; Herod. 4, 12, 3—13, 2. HA *Caracalla* 6, 6; HA *Macrinus* 4, 7—8. Recently A. Luther (*Marcopolis in Osrhoene und der Tod des Kaisers Karakalla*. In: *The Roman Near East and Armenia*. Ed. E. Dąbrowa. "Electrum". Vol. 7. Kraków 2003, pp. 101—110) made an attempt to identify the place of the assassination, he suggests that it could have happened at the town, called *Marcopolis* under Gordian III perhaps in honour Caracalla (Marcus Aurelius Antoninus).

[103] So: H.J. Bassett: *Macrinus...*, pp. 19—21; H. v. Petrikovits: *M. Opellius Macrinus...*, col. 543—545; A. Calderini: *I Severi. La crisi dell'impero nel III secolo*. Bologna 1949, p. 98; D. Magie: *Roman Rule in Asia Minor to the End of the Third Century after Christ*. Vol. 1. Princeton 1950, p. 686; H.M.D. Parker: *A History of the Roman World from A.D. 138 to 337*. Revised with additional notes by B.H. Warmington. London 1969, p. 96; P. Cavuoto: *Macrino...*, pp. 17—20; M. Cary, H.H. Scullard: *Dzieje Rzymu. Od czasów najdawniejszych do Konstantyna*. T. 2. Warszawa 1992, p. 314; D. Baharal: *Victory of Propaganda...*, p. 44. About the date, description and circumstances of Caracalla's death in the sources, see also: E. Hohl: *Das Ende Caracallas...*, pp. 276—293; F. Kolb: *Literarische Beziehungen...*, pp. 118—135.

[104] H. Mattingly: *The Reign of Macrinus...*, pp. 963—965; A. Krawczuk: *Poczet cesarzy rzymskich. Pryncypat*. Warszawa 1986, p. 308.

"father", thus emphasizing the "legality" of the usurpation.[105] Second, another surprising fact is the excessive amount of details cited by the sources.[106] One should remember that all of them come from the period after the year 218, i.e. from the times when the memory of Macrinus was subjected to *damnatio memoriae*, and most of the people involved in the conspiracy or knowing anything about it were already dead. Martialis was killed right after the murder of the emperor.[107] The fate of Apollinaris and Nemesianus is unknown — they disappear from the sources, though perhaps Herodianuss remark of the tribunes who had participated in the plot and had been punished after Macrinus' death, refers to them.[108] Ulpius Iulianus was murdered by the rebellious soldiers during the siege of the camp at Raphanea.[109] Moreover, Maternianus was sentenced to death by Macrinus[110] — maybe that predestined him to play the part ascribed to him by the propaganda. As for Macrinus, he was the main accused and therefore he could not defend himself. Therefore, it had not been possible any more at the time to verify the contents disseminated by the propaganda, and the details such as the content of the letters as well as the arrangements made among the conspirators were easy to fabricate. Suitably passed to public knowledge they became with time the only valid "truth". Third, it may be surprising to see the ineptitude with which Maternianus wanted to inform Caracalla about the attempt being prepared by Macrinus. Maternianus, who was staying in Rome at the time, must have known the customs of the court, and therefore he must have known that the correspondence directed to the emperor was usually handled by one of the prefects, Macrinus at that time. Therefore, it would be unreasonable to write an official letter to the emperor with the accusations against Macrinus, as it would have reached him anyway. There were other, and safer, ways of informing the emperor. It would have been possible, for example, to send a letter through a messenger, who would deliver it directly to the ruler or the other prefect. Besides, it would have been certain to find someone among *familia imperatoris*, at Caracalla's court, to hand over such a letter to the emperor, even if it contained false accusations. Fourth, there is no information in the sources about the disclosing of the conspiracy by Iulia Domna, who — accord-

---

[105] Compare the opinion of F. Kolb (*Literarische Beziehungen...*, pp. 134—135), who believes that the account of Cassius Dio was a source of information for Herodianus and *Historia Augusta*. However, it does not exclude the fact that Dio could quote only the official version of the events propagated by Elagabalus and Severus Alexander.

[106] They were certainly not discussed by the conspirators, not to mention by Macrinus — a public acknowledgement of the responsibility for the murder of the emperor beloved by the soldiers would have brought tragic consequences for them.

[107] Cass. Dio 79(78), 5, 5; Herod. 4, 13, 6.

[108] Herod. 44, 14, 2—3.

[109] Cass. Dio 79(78), 32, 3 and 34, 4; Herod. 5, 4, 3—4.

[110] Cass. Dio 79(78), 15, 3.

ing to Dio — knew about it.[111] Such information, even a rumor, passed to the soldiers by the mother of the murdered emperor, could deprive Macrinus of power as early as in the summer of 217. Finally, the information concerning the organization of the conspiracy and any actions of the conspiracy members were kept secret; as revealing of anything was a deadly threat to everybody involved in the matter. The conspiracy's traces in the form of letters, witnesses, etc., therefore had to be removed (Martialis' fate!) and surely nobody saved them; neither made a show of their part in such an undertaking.

It is comprehensible, however, that the events of the day of Caracalla's death were well-known, as there were many witnesses of that event and therefore the circumstances of the death of Severus' son do not raise much doubt. The course of the attempt on Caracalla did not have to be distorted by propaganda, as it ideally agreed with its requirements; nor did it disturb the view of the conspiracy created thereby. Moreover, it was easy to get rid of several real or alleged conspirators, and still harder meanwhile to remove the numerous members of Caracalla's retinue acompanying the ruler on his last day, as it would be highly suspicious and would arouse unnecessary interest in the events of that day, which was certainly not desired. Finally, Macrinus' presence by the ruler at the moment of his death, a fact known by many, rendered more probable the contents promoted later by the hostile propaganda, which could portray him as the conspirators' main leader.

One should also wonder here whether Macrinus, if he actually led the conspirators, would dare, three days later, to accept by imperial acclamation the title of Severus in the presence of the army venerating the murdered ruler,[112] and thus propagate his relations with the dynasty of Antonines-Severi and their political program.[113] It is not very likely, because such an act would make him an exceptionally perfidious malefactor — usurper of the good name of his direct predecessors, which he had profaned that way and which he desired to make an additional use of in his own interest. However, such a representation of Macrinus' conduct was in the interest of the propaganda hostile to him and perhaps it was promoted by that propaganda.

---

[111] Cass. Dio 79(78), 4, 2—3.

[112] His acceptance is confirmed by all kinds of sources: Cass. Dio 79(78), 16, 2; 37, 5 (cf.: HA *Macrinus* 2, 1; 3, 6; 5, 6—7; 11, 2); RIC IV/2 (*Macrinus*), Nos. 1—98, 119—210; P. S a l a m a: *L'empereur Macrin Parthicus Maximus...*, after p. 340 (inventory of inscriptions). See also: M. H a m m o n d: *Imperial Elements in the Formula of the Roman Emperors during the First Two and a Half Centuries of the Empire.* "Memoirs of the American Academy at Rome", Vol. 25 (1957), p. 36; H. G e s c h e: *Die Divinisierung der römischen Kaiser in ihrer Funktion als Herrschaftslegitimation.* "Chiron", Bd. 8 (1978), p. 387; P. C a v u o t o: *Nome e titoli di Macrino e Diadumeniano...*, pp. 335—336; P. C a v u o t o: *Macrino...*, pp. 22—23; PIR² O 108 (p. 448).

[113] On Antoninian-Severan imitations in Macrinus' policy, see: D. B a h a r a l: *The Emperor Marcus Opellius Macrinus...*, pp. 415—432; E a d e m: *Victory of Propaganda...*, pp. 43—51, 96—98.

Though in the light of the known sources it is not possible therefore to absolve the emperor Macrinus explicitly from the accusation of organizing the conspiracy against Caracalla, it should be acknowledged that its representation handed down by the ancient sources is warped. Most probably, this has been caused by the propaganda of Macrinus' direct successors. The reconstruction of the conspirators' actions related in the sources is not free from contradictions and arouses justified doubts, and moreover it ideally fits the representation created on purpose for the needs of the propaganda. The figures of the conspirators acquire the features of exceptionally tricky, unscrupulous traitors and killers, whose primary objective was to slay the emperor. The propaganda was very effective in blurring the real course of the events, in which Macrinus did not necessarily have to play the role of the conspiracy leader, directing actions of the rest of the perpetrators, which was attributed to him by the sources.

Translated by Marcin Fijak

Przemysław Dyrlaga

CESARZ MAKRYN I SENAT
Z SUPLEMENTEM:
MAKRYN — MORDERCĄ KARAKALLI
PRAWDA CZY FAŁSZERSTWO PROPAGANDY
ELAGABALA I SEWERA ALEKSANDRA?

Streszczenie

W artykule szczegółowo przedstawiono relacje cesarza Makryna z senatem. Zwrócono uwagę, że w źródłach brak śladów rywalizacji czy konfliktu między nimi, wręcz przeciwnie — można znaleźć wiele śladów współpracy i wzajemnego poszanowania. Cesarz nie dążył do konfrontacji z *patres*, widział w nich raczej sojuszników w walce o uzdrowienie sytuacji w państwie i ugruntowanie swej władzy. Dbał o formalną stronę stosunków z senatem, korzystał z poparcia i przychylności tej instytucji oraz wykorzystywał splendor, który ją otaczał, i prestiż, którym cieszyła się ona w społeczeństwie. W korespondencji kierowanej do *patres* Makryn formalnie informował ich o różnych, nie zawsze najważniejszych dla państwa sprawach, oczekując z ich strony aprobaty swych działań, jednak ostatnie słowo zwykle należało do niego. Poczynione na rzecz senatu ustępstwa w niczym nie uszczuplały jego imperatorskich prerogatyw, choć dla członków kurii mogły mieć istotne znaczenie prestiżowe. Wzmacniały bowiem poczucie współodpowiedzialności za losy imperium, podnosiły autorytet instytucji jako drugiego, oprócz cesarza, choć tylko nominalnego, decydenta w państwie oraz przywracały porządek z czasów Antoninów, cieszących się powszechnym szacunkiem i dobrą pamięcią wśród członków *ordo senatorius*.

Podkreślono, że generalnie w postępowaniu z *patres* Makryn wykazał się niewątpliwie nie-małym talentem dyplomatycznym, dzięki któremu zdołał jednocześnie zyskać sobie ich poparcie i aprobatę oraz potrafił stawiać na swoim, nie wzbudzając przy tym większego oburzenia, nie mówiąc już o nastrojach opozycyjnych.

Na koniec zwrócono jeszcze uwagę na pewien paradoks — zaliczenie Makryna przez późnoantyczną historiografię, mimo jego dobrych stosunków z senatem, do grona „złych cesarzy". Za powód tego uznano pośmiertne *damnatio memoriae* oraz wpływ wrogiej propagandy następ-ców, Elagabala i Sewera Aleksandra, zmuszonych do zdyskredytowania poprzednika w celu legalizacji własnej uzurpacji.

W apendyksie dokonano analizy źródeł dotyczących przebiegu spisku przeciw cesarzowi Karakalli, którego finałem było zabójstwo imperatora. Źródła, a w ślad za nimi większość badaczy, uważają za głównego inspiratora i prowodyra zamachowców Marka Opeliusza Makryna, następcę zamordowanego władcy. Wnikliwa analiza problemu wykazała jednak wiele mankamen-tów dotyczącej owych wydarzeń tradycji źródłowej i pozwoliła na wysunięcie określonych wątpliwości odnośnie do przekazanego przez nią obrazu wydarzeń. Chociaż nie można jedno-znacznie uwolnić cesarza Makryna od zarzutu zorganizowania spisku przeciw Karakalli, to jednak w związku z tym trzeba stwierdzić, iż przekazany przez starożytnych historyków jego obraz jest wypaczony. Najprawdopodobniej przyczyniło się do tego postępowanie bezpośrednich następców Makryna, wspomnianych wyżej — Elagabala i Sewera Aleksandra. Przekazana w relacjach rekonstrukcja poczynań spiskowców jest niewolna od sprzeczności, a ponadto idealnie pasuje do obrazu stworzonego celowo na potrzeby propagandy. Postacie spiskowców, zwłaszcza Makryna, uzyskały w wyniku jej działań cechy wyjątkowo podstępnych, pozbawionych wszelkich skrupułów zdrajców i zabójców, których głównym celem było zamordowanie cesarza. Propaganda ta bardzo skutecznie zatarła rzeczywisty bieg wydarzeń, w którym Makryn nie musiał koniecznie odegrać przypisanej mu przez relacje roli przywódcy spisku, kierującego poczynaniami reszty zamachow-ców.

Przemysław Dyrlaga

L'EMPEREUR MACRIN ET LE SÉNAT
AVEC LE SUPPLÉMENT:
MACRIN — L'ASSASSIN DE CARACALLA
LA VÉRITÉ OU LA MENTERIE DE LA PROPAGANDE D'ELAGABAL
ET D'ALEXANDRE SÉVÈRE?

Résumé

Dans l'article nous avons minutieusement présenté la relation de l'empereur Macrin avec le sénat. Nous avons attiré l'attention sur le fait que dans les sources il n'y a point des traces d'une rivalité ou du conflit entre eux, contrairement, nous pouvons trouver des signes de coopération et du respect mutuel. L'empereur ne visait pas à la confrontation avec les *patres*, il voyait en eux plutôt des alliés dans la lutte de l'assainissement de la situation de l'état et dans la consolidation de son pouvoir. Il s'occupait du côté formel des rapports avec le sénat, il bénéficiait de l'assistance et de l'approbation de cette institution et profitait de la gloire qui l'entourait ainsi que le prestige que le sénat avait auprès de la société. Dans la correspondance adressée aux *patres*, Macrin les informait formellement de différentes questions, pas toujours les plus importantes pour l'état, en attendant de leur part une approbation pour ses actions, pourtant la décision finale d'habitude n'appartenait qu'à lui-même. Les concessions au profit du sénat ne modéraient en rien ses prérogatives impériales bien que pour les membres de la curie elles aient pu avoir un poids de prestige. Elles renforçaient le sentiment d'une responsabilité commune pour le destin de l'empire, confirmaient l'autorité de l'institution comme le second responsable de l'état — bien que seulement nominal, et rétablissait l'ordre de l'époque des Antonins, entourés du respect et si bien conservés dans les souvenirs des membres d'*ordo senatorius*.

Nous avons souligné que dans les relations avec *patres*, Macrin démontrait sans doute un grand talent diplomatique qui lui permettait de garder leur soutenance et leur approbation, ainsi tout en réalisant en même temps ses objectifs personnels, il ne suscitait jamais des protestations sans parler de l'opposition.

Nous avons finalement démontré un paradoxe — l'historiographie antique tardive classe Macrin dans le cercle «des mauvais empereurs» malgré ses bonnes relations avec le sénat. Cette position est justifiée par la *damnatio memoriae* après la mort et l'influence de la propagande de ses successeurs, Elagabal et Alexandre Sévère, forcés à discréditer leur prédécesseur en vue de légaliser leur usurpation.

Dans l'appendice nous avons analysé les sources concernant le complot contre l'empereur Caracalla, dont la fin était l'assassinat de l'empereur. Les sources, et ensuite la plupart des savants, considèrent comme l'inspirateur et le dirigeant des comploteurs Marcus Opelius Macrinus, le successeur du gouverneur tué. Cependant une analyse détaillée du problème démontre de nombreuses inexactitudes concernant cette tradition historiographique et permet de formuler des doutes sur cette version des évènements. Bien qu'on ne puisse pas libérer l'empereur Macrin du reproche d'organiser le complot contre Caracalla, il faut remarquer que l'image transmise par les historiens antiques est déformée. Il est bien possible que c'est justement le résultat de la propagande des successeurs directs de Macrin — Elagabal et Alexandre Sévère. La reconstruction des actions des comploteurs, transmise dans des relations, n'est pas libre des contradictions, et en plus est parfaitement conforme à l'image forgée pour la propagande. En conséquence les personnages des comploteurs, surtout celui de Macrin, gagnaient des traits des traîtres et des assassins particulièrement odieux dont l'objectif était de tuer l'empereur. Cette propagande a falsifié de manière bien efficace la véritable course des évènements où Macrin ne devaient pas jouer le rôle du comploteur dirigeant, imposé par la relation historique.

AGATA A. KLUCZEK

Empereur invaincu et barbares
Les représentations des barbares dans
le monnayage romain
de l'époque impériale (235—284 apr. J.-C.)

Pour les Romains, la notion de barbare avait à la fois un sens ethnique et un sens éthique; la question était très complexe, «il pouvait exister des barbares intérieurs, et des Romains pouvaient se conduire de manière barbare»[1]; il y avaient aussi des barbares extérieurs qui étaient les habitants de toutes les régions extérieures à l'*Imperium Romanum*. Pour nos considérations les barbares sont seulement les peuples extérieurs d'en dehors

S. P. Q. R.

[1] H. I n g l e b e r t : *Citoyenneté romaine, romanités et identités romaines sous l'Empire*. Dans: *Idéologie et valeurs civiques dans le monde romain. Hommage à Claude Lepelley*. Textes réunis par H. I n g l e b e r t. Paris 2002, p. 249—250; cf. plus largement p.ex. K. C h r i s t : *Römer und Barbaren in der hohen Kaiserzeit*. „Saeculum" 1959, Bd. 10, p. 277—280; J. G a u d e - m e t : *L'Étranger dans le monde romain*. „Studii Classice" 1965, t. 7, p. 37—47; I d e m : *Les Romains et les „autres"*. Dans: *La nozione di „romano" tra cittadinanza e universalità*. Napoli 1984, p. 7—37; Y.A. D a u g e : *Le Barbare. Recherches sur la conception de la barbarie et de la civilisation*. Bruxelles 1981; E. D e m o u g e o t : *L'image officielle du barbare dans l'Empire romain d'Auguste à Théodose*. „Ktèma" 1984, t. 9, p. 123—143; E. C i z e k : *L'image de l'autre et les mentalités romaines du Ier au IVe siècle de notre ère*. „Latomus" 1989, t. 48, p. 360—371; A. C h a u v o t : *Opinions romaines face aux barbares au IVe siècle ap. J.-C.* Paris 1998, p. 17—20; Y. P e r r i n : *À propos de Sénèque. Modernité de la question de l'étranger à Rome au Haut-Empire*. Dans: *Le barbare, l'étranger: images de l'autre*. Textes réunis et présentés par D. N o u r i s s o n et Y. P e r r i n. Saint-Etienne 2005, p. 123—136.

de l'Empire romain[2]. Quelquefois ils étaient des individus sauvages ou in-
cultivés, toujours étrangers et surtout ennemis de l'État romain. C'étaient aussi
bien les Perses organisés politiquement que les Romains, et les peuples de
tribus demeurant la région outre un *limes* en Europe et en Afrique. Le barbare
restait ennemi avec lequel il fallait lutter et qu'il fallait assujettir, il était
« l'obstacle, l'adversaire, le défi, le mal, la menace permanente, et aussi la
matière rebelle à traiter et à transformer : cette omniprésence est donc dan-
gereuse et stimulante en même temps »[3]. Le motif du barbare était très repandu
dans l'art romain. Les ennemis luttant contre les Romains, les prisonniers de
guerre les mains liées ou les barbares rendant l'hommage à l'*imperator* sont
présentés dans les sculptures ornant arcs de triomphe, colonnes, temples,
sarcophages et autres monuments[4]. Telles représentations apparaissaient aussi
dans le monnayage impérial.

Dans les années 235—284 qui couvrent la période dite de la crise du IIIe
siècle, les monnaies impériales gagnent une grande importance dans les
recherches sur les différents aspects de l'histoire de l'Empire romain. Leurs
représentations nous apprennent l'attitude des Romains envers les peuples
étrangers et le caractère de leurs relations réciproques. Celles-là sont ainsi un
complément des sources littéraires parmi lesquelles peu nombreux sont les
témoignages contemporains aux événements décrits[5]. Les contenus des mon-

---

.   [2] Cf. P. T r o u s s e t : *La frontière romaine, concepts et représentations.* Dans : *Frontières
d'empire. Nature et signification des frontières romaines.* Éd. P. B r u u n, S. v a n d e r L e e u w,
C.R. W h i t t a k e r. Nemours 1993, p. 115—120. Il n'y avait pas de frontière officielle de l'Empire
romain ; *limes* et *ripa* étaient la frontière *de facto* ; il y avait aussi la frontière invisible des peuples
plus ou moins vassaux, ces *fines imperii* faisaient lc limite insaisissable et flottante à la périphérie de
l'orbis Romanus. Mais en sens idéologico-propagandiste les limites de l'*imperium populi Romani* se
confondaient avec celles de l'*orbis terrarum.*

[3] Y.A. D a u g e : *Le Barbare...,* p. 20.

[4] P.ex. P. B i e ń k o w s k i : *De simulacris barbararum gentium apud Romanos.* Cracoviae
1900 ; K. C h r i s t : *Antike Siegesprägungen.* „Gymnasium" 1957, 64, p. 509—529 ; A. G r a b a r :
L'empereur dans l'art byzantin. London 1971, p. 31—45 ; J.A. O s t r o w s k i : *Simulacra gentium et
fluminum. Propagandowe aspekty sztuki rzymskiej.* W : *Studia classica et byzantina Alexandro
Krawczuk oblata.* Red. M. S a l a m o n, Z.J. K a p e r a. Kraków 1996, p. 129—138 ; *The Colloquia
of the XIII International Congress of Prehistoric and Protohistoric Sciences.* Forlí (Italia) 8—14
september 1996, 13 : *The Roman Period (in the Provinces and the Barbaric World).* Colloquium
XXV : *The Symbolic and Ideological Significance of the Representations at the Barbarians in
Classical Art.* Eds. B. L u i s e l l i, P. P e n s a b e n e. Forlí 1996 ; I.M. F e r r i s : *Enemies of Rome,
Barbarians Through Roman Eyes.* Stround 2000 ; I d e m : *The Hanged Men Dance : Barbarians in
Trajanic Art.* In : *Roman Imperialism and Provincial Art.* Eds. S. S c o t t, J. W e b s t e r. Cambridge
2003 ; J. C o u l s t o n : *Overcoming the Barbarian. Depictions of Rome's Enemies in Trajanic
Monumental Art.* In : *The Representation and Perception of Roman Imperial Power.* Ed. L. D e
B l o i s et al. Amsterdam 2003, p. 389—424. À propos du motif de la victoire de l'empereur romain
dans la littérature antique, cf. T. K o t u l a : *Barbarzyńcy i dworzanie. Rzym a barbarzyńcy
w dworskiej literaturze późnorzymskiej.* Kraków 2004, p. 34—112.

[5] À propos de la littérature au IIIe siècle cf. p.ex. D. F l a c h : *Einführung in die römische
Geschichtsschreibung.* Darmstadt 1985, p. 259—262 ; H. B r a n d t : *Dexipp und die Geschichts-*

naies impériales reflètent aussi la condition de l'*Imperium Romanum*, et leurs représentations peuvent être traitées comme transposition en langue de la propagande de la situation concrète de l'État romain de l'époque et de ses problèmes les plus graves[6]. Au IIIe siècle une nouvelle situation aux frontières entre l'Empire et ses ennemis barbares, et dans les relations de l'Empire et de ses voisins est apparue; d'après Jerzy Kolendo dans ce temps a eu lieu une violation de l'équilibre entre l'*Imperium Romanum* et le monde extérieur peuplé des barbares[7]. Cette situation a dû influencer les demarches des empereurs romains dans le domaine de la propagande politique. En outre, certains phénomènes de l'époque de la crise comme l'affaiblissement de l'autorité du souverain et de son pouvoir et les usurpations provoquaient que le motif de l'ennemi-captif était souvent utilisé pour construire l'image propagandiste de l'empereur donné comme fort et vainqueur et même charismatique par ses valeurs du guerrier-vainqueur[8].

Dans «la propagande de la victoire» de l'époque de la crise du IIIe siècle, se propageait le courant dont l'essence était de lancer la conviction de l'empereur romain s*emper invictus* et *semper triumphator*[9]. Dans les guerres avec les barbares, il était soutenu par les dieux[10]. Ils étaient garants de la victoire

schreibung: des 3. Jh.n.Chr. In: *Geschichtsschreibung und politischer Wandel im 3.Jh.n.Chr. Kolloquium zu ehren von Karl-Ernst Petzold (Juni 1998) Anlässlich seines 80. Geburtstags.* Hrsg. v. M. Z i m m e r m a n n. Stuttgart 1999, p. 169—181; T. H i d b e r: *Zeit und Erzählperspektive in Herodians Geschichtswerk.* In: *Geschichtsschreibung...,* p. 145—167; M. Z i m m e r m a n n: *Herodians Konstruktion der Geschichte und sein Blick auf das stadtrömische Volk.* In: *Geschichtsschreibung...,* p. 119—143.

[6] À propos de la propagande monétaire au IIIe siècle cf. p.ex. H. T h i e r f e l d e r: *Die römische Reichspolitik von Septimius Severus bis zum Senatskaisertum (193—238 n.Chr.) im Spiegel der Münzen.* „Wissenschaftliche Zeitschrift der Karl-Marx-Universität Leipzig” 1956/1957, H. 3: *Gesellschafts- und Sprachwissenschaftliche Reihe,* p. 282—284; W. K a c z a n o w i c z: *Aspekty ideologiczne w rzymskim mennictwie lat 235—284 n.e.* Katowice 1990.

[7] J. K o l e n d o: *Les invasions des Barbares sur l'Empire romain dans la perspective de l'Europe centrale et orientale.* „Cahiers du Centre Gustave-Glotz” 1995, t. 6, p. 81—99.

[8] S.P. M a t t e r n: *Rome and the Enemy.* Berkeley—Los Angeles—London 1999, p. 171—202; N. H a n n e s t a d: *Rome and her Enemies: Warfare in Imperial Art.* In: *War as a Cultural and Social Force. Essays on Warfare in Antiquity.* Eds. T. B e k k e r - N i e l s e n, L. H a n n e s t a d. Kongelige Danske Vindenskabernes Selskab, Historisk-filosofiske Skrifter 2001, t. 22, p. 146—154.

[9] M. I m h o f f: *Invictus.* „Museum Helveticum” 1957, Bd. 14, p. 197—215; R.H. S t o r c h: *The „Absolutist” Theology of Victory: Its Place in the Late Empire.* „Classica et mediaevalia” 1968, vol. 28, p. 200—203; *Pius Felix Invictus Augustus. Una titolatura imperiale tra tradizione pagana e innovazione cristiana.* A cura di S. L a c o n i. Roma 2003, p. 45—55; K. B a l b u z a: *Triumfator. Triumf i ideologia zwycięstwa w starożytnym Rzymie epoki Cesarstwa.* Poznań 2005, p. 189—194, 229—233; S. B e n o i s t: *Rome, le prince et la Cité. Pouvoir impérial et cérémonies publiques (Ier siècle av.-début du IVe siècle apr. J.-C.).* Paris 2005, p. 211—228, 241—272.

[10] Voir p.ex. Y.A. D a u g e: *Le Barbare...,* p. 302: «*Sol Invictus* représentait [...] pour tous les Romains la puissance „anti-barbare” par excellence...». Cf. G.Ch. P i c a r d: *Les trophées romains. Contribution à l'histoire de la religion et de l'art triomphal de Rome.* Paris 1957,

romaine. Leur puissance surnaturelle soutenait la *virtus invicta* incarnée par l'empereur, lui garantissait la chance, la victoire perpétuelle et universelle. L'épithète *invictus* comprenait toutes ces valeurs du souverain romain. Il apparaissait dans la titulature impériale depuis le temps de Commode au déclin du IIe siècle et dans les années 235—284 il a trouvé sa place dans la pratique épigraphique et sur les monnaies impériales d'un grand groupe d'empereurs[11]. Dans l'usage, de plus en plus répandu, d'adopter le qualificatif invaincu, il est possible d'apercevoir les signes idéologiques de l'époque de la crise du IIIe siècle qui se démontraient par le développement des tendances absolutistes et l'omniprésence des sujets de guerre. Celle-ci surgissait de la nécessité de mener presque constamment des guerres contre les barbares et contre les concurrents au pourpre impérial. Ces changements idéologiques et la pratique des certains sujets se sont reflétés dans l'art numismatique. Annalina Caló Levi et Emilienne Demougeot parlent de la présence des barbares dans le monnayage romain et attirent attention à cette manière de célébrer et de propager les victoires romaines[12]. Les représentations des barbares comme les adversaires vaincus ou attaqués par l'empereur, dans l'iconographie monétaire exprimaient aussi bien l'épithète *invictus* de l'*imperator* romain. Il semble qu'il vaut bien analyser les représentations monétaires avec les barbares dans ce contexte plus étendu de l'un des courants principaux de la propagande impériale et d'assigner des étapes de l'usage du motif du barbare pour définir son importance et son lieu dans la propagande concentrée autour du thème de l'empereur invincible.

Les monnaies impériales frappées dans les années 235—284, sur lesquelles apparaissent des éléments graphiques faisant référence à des peuples et des pays «extérieurs à l'Empire» feront l'objet de notre analyse. Sur les revers monétaires les barbares apparaissent à côté de l'empereur, divinités romaines ou symboles de la puissance romaine comme Victoire ou trophée[13]. Dans le

---

p. 471—481; J.R. F e a r s: *The Theology of Victory at Rome: Approaches and Problems.* In: *Aufstieg und Niedergang der römischen Welt. Geschichte und Kultur Roms im Spiegel der neueren Forschung.* Abt. II, Bd. 17/2. Berlin—New York 1981, p. 822.

[11] La liste des empereurs voir R.H. S t o r c h: *The „Absolutist" Theology...*, p. 197—206; M. P e a c h i n: *Roman Imperial Titulature and Chronology, A.D. 235—284.* Amsterdam 1990, p. 106—493. Cf. aussi S. B e r r e n s: *Sonnenkult und Kaisertum von den Severern bis zu Constantin I. (193—337 n.Chr.).* Stuttgart 2004, p. 184—198.

[12] A. C a l ó L e v i: *Barbarians on Roman Imperial Coins and Sculpture.* New York 1952; E. D e m o u g e o t: *L'image...*, p. 126—128.

[13] Les représentations qui servent à la propagande politico-religieuse liée à Mars ou *Sol Invictus*, sont omises. Cependant elles sont incluses dans le tableau n° 1 pour avoir une liste complète de monnaies impériales au motif du barbare. Les références seront données d'après les catalogues suivants: F. G n e c c h i: *I medaglioni romani.* Vol. 1—3. Milano 1912 (abrégé en Gnecchi); *The Roman Imperial Coinage.* Vol. IV/2—V/2. Eds. H. M a t t i n g l y et al. London 1968 (cité ici RIC); P. B a s t i e n: *Le monnayage de bronze de Postume.* Wetteren 1967 (cité ici Bastien);

monnayage impérial les barbares sont toujours un élément secondaire et constituent un ensemble peu logique ; il lui manque de structure et de hiérarchie. En général, les représentations des barbares n'ont pas de traits ethniques individuels. Leurs silhouettes sont unifiées et simplifiées. Grâce à cela ils deviennent un symbole universel des ennemis et en constituant un élément secondaire du dessin, leurs personnages servent surtout à la caractéristique de l'empereur victorieux, de l'Empire romain et des dieux romains. Néanmoins, dans l'iconographie monétaire les barbares réalisent des fonctions importantes. Ils suggèrent le sens de déchiffrer la signification des éléments principaux de l'iconographie et parfois ils changent la signification de la représentation par le seul fait d'être présent même d'une façon passive près des symboles de la puissance romaine et aux pieds du souverain ou du dieu. Entre les représentants de la partie romaine et les barbares, un certain discours se déroule. Dans l'iconographie il est annoncé par la pose des personnages, leurs tailles et gestes. Les représentants et symboles de la puissance romaine restent toujours les éléments centraux. Les barbares ont de l'humilité envers l'empereur ou le dieu. Le souverain et les dieux romains sont souvent de taille plus grande que les barbares, on dirait que ceux-là les écrasent par leur présence[14]. Le caractère des relations entre l'Empire romain et les barbares est illustré par la demonstration de l'hostilité avec laquelle ceux qui représentent les forces romaines traitent ceux qui représentent le monde des barbares. L'empereur ou le dieu les foule, l'empereur lance une haste contre eux, ils sont foulés par les chevaux[15].

B. S c h u l t e: *Die Goldprägung der gallischen Kaiser von Postumus bis Tetricus.* Aarau-Frankfurt a.M.-Salzburg 1983 (cité ici Schulte); M. A l r a m: *Die Münzprägung des Kaisers Maximinus I Thrax (235—238).* Wien 1989 (cité ici Alram); R. G ö b l: *Die Münzprägung des Kaisers Aurelianus (270—275).* Wien 1993 (abrégé en Göbl 1993); I d e m: *Die Münzprägung der Kaiser Valerianus I./Gallienus/Saloninus (253—268), Regalianus (260) und Macrianus/Quietus (260/262).* Wien 2000 (abrégé en Göbl 2000); H.-J. S c h u l z k i: *Die Antoninianprägung der gallischen Kaiser von Postumus bis Tetricus (AGK). Typenkatalog der regulären und nachgeprägten Münzen.* Bonn 1996 (cité ici Schulzki). On ajoutera les autres publications complémentaires mentionnées ci-dessous. Ces matériaux numismatiques ont servi à construire le tableau n° 1. La discussion sur la chronologie et la provenance des émissions a été omise ; les différents points de vue des chercheurs à ce propos n'ont pas d'importance primordiale pour le sujet du présent article et ne changent pas les remarques y faites.

[14] Cf. la dénomination 'small barbarians' utilisée par A. C a l ó L e v i: *Barbarians...,* p. 25—40.

[15] Telles idées apparaissaient auparavant mais au IIIe siècle elles dominent ; il n'y a pas dans l'art romain des images connues plus récentes de la *humanitas* de barbares ni de la *clementia* impériale leur accordée, cf. J. G a g é: *La théologie de la Victoire impériale.* „Revue Historique" 1933, t. 58, p. 30 ; E. D e m o u g e o t: *L'image...,* p. 127—128 ; G.Ch. P i c a r d: *Les trophées...,* p. 475—476. Sur l'évolution des représentations des barbares dans l'art romain voir aussi R. B r i l l a n t: *The Pax Romana, Bridge or Barrier between Romans and Barbarians.* In: *Gegenwelten zu den Kulturen Griechenlands und Roms in der Antike.* Hrsg. v. T. H ö l s c h e r. München—Leipzig 2000, p. 399—403.

Les barbares ont souvent des mains liées[16], restent debout ou assis aux pieds du souverain ou du dieu romain. Les représentations où ils rendent hommage à l'empereur apparaissent sporadiquement. Ces juxtapositions des barbares, des représentants et des symboles de l'Empire romain désignent leurs principale importance idéologique et propagandiste. Elles touchent surtout le domaine de la guerre[17].

La liaison de l'image du souverain romain construite à l'aide du motif du barbare au domaine de la guerre est annoncée par les représentations des monnaies qui comprennent sur les revers l'inscription du *cursus* impérial, un élément peu explicite au niveau idéologique et propagandiste. Sur les monnaies de ce type émises au nom de Philippe le Jeune[18] et de Probus[19], le souverain reste debout au-dessus du captif assis à terre dans l'attitude de la tristesse. Pourtant sur les monnaies de Valérien I et de Gallien, c'est la déesse Victoire qui reste le personnage principal du dessin. Elle est debout au-dessus du captif ou va dans un quadrige et tire la main vers les empereurs, pendant que Mars suit le char et deux barbares sont terrassés[20]. D'autre part les *aurei* de Postume sont illustrés d'un trophée entouré de deux prisonniers[21]. Sur les monnaies « des successeurs du trône », Philippe le Jeune, Salonin et Carin, avec le titre *princeps iuventutis*, un petit captif barbare (ou une petite captive) construit l'image du prince fort et vainqueur[22]. Dans les cas mentionnés ci-dessus, les traits du portrait propagandiste du souverain-guerrier ne sont déterminés que par l'iconographie monétaire.

Le motif du barbare a servi à souligner la puissance de l'empereur invaincu sur les représentations des monnaies dont les légendes concernent les différents aspects de son activité cependant l'affaire de la guerre apparaît toujours au

---

[16] Voir J.A. Ostrowski: „*Cum restrictis ad terga manibus*", wizerunki jeńców wojennych jako element rzymskiej propagandy politycznej. W: *Niewolnictwo i niewolnicy w Europie od starożytności po czasy nowożytne*. Red. D. Quirini-Popławska. Kraków 1998, p. 41—47.

[17] Cf. p.ex. J. Gagé: *La théologie...*, p. 26—31; T. Hölscher: *Images of War in Greece and Rome: Between Military Practice, Public Memory, and Cultural Symbolizm*. „The Journal of Roman Studies" 2003, vol. 93, p. 1—17.

[18] RIC IV/3 (Philip II), n° 237. Pour simplifier, on admet dans cet article que toutes les monnaies avec l'inscription de la titulature impériale appartiennent au même type. De même la formule *senatus consultum* (*SC*) ne fait pas de nouveau type de revers.

[19] RIC V/2 (Probus), n° 245—246.

[20] RIC V/1 (Valerianus), n° 231; Gnecchi II, p. 105, n° 5—6, pl. 112,8; C.E. King: *Dated issues of Valerian and Gallienus from the mint of Rome, A.D. 253—260*. In: *Essays in honour of R. Carson and K. Jenkins*. Eds. M. Price et al. London 1993, p. 217, n° 35; Göbl 2000, n° 813, 839.

[21] RIC V/2 (Postumus), n° 3; Schulte (Postumus), n° 43—46.

[22] RIC IV/2 (Philip II), n° 219; RIC V/1 (Saloninus), n° 11, 28, 32—34; Gnecchi II, p. 111, n° 3, pl. 116,5 (fig. 7); Gnecchi III, p. 61, n° 5, 12, 14; Göbl 2000, n° 269, 272, 274, 276, 323, 941—942; RIC V/2 (Carinus), n° 181—182, 302.

fond. Sur les médaillons de Gallien[23] et de Probus[24] qui acclament le slogan *adlocutio*, la scène où l'empereur (ou deux empereurs) reste debout, accompagné du préfet du prétoire, entouré de ses soldats qu'il harangue, est complétée par les prisonniers, les mains liées derrière le dos. De même les émissions annonçant l'arrivée de l'empereur vainqueur de guerre comme sur les antoniniens de Gordien III, du type *fortuna redux* qui présentent Victoire et un captif barbare[25]. Les émissions du type *adventus* gagnaient cette dimension plus souvent et plus couramment. Sur les médaillons du type *ADVENTVS AVGG* trois cavaliers précédés de la déesse Victoire qui tient une couronne sont représentés ; dans le cortège il y a aussi les soldats, devant les chevaux sont assis des prisonniers. Ces médaillons étaient frappés dans les années du règne de Philippe l'Arabe[26], puis dans les années du règne conjoint de Valérien I et de Gallien[27]. Plus souvent le captif barbare, parfois foulé, complétait le simple schéma de l'empereur à cheval, en absence de la Victoire, propre aux émissions du type *adventus*. C'était caractéristique pour le monnayage de Gallien[28], d'Aurélien[29] et de Probus[30]. Ces émissions glorifiaient l'entrée de l'empereur à Rome, mais aussi dans de différentes villes de l'Empire romain. Il est significatif qu'il s'agit d'un *adventus* militaire et triomphal, du retour de guerre en gloire.

D'habitude l'alliance du motif du barbare au domaine de la guerre est exprimée dans les représentations monétaires par son placement à côté de la légende parlant de l'idée *victoria*. Dans ce cas-là, le sujet de l'empereur vainqueur gagnait sa signification principale, la plus importante. Le souverain

---

[23] Gnecchi II, p. 106, n° 1—2, pl. 113,4—5 (fig. 4); Göbl 2000, n° 301—302, 771.

[24] Gnecchi I, p. 9, n° 1; Gnecchi II, p. 115, n° 1, pl. 119,1 (fig. 14); RIC V/2 (Probus), n° 320—322, 580—581; K. Pink: *Die Medaillonprägung unter Kaiser Probus.* „Numismatische Zeitschrift" 1955, Bd. 76, p. 17, n° 1.

[25] RIC IV/3 (Gordian III), n° 247A.

[26] F. Gnecchi (Gnecchi II, p. 100, n° 3, pl. 109,10) et P. Dufraigne (*Adventus Augusti, Adventus Christi. Recherches sur l'exploitation idéologique et littéraire d'un cérémonial dans l'antiquité tardive.* Paris 1994, p. 70) admettent que l'iconographie montre Philippe l'Arabe, Philippe le Jeune et Lucius Priscus.

[27] F. Gnecchi (Gnecchi I, p. 55, n° 1, pl. 27,10) et P. Dufraigne (*Adventus Augusti...,* p. 70) admettent qu'ils concernent Gallien, Valérien le Jeune et Salonin. Mais ces princes ne portaient pas les titres au même temps, cf. A.A. Kluczek: *Polityka dynastyczna w Cesarstwie Rzymskim w latach 235—284.* Katowice 2000, p. 49—51. Ce seraient Valérien I, Gallien I et soit Valérien le Jeune soit Salonin, comme l'admet P.H. Webb, RIC V/1 (Gallienus and Saloninus), n° 1. À propos de ces monnaies cf. aussi J. Gagé: *La théologie...,* p. 26—27; R. Brilliant: *Gesture and Rank in Roman Art. The Use of Gestures to Denote Status in Roman Sculpture and Coinage.* Copenhagen 1963, p. 173—176.

[28] RIC V/1 (Gallienus, Sole Reign), n° 551; Göbl 2000, n° 1422.

[29] RIC V/1 (Aurelian), n° 42—43; Göbl 1993, n° 108.

[30] RIC V/2 (Probus), n° 2, 19—20, 63—64, 133, 154—167, 624—636, 836—837, 903—904 (fig. 15); Gnecchi III, p. 67, n° 46, p. 69, n° 65.

romain qui à l'époque de la crise du IIIe siècle devait souvent partir lui même
à la guerre contre les voisins barbares qui attaquaient les provinces de l'Empire, gagnait aussi de la toute gloire pour le développement propice des actions
de guerre[31]. L'exagération des succès militaires était symptomatique pour
cette époque. Par conséquent on profitait de chaque bataille gagnée, même
«menue» et sans grande importance politique ou stratégique à construire le
mythe de l'*imperator semper invictus*. Aux origines de ce mythe il y avait
parfois des faits fortunés comme un succès militaire. Quelquefois malgré les
faits infortunés comme une défaite romaine la propagande persuadait que
l'empereur auquel elle a ajouté les traits du guerrier-vainqueur, participait aux
luttes victorieuses avec des adversaires réels. Au fait, de nombreuses émissions
monétaires des empereurs des années 235—284 dans une légende désignent
l'ennemi. Néanmoins, les contenus de ces émissions ne se rapportent qu'aux
adversaires européens et asiatiques; il y manque de rapports aux batailles avec
les peuples libyens en Afrique romaine. En numismatique du IIIe siècle il
y a seulement deux grands adversaires du Nord et de l'Est, des terres au-delà
du Rhin et du Danube ou du Tigre et de l'Euphrate.

Dans l'histoire des rencontres guerrières de Rome avec ses voisins européens d'en dehors du Rhin et du Danube, les noms des peuples barbares sont
nombreux. Les frontières romaines étaient attaquées par les Francs germains,
Alamans, Saxons, Vandales, Hasdings, Juthunges, Quades, Goths, et Hérules
et Gépides apparentés à eux, Sarmates Iazyges, Sarmates Roxolans, Carpes,
Taïfales, et les autres barbares[32]. Dans le lexique monétaire seulement certains
d'entre ces noms ont apparu.

Sans prendre soin de différences linguistiques ni culturelles, presque toute
la population barbare sur la rive droite du Rhin a été appelée Germains[33].
Les rapports aux guerres avec eux sur les légendes des monnaies impériales et
les représentations des barbares dans l'iconographie, pouvaient prendre des
formes diverses, comprenant un déterminant ethnique *Germanica* ou *Germa-*

---

[31] J. Gagé: *La théologie...*, p. 21—34.

[32] À propos des guerres avec les barbares aux années 235—284 voir p.ex. E. Demougeot:
*La formation de l'Europe et les invasions barbares. I. Des origines germaniques à l'avènement de
Dioclétien.* Paris 1969, p. 391—534; K.-P. Johne: *Die Krise des 3. Jahrhunderts (193—306).* In:
*Die Römer an Rhein und Donau. Zur politischen, wirtschaftlichen und sozialen Entwicklung in
den römischen Provinzen an Rhein, Mosel und oberer Donau im 3. und 4. Jahrhundert.* Hrsg. v.
R. Günther, H. Köpstein. Berlin 1975, p. 59—98; voir aussi T. Kotula: *Kryzys III wieku
w zachodnich prowincjach cesarstwa rzymskiego.* Wrocław 1992, p. 11—41; M. Christol:
*L'Empire romain du III siècle, Histoire politique (de 192, mort de Commode à 323, concile de
Nicée).* Paris 1997, p. 81—185; J.-M. Carrié, A. Rousselle: *L'Empire romain en mutation des
Sévères à Constantin, 192—337.* Paris 1999, p. 94—109 (avec bibl. antérieure).

[33] Voir A. Chastagnol: *La signification géographique et ethnique des mots Germani et
Germania dans les sources latines.* „Ktèma" 1984, t. 9, p. 97—101. Cf. Y.A. Dauge: *Le Barbare...*, p. 468—481.

nicus. Pour la première fois à l'époque de la crise du IIIe siècle, le sujet de la victoire romaine sur les Germains illustré du motif du barbare est apparu dans les années du règne de Maximin le Thrace, sur les monnaies et médaillons du type *VICTORIA GERMANICA (SC)*[34]. Il y avait trois variantes de dessins de ces émissions : le prisonnier barbare aux pieds de la déesse Victoire ; l'empereur au-dessus de qui la Victoire surmonte une couronne et le captif aux pieds de celui-ci ; l'empereur à cheval au galop, précédé par la Victoire avec une couronne, écrasant deux ennemis, un soldat le suit. Les mêmes reprises des guerres avec les Germains ont réapparu sous le règne conjoint de Valérien I et de Gallien et sous le règne seul de Gallien. Le slogan principal *victoria Germanica* était alors modifié ; la propagande de la victoire germaine était liée aux deux souverains ou le superlatif *maximus* ou *maxima* soulignait la grandeur et l'importance du succès romain[35]. Sur les monnaies de Claude II le Gothique deux variantes des légendes monétaires ont été reprises. Elles acclamaient soit *victoria Germanica*, soit *victoria Germanica maxima*[36]. Dans le monnayage des autres souverains — Tétricus I[37], Probus[38] et Carin[39] — on s'est limité au slogan *victoria Germanica*. Depuis les années 50 du IIIe siècle, trois schémas iconographiques étaient répétés : la déesse Victoire représentée à côté du prisonnier germain ou des prisonniers germains ; rarement — sur les émissions de Gallien et de Tétricus I — elle couronne l'empereur ; ou un trophée flanqué à sa base par des captifs. Selon Gilbert Charles Picard[40], ce

---

[34] RIC IV/2 (Maximinus I), n° 23 (fig. 2), 70—73, 90—94, 115—116; RIC IV/2 (Maximinus and Maximus), n° 121 (fig. 1); Alram, n° 18—5/C, 6/C, 19—6/C, 26—5,7, 27—1—7, 32, 47—11; 48—11; Gnecchi II, p. 86, n° 4, pl. 102,5, p. 87, n° 4, pl. 102,9; Gnecchi III, p. 46, n° 6, pl. 153,11. Cf. R. Brilliant: *Gesture...*, p. 182.

[35] RIC V/1 (Valerianus), n° 129—130, 132, 181, 203, 263—265; RIC V/1 (Gallienus, Joint Reign), n° 3, 44—52 (fig. 5), 61—63, 95—98, 173—175, 177, 180—180a, 194—195, 245, 283—285, 404, 406, 429—430; RIC V/1 (Gallienus, Sole Reign), n° 307—308, 400—402, 436—437; Gnecchi II, p. 109, n° 33, pl. 115,1; Gnecchi III, p. 56, n° 77—78, pl. 155,2, p. 57, n° 95—96, p. 58, n° 103—104; Göbl 2000, n° 35, 37, 78—82, 116—118, 146—148, 187—188, 307, 415, 429, 442, 447, 451, 454, 793, 845, 848, 873—874, 892—893, 960—961; *Roman Imperial Coins in the Hunter Coin Cabinet University of Glasgow* (cité ici HCC), IV: *Valerian I to Allectus*. Ed. A.S. Robertson. Oxford 1978, (Gallienus, Joint Reign), n° 19.

[36] RIC V/1 (Claudius Gothicus), n° 108, 247—250; Ph. Gysen: *À propos des ateliers de Smyrne et de Cyzique sous Claude II le Gothique.* „Cercle d'études numismatiques, Bulletin" (cité ici: CENB) 1999, t. 36, p. 32, fig. 4; D. Hollard: *Variété inédite d'un antoninien de Claude II frappé à Rome pour célébrer la victoire du lac de Garde.* „Bulletin de la Société française de Numismatique" (cité ici BSFN) 1998, t. 53, p. 83—87.

[37] RIC V/2 (Tetricus I), n° 38 (fig. 10); Schulte (Tetricus I), n° 2.

[38] RIC V/2 (Probus), n° 141—142, 149, 217—223 (fig. 17), 254—259, 268—269, 272—278, 299—300, 425; Gnecchi III, p. 70, n° 76, pl. 157,12, p. 70, n° 77—78, pl. 157,13, p. 71, n° 95, p. 72, n° 99, p. 71, n° 96, p. 72, n° 100—108, pl. 157,19—20.

[39] RIC V/2 (Carinus), n° 319—320. Cf. K. Pink: *Die Goldmünzen des Carus und seiner Söhne.* „Mitteilungen der Numismatischen Gesellschaft in Wiener Münzkabinett" 1928, p. 61.

[40] G.Ch. Picard: *Les trophées...*, p. 472—476.

dernier modèle a enrichi l'iconographie numismatique après des années d'absence dans le monnayage officiel de Macrin à Gallien, et il a pris la significance importante dans l'art triomphal. Le dessin sur les *aurei* de Carin se fait distingué. Ici, la représentation de l'ennemi sous les chevaux accompagne la présentation de la déesse Victoire qui va dans une *biga*, et tient une palme et une couronne. D'autre part l'idée de la victoire sur les Germains était aussi lancée par les légendes de revers monétaires qui rappelaient le surnom vainqueur de l'empereur, *Germanicus maximus*. L'image d'un trophée avec deux captifs y a été jointe dans le monnayage de Valérien I et de Gallien[41] et dans le monnayage de Postume[42].

Les Goths étaient le deuxième adversaire mentionné sur les légendes monétaires et symbolisé dans l'iconographie par le motif du barbare. Ils ont apparu dans le monnayage de l'époque de la crise depuis le temps de Claude II. Cet empereur a gagné le surnom *Gothicus maximus* menant les batailles célèbres contre eux[43]. Ses antoniniens du type *VICTORIA GOTHIC* et *VICTORIAE GOTHIC SPQR* représentent les Goths battus à côté du trophée[44]. Dans les années suivantes cette représentation a été reprise sur les antoniniens de Quintille[45] et d'Aurélien[46]. Sur les *aurei* de Tacite[47], de Florien[48] et de Probus[49], le sujet *victoria Got(t)hica* était commenté par le prisonnier de guerre et la déesse Victoire avec une couronne et une palme.

Sur le médaillon de Numérien l'image est nouvelle, mais le thème idéologique est ancienne et concerne une cérémonie symbolique du triomphe impérial. L'iconographie du médaillon présente les co-souverains — Numérien et Carin allant dans un quadrige, la déesse Victoire tenant une couronne figure en tête du cortège triomphal; sur le second plan on peut reconnaître les soldats et le trophée au pied duquel sont assis deux prisonniers, à l'exergue on peut

---

[41] RIC V/1 (Valerianus), n° 9—9a; RIC V/1 (Gallienus, Joint Reign), n° 17—19, 60, 141—142, 382—383; RIC V/1 (Gallienus, Sole Reign), n° 200; Gnecchi III, p. 56, n° 84; Göbl 2000, n° 93, 840, 872, 883.

[42] RIC V/2 (Postumus), n° 63, 129, 199; Bastien, n° 301—302; Schulzki (Postumus), n° 118.

[43] Voir l'ouvrage de T. K o t u l a: *Cesarz Klaudiusz II i Bellum Gothicum lat 269—270*. Wrocław 1994, p. 79—108.

[44] RIC V/1 (Claudius II), n° 251—252 (fig. 9); Ph. G y s e n: *À propos des ateliers...*, p. 31—32, fig. 3.

[45] RIC V/1 (Quintillus), n° 87.

[46] RIC V/1 (Aurelian), n° 339—340; Göbl 1993, n° 295—296.

[47] RIC V/1 (Tacitus), n° 110; S. E s t i o t: *L'or romain entre crise et restitution, 270—276 ap. J.-C., II. Tacite et Florien*. „Journal des Savants" 1999, fasc. 2, Tacite, n° 92—94.

[48] Ibidem, Florien, n° 9, 18: *Victoria Gotthica SC* et *Victoria Ghottica*.

[49] RIC V/2 (Probus), n° 10. La légende *Victoria Gothic* et *Victoria Gutthica*, cf. S. E s t i o t, Ph. G y s e n: *Probus Invictus Augustus: bustes inédits ou rares de l'empereur Probus*. BSFN 2004, t. 59, p. 82—84.

distinguer aussi les captifs enchaînés, assis en sens contraire. Ces barbares
— Quades — sont identifiés par l'inscription de revers : *TRIVNFV QVADOR*[50].

Le motif du barbare a également apparu sur les émissions dont les légendes
démontrent la victoire sur les Germains et simultanément sur les Carpes
transdanubiens. Sur les médaillons de bronze du type *GERM MAX CARPICI
MAX III ET II COS*, se rapportant au *processus consularis* de Philippe l'Arabe
et de Philippe le Jeune, les prisonniers barbares étaient présentés dans la scène
où la déesse Victoire va dans un quadrige, les deux souverains et Mars la
suivent à pied[51].

La représentation du prisonnier de guerre a aussi trouvé une place sur les
monnaies dont la légende de revers propage l'idée du succès militaire sur l'ennemi asiatique de Rome, la monarchie perse des Sassanides. Dans les années
du règne conjoint de Valérien I et Gallien les antoniniens du type *VICTORIA
PART(ICA)* ont été émis[52]. Sur leurs revers on voit la déesse Victoire tenant
une palme et une couronne, et le captif humilié à ses pieds.

Sur les représentations des autres monnaies qui clament l'idée *victoria
Augusti* ou *victoria Augustorum*, l'ennemi barbare reste sans nom, il est seulement symbolisé par un dessin schématique de revers. Ces monnaies étaient
très populaires dans les années 235—284. Sur les émissions de Gordien III,
l'empereur assis sur une *sella*, est couronné par la Victoire debout qui tient une
palme, devant lui un soldat (ou le dieu Mars ?) est debout tenant une haste, et
un captif supplie à genoux[53]. Dans le monnayage d'Aurélien[54] et de Probus[55]
l'image du trophée accosté de deux prisonniers de guerre a été exploitée. Sur les
monnaies de Postume, l'empereur reste debout à côté du trophée entouré de
deux captifs barbares[56]. Dans le monnayage de Valérien I[57], Gallien[58], Clau-

---

[50] Gnecchi II, p. 123, n° 11, pl. 123,8 (fig. 24) ; K. P i n k : *Die Medaillonprägung unter Carus
und seinen Söhnen.* In: *Centennial Publication of the American Numismatic Society.* Ed. H. I n -
g h o l t. New York 1958, p. 558, n° 12.

[51] Gnecchi II, p. 97, n° 4, pl. 109,1. Cf. aussi RIC IV/3 (Philip I), n° 66: *VICTORIA
CARPICA* ; Ch. K ö r n e r : *Philippus Arabs, Ein Soldatenkaiser in der Tradition des antoninisch-
severischen Prinzipats.* Berlin—New York 2002, p. 150, 155—157.

[52] RIC V/1 (Valerianus), n° 22, 262 ; Göbl 2000, n° 846—847, 881.

[53] Gnecchi II, p. 92, n° 44—47, pl. 105,9—10, 106,1 (fig. 3) ; K. P i n k : *The bronze medallions
of Gordianus III.* „Numismatic Chronicle (cité ici NC) 1931, vol. 11, S. 5, p. 259, n° 55—58 ;
HCC III: *Pertinax to Aemilian.* Ed. A.S. R o b e r t s o n. London—Glasgow—New York 1977,
(Gordian III), n° 164 ; H. D r e s s e l : *Die römischen Medaillone des Münzkabinetts der Staatlichen
Museen zu Berlin, bearbeitet von K. Regling.* Dublin—Zurich 1973, p. 224—225, n° 131, pl. XVI 3:
peut-être Mars au lieu du soldat.

[54] RIC V/1 (Aurelian), n° 354 ; Göbl 1993, n° 321. Cf. H.-G. P f l a u m : *Monnaie inédite
d'Aurélien, de Cyzique.* BSFN 1963, t. 18, p. 269—270.

[55] RIC V/2 (Probus), n° 291, 423—424 ; Gnecchi III, p. 70, n° 75, pl. 157,11.

[56] RIC V/2 (Postumus), n° 176, 235 ; Bastien, n° 150—151, 163, 174.

[57] RIC V/1 (Valerianus), n° 21, 260, 288—290 ; Göbl 2000, n° 842, 1565.

[58] RIC V/1 (Gallienus, Sole Reign), n° 80, 520 ; Göbl 2000, n° 113, 953—954.

de II le Gothique[59], Aurélien[60], Probus[61], Postume[62], Tétricus I[63], Carus et Carin[64], et Numérien[65], la représentation de la déesse Victoire à côté des prisonniers était l'élément principal de l'iconographie. Juste le nombre de barbares et les attributs de la déesse changeaient. Tantôt elle surmontait trophée, palme ou couronne, tantôt elle était présentée debout sur un globe, ou deux Victoires tenaient un bouclier. Sûrement ces légendes étaient énigmatiques et ces images étaient construites selon un schéma simple. Néanmoins, ces représentations, constamment répétées dans la propagande de l'époque de la crise du IIIe siècle avaient une grande importance à lancer la conviction de l'empereur romain invaincu. Sans préciser les faits, demeurant dans le monde d'illusions, de mythes, d'idées — bien qu'il faut admettre que dans certains cas elles aient un point commun avec les actions effectives et les résultats des actions d'un tel empereur — elles contribuaient à créer l'image de l'*imperator* invincible.

Dans la propagande monétaire de certains souverains on essayait de rendre l'idée générale *victoria Augusti* plus personnelle et distinguer le personnage donné. Pour atteindre ce but, on modifiait les légendes des revers monétaires. Sur les monnaies de Gallien un numéro a été attribué à la victoire[66]. La légende a été enrichie par le nom du souverain, sur les *antoniniani* de Gallien elle a pris la forme *VICT GALLIENI AVG*[67], sur les *antoniniani* de Postume: *VIC POSTVMI AVG*[68], et sur les *aurei* de Probus: *VICTORIA PROBI*

---

[59] RIC V/1 (Claudius Gothicus), n° 9 (fig. 8), 119, 170; Gnecchi III, p. 64, n° 18; H. Huvelin: *L'atelier de Siscia sous Claude II le Gothique.* BSFN 1985, t. 40, p. 723.

[60] RIC V/1 (Aurelian), n° 72—73 (fig. 12), 55, 96; Göbl 1993, n° 126, 139, 135A; Gnecchi III, p. 65, n° 18; S. Estiot: *Or et billon: l'atelier de Milan sous Aurélien (270—274 A.D.)* Dans: *Ermanno A. Arslan studia dicata. P. 2: Monetazione romana repubblicana ed imperiale.* Ed. R. Martini, N. Vismara. Milano 1991, n° 31, 34, 41—43; S. Estiot: *L'or romain entre crise et restitution, 270—276 ap. J.-C., I. Aurélien.* „Journal des Savants" 1999, fasc. 1, n° 50, 54—57, 62—64.

[61] RIC V/2 (Probus), n° 271, 599—600; Gnecchi III, p. 72, n° 98.

[62] RIC V/2 (Postumus), n° 39—40, 89, 103, 166—172, 174—175, 230—231, 233—234, 236, 251; Bastien, n° 3, 33—46, 91—102, 152, 162, 166, 175, 179, 184, 188, 193, 194a, 219, 229, 246, 252, 255, 259—260, 272—273, 287, 296, 298, 321, 328—329, 356, 366; Schulte (Postumus), n° 10; Schulzki (Postumus), n° 97a, b, c; J.-P. Carlot, D. Gricourt, P. Leclercq: *Une nouvelle série d'émission de doubles sesterces de Postume à titulature courte.* BSFN 1982, t. 37, p. 205—208; H.-J. Gilljam: *A New Gold Coin of Postumus.* NC 1993, vol. 153, p. 205—206; C. Poncelet: *Deux monnaies de bronze au nom de Postume.* CENB 1993, t. 30, p. 14—15, n° 1.

[63] RIC V/2 (Tetricus I), n° 33—34; Schulte (Tetricus I), n° 19.

[64] RIC V/2 (Carus), n° 18—19, 23—26; RIC V/2 (Carus and Carinus), n° 142 (fig. 23).

[65] RIC V/2 (Numerianus), n° 358.

[66] RIC V/1 (Gallienus, Sole Reign), n° 85, 399, 526; Göbl 2000, n° 955.

[67] RIC V/1 (Gallienus, Joint Reign), n° 38.

[68] Schulzki (Postumus), n° 96.

AVG[69]. Parfois on rendait les dessins qui accompagnaient les légendes clamant l'idée *victoria Augusti* plus originaux. À part les idées mentionnées ci-dessus, dans le monnayage de Probus on s'est servi de l'illustration sur laquelle l'empereur à cheval lance un javelot contre un ennemi terrassé[70]. Sur ses médaillons du type *VICTORIAE AVGVSTI*, deux Victoires restent debout face à face tenant entre elles un bouclier sur lequel on écrit : VOT X, à un palmièr auprès duquel sont deux captifs assis, les mains attachées derrière le dos[71].

La formule *victoria Augustorum* était parfois accompagnée des dessins originaux. Dans l'iconographie des médaillons des années du règne du premier souverain de l'époque de la crise du IIIe siècle Maximin le Thrace, l'empereur en habit militaire et son fils, césar Maxime en toge tiennent une *victoriola* ; au fond on aperçoit des soldats, et aux pieds des personnages principaux il y a deux prisonniers de guerre[72]. Dans le monnayage des derniers souverains de l'époque de la crise du IIIe siècle, Carin et Numérien, des représentations intéressantes ont aussi apparu : la déesse Victoire offre une couronne à l'*imperator*, deux captifs barbares sont assis à leurs pieds[73].

Les proportions du nombre de rapports dans le monnayage impérial aux victoires romaines sur les ennemis de l'est et de ceux qui signalent les succès militaires sur les barbares en Europe, surtout sur les Germains, sont caractéristiques. À part le cas décrit des antoniniens de Valérien I, les autres monnaies lançant l'idée *victoria Parthica*, émises au nom de cet empereur et des autres aussi[74], ne montrent pas l'ennemi vaincu. L'adversaire de l'est, la monarchie de Sassanides dont le voisinage aggressif menaçait les territoires romains surtout dans les années du règne du roi perse Sapor I, n'est pas devenu l'objet de transposition plus large en image de l'ennemi ou du captif sur les représentations monétaires. Cela est d'autant plus troublant que les empereurs romains admettaient les *cognomina Persicus* et *Parthicus*[75]. Pourtant la re-

---

[69] RIC V/2 (Probus), n° 11, 898.

[70] Gnecchi III, p. 68, n° 57.

[71] RIC V/2 (Probus), n° 601 (fig. 18) ; Gnecchi I, p. 10, n° 8, pl. 4,3 ; S. E s t i o t : *À propos du multiple d'or de Probus de la collection Duquénelle (Catalogue Journées Numismatiques Reims n° 55)*. BSFN 1992, t. 47, p. 342—344, n° 8.

[72] Gnecchi II, p. 86—87, n° 3, pl. 102,8 ; RIC IV/2 (Maximinus and Maximus), n° 120 ; Alram, n° 33—5 ; 50—12. Voir aussi RIC IV/2 (Maximinus I), n° 89 ; cf. Alram, n° 33—5, p. 83, n. 14.

[73] RIC V/2 (Carinus), n° 204 ; RIC V/2 (Numerianus), n° 443. Cf. K. P i n k : *Die Goldmünzena...*, p. 64.

[74] RIC V/1 (Valerianus), n° 291 ; RIC V/1 (Gallienus, Joint Reign), n° 453 ; RIC V/1 (Gallienus, Sole Reign), n° 310 ; RIC V/1 (Valerian II), n° 54 ; Göbl 2000, n° 1604 ; RIC V/1 (Aurelian), n° 240 ; Göbl 1993, n° 208.

[75] La titulature impériale avec des *cognomina devictarum gentium*, voir P. K n e i s s l : *Die Siegestitulatur der römischen Kaiser. Untersuchungen zu den Siegerbeinamen der ersten und zweiten Jahrhunderts*. Göttingen 1969, p. 174—178, 232—238 ; M. P e a c h i n : *Roman Imperial Titulature...*, p. 106—493.

présentation explicite des ennemis «nommés» d'en dehors du Rhin ou du Danube se trouvait dans le monnayage de treize souverains de l'époque de la crise du IIIe siècle. Dans cette dimension le contenu des slogans monétaires est moins diversifié et plus modeste que la titulature de l'épigraphie et des légendes du droit des monnaies qui donne parfois une longue liste *cognomina ex virtute* (surnoms de peuples vaincus) pour l'empereur donné. Le cas du monnayage de Claude II le Gothique et de Probus est exceptionnel; on y voit la pratique cumulative des déterminants ethniques de la victoire. Sur leurs monnaies le motif du barbare illustre l'idée *victoria* qui est complétée par les deux adjectifs: *Germanica* et *Gothica*. Par contre sur les monnaies de Philippe l'Arabe, Quintille et Tacite il n'apparait point avec le slogan très général *victoria Augusti* mais il est présent là où l'identité des ennemis est donnée.

Dans la plupart de cas décrits ci-dessus, les barbares — nommés dans les légendes des revers — contribuent à créer la représentation là où la victoire est déjà atteinte. Il y a des adversaires vaincus, enchaînés, humiliés, jetés à terre, l'empereur couronné par Victoire. Il y a peu d'images de l'empereur en combat sauf le monnayage de Probus. Les barbares sont, en général, un élément de représentations statiques, qui créent la conviction que la lutte est déjà finie, la victoire atteinte et que l'empereur triomphe. L'émission mentionnée du type *TRIVNFV QVADOR* en persuade parfaitement.

La vertu impériale qui exprime le mieux l'idée de l'invincibilité de l'empereur romain était *virtus Augusti*. Elle comprenait ses avantages de brave guerrier, dangereux aux ennemis: courage, vaillance et pouvoir de gagner[76]. En numismatique, elle exprimait sous la forme graphique le trophée, Mars, Hercule, ou la Victoire; mais aussi les représentations des captifs barbares à genoux ou assis à terre, les mains liées derrière le dos, et celles qui accompagnaient les présentations de l'empereur en combat contre l'ennemi pouvaient être sa correspondance graphique[77].

Le motif du barbare était très populaire dans l'iconographie des monnaies impériales clamant l'idée *virtus Augusti*. Dans ce contexte il apparait dans le monnayage de douze souverains. Au début de l'époque de la crise du IIIe siècle

---

[76] Voir p.ex. J. G a g é: *La „virtus" de Constantin, à propos d'une inscription discutée.* „Revue des Etudes Latines" 1934, t. 12, p. 398—405; W. E i s e n h u t: *Virtus Romana.* München 1973; H.L. A x t e l l: *The Deification of Abstract Ideas in Roman Literature and Inscriptions.* New York 1987, p. 25—26; S. L a c o n i: *Virtus, Studio semantico e religioso dalle origini al Basso Impero.* [Cagliari] 1988, p. 13—107; F. H e i m: *Virtus, Idéologie politique et croyances religieuses au IVe siècle.* Berne—Frankfurt a.M.—New York 1991, p. 175—184.

[77] À propos des représentations de la *virtus* dans le monnayage romain voir F. G n e c c h i: *Le personificazioni alegoriche sulle monete imperiali.* „Rivista Italiana di Numismatica e scienze affini" 1905, vol. 18, p. 387—388; I d e m: *The Coin-Types of Imperial Rome.* Chicago 1978, p. 63—64; F. S c h m i d t - D i c k: *Typenatlas der römischen Reichsprägung von Augustus bis Aemilianus.* Bd. 1: *Weibliche Darstellungen.* Wien 2002, p. 133—136.

les barbares apparaissent sur les médaillons de Gordien III. Le slogan *VIRTVS AVGVSTI* est accompagné par les scènes qui montrent l'empereur recevant le globe du dieu *Sol*, ou couronné par la déesse Victoire, à côté d'eux il y a des soldats ou *Virtus* personifiée[78]. Sur ses sesterces du même type on a représenté l'empereur à cheval, perçant de sa haste un ennemi terrassé[79]. Depuis les années 50 du IIIe siècle la liaison de l'idée *virtus Augusti* au motif du barbare est devenue plus populaire, la césure est mise par la période du règne conjoint de Valérien I et Gallien. Ça vaut la peine de souligner que dans le monnayage de Valérien I ce motif n'a pas du tout apparu sur les émissions du type *virtus Augusti* pendant que dans le monnayage de Gallien il apparaissait souvent et dans diverses combinaisons iconographiques: empereur foulant ennemi; souverain à cheval, des ennemis sous le cheval; souverain en cavalier enfilant des ennemis sur sa lance; empereur et femme suppliante, au-dessous prisonnier; captif aux pieds de Mars tropaeophore; trophée et prisonniers; Victoire qui couronne empereur, trophée entouré de deux prisonniers à côté[80]. Par la modification de la légende de revers on essayait quelquefois de donner une valeur particulière à la virilité dans la propagande de Gallien. De nombreuses monnaies qui lancent cette vertu l'unient à ce personnage: *VIRT(VS) GALLIENI AVG*[81]. Voyant la monotonie de la représentation de l'idée *virtus Augusti* dans le monnayage des souverains des années suivantes — Quintille[82], Tétricus I[83], Florien[84], Carin[85] — certains cas où les tendances à individualiser cette vertu et à mettre dans les représentations monétaires des modèles iconographiques plus originaux, se font distinguer. Dans le monnayage de Postume et de Claude II le Gothique à part l'idée primordiale *virtus Augusti*, les slogans *VIRTVS POSTVMI SC*[86] et *VIRTVS CLAVDI AVG*[87] sont

---

[78] Gnecchi I, p. 48, n° 11, pl. 24,3; Gnecchi II, p. 93, n° 50, pl. 106,10, p. 93, n° 56—59, pl. 106,8—10; K. Pink: *The bronze medallions...*, p. 257, n° 40—42, p. 260, n° 61.

[79] RIC IV/3 (Gordian III), n° 327.

[80] Gnecchi II, p. 109, n° 34, 36, pl. 115,2—3; Gnecchi III, p. 58—59, n° 110; RIC V/1 (Gallienus, Sole Reign), n° 323, 538, 589—593, 674—675; Göbl 2000, n° 779, 965, 1405—1406, 1450, 1555.

[81] RIC V/1 (Gallienus, Joint Reign), n° 38, 53—55 (fig. 6), 64; RIC V/1 (Gallienus, Sole Reign), n° 88, 149, 312—315, 378, 403, 529—530a; Gnecchi I, p. 54, n° 31; Gnecchi III, p. 58, n° 105; HCC IV (Gallienus, Sole Reign), n° 3; Göbl 2000, n° 890, 896, 966—969.

[82] RIC V/1 (Quintillus), n° 81.

[83] RIC V/2 (Tetricus I), n° 40—43 (fig. 11); Schulte (Tetricus I), n° 33—35, 73; D. Hollard: *Aurei méconnus de l'empire gaulois conservés au Cabinet des Médailles de Paris*. BSFN 1994, t. 49, p. 926, n° 4.

[84] RIC V/1 (Florian), n° 13, 16, 24, 44, 108.

[85] RIC V/2 (Carinus), n° 169—170, 287; Gnecchi III, p. 76, n° 29.

[86] RIC V/2 (Postumus), n° 185; Bastien, n° 22. Cf. sans nom d'empereur dans la légende de revers, RIC V/2 (Postumus), n° 94, 181—182, 252, 331—332; Bastien, n° 4, 106, 210; Schulzki (Postumus), n° 104—105.

[87] RIC V/1 (Claudius Gothicus), n° 227. Cf. sans nom d'empereur dans la légende de revers, ibidem, n° 255.

clamés. De même sur les émissions de Probus, la forme de la légende *virtus Augusti*[88] a été complété par la dénomination de l'empereur : *VIRTVS AVGV(STI) N(OSTRI)*[89] et de son nom : *VIRTVS PROBI AVG(VSTI)*[90], ou par souligner sa valeur d'invincibilité : *VIRTVS INVICT(I) AVG*[91]. Le trait particulier des représentations de ces monnaies de Probus était le fait que souvent elles montraient l'empereur à cheval en combat contre les barbares. Mais dans l'iconographie du médaillon de type *VIRTVS AVG*, avec la mention *Triumfum Gotthicum* qui est gravée à l'exergue, la lutte est déjà finie ; on y voit l'empereur à cheval, suivi par une Victoire qui le couronne ; devant lui un trophée et deux prisonniers, l'un assis, l'autre debout[92]. Les captifs aux pieds de Mars ou de la déesse Victoire ou aux pieds du Soleil Invincible qui couronne l'empereur apparaissaient plus rarement dans le monnayage impérial de Probus. Le monnayage d'Aurélien est différent au niveau de l'iconographie des monnaies du type *virtus Augusti*. Sur ses émissions les modèles connus qui montrent l'empereur à cheval foulant l'adversaire, galopant contre des ennemis, lançant sa haste vers l'ennemi, Mars portant le trophée et le captif assis à ses pieds, ou le trophée flanqué à sa base par des captifs, ont été reprises[93]. En outre, on a démontré que la *virtus* d'Aurélien est soutenue par les dieux.

---

[88] RIC V/2 (Probus), n° 12, 54—56, 225, 233, 235, 243, 283—286, 446—450, 602—603, 803—808 ; Gnecchi II, p. 120, n° 45 ; Gnecchi III, p. 68, n° 56, p. 68, n° 58, pl. 157,5 (fig. 20), p. 73, n° 113—115, pl. 157,22, p. 7, n° 116 ; K. P i n k : *Die Medaillonprägung unter Kaiser...*, p. 24, n° 39, p. 25, n° 40 ; H.-G. P f l a u m : *Deux antoniniani de Probus de trésor de Fresnoy-lès-Roye frappés à l'atelier de Ticinum.* BSFN 1969, t. 24, p. 346 ; cf. A. C a l ó L e v i : *Barbarians...*, p. 44. Sur la propagation de la *virtus* dans le monnayage de Probus, aussi dans les légendes du droit, voir H.-G. P f l a u m : *Bustes de parade frappés à Lyon en honneur de l'empereur Probus.* Dans : *Mélanges de travaux offerts à Maître Jean Tricou.* Lyon 1972, p. 253—260 ; W. K a c z a n o w i c z : *Probus the Emperor 276—282 AD, A Biographical Study.* Cieszyn 2003, p. 68—70, 80—82 ; P. B a s t i e n : *Le buste monétaire des empereurs romains.* Vol. 2. Wetteren 1993, p. 461—489.

[89] RIC V/2 (Probus), n° 809 ; Gnecchi II, p. 120, n° 43—44, pl. 121,10 (fig. 21) ; K. P i n k : *Die Medaillonprägung unter Kaiser...*, p. 24, n° 38.

[90] RIC V/2 (Probus), n° 13, 287, 312, 604—605, 810—822, 877—889 (fig. 19), 899—900, 912—913 ; Gnecchi III, p. 68, n° 61, pl. 157,6 (fig. 22), p. 73, n° 118 ; K. P i n k : *Die Medaillonprägung unter Kaiser...*, p. 25, n° 41 ; Ph. G y s e n : *Légende d'avers inédite d'antoniniens de Cyzique pour Probus en 281.* CENB 1997, t. 34, p. 56.

[91] RIC V/2 (Probus), n° 451—456 ; L. B e l l e s i a : *Nota su tre monete romane imperiali inedite: I. Denario di Marco Aurelio. II. Dupondio di Lucio Vero. III. Antoniniano di Probo.* „Annotazioni Numismatiche" 1997, vol. 7, n° 27, p. 602.

[92] S. E s t i o t, Ph. G y s e n : *Probus...*, p. 82—84. Cf. E. P e g a n : *Ein Bronzemedaillon des Probus auf den Triumph über die Goten im Jahr 278 in Pannonien.* „Numizmatičar" 1980, 3, p. 47—56.

[93] RIC V/1 (Aurelian), n° 15, 99 (fig. 13), 181—183, 210 ; Göbl 1993, n° 127, 164—166, 337A ; S. E s t i o t : *La première émission d'or au nom d'Aurélien à Siscia (270 A.D.).* Dans : *Proceedings of the XIth International Numismatic Congress, Bruxelles.* Vol. 2. Ed. T. H a c k e n s et al. Louvain-la-Neuve 1993, p. 324, n° 2, 16—18, p. 330—331, n° 1 ; S. E s t i o t : *Or et billon...*, n° 32, 37—39 ; E a d e m : *L'or romain...*, 1, n° 51, 58—60, 90—91, 98, 102, 125—136, 160.

Sur ses monnaies *Sol Invictus* remet le globe à Hercule, à leurs pieds un captif assis, ou c'est l'empereur qui reçoit le globe du dieu *Sol Invictus* et le captif accompagne cette scène[94]. L'iconographie des médaillons frappés à l'effigie de Numérien, du type *VIRTVS AVGVSTORVM* est différente et elle donne l'image très pittoresque. Deux Victoires couronnent Carin et Numérien co-souverains, et les empereurs en cavalier attaquent un groupe d'ennemis[95]. Sur les autres monnaies de Numérien, du type *VIRTVS AVGG* l'empereur est aussi présenté en combat[96]. Le motif de la déesse Victoire couronnant l'*imperator* était déjà connu dans le monnayage de Postume, il a été repris sur les *aurei* de Victorin, du type *VIRTVS AVG*[97]. Sur ses autres monnaies d'or, le motif du barbare a été lié aux slogans qui exprimaient l'invincibilité de Victorin, *INVICTVS AVG* et *DEFENSOR ORBIS*. Leur iconographie montre l'ennemi foulé par l'empereur chevauchant ou les barbares attaqués par l'empereur et le dieu Mars[98].

Le trait d'invincibilité du souverain romain — comme en persuadent les représentations monétaires — avait une signification plus large. Les barbares apparaissaient également sur les monnaies sur lesquelles les souverains étaient dotés du titre *restitutor* et *pacator* et aussi ils étaient définis comme donateurs de la paix et de la félicité. Dans l'iconographie les ennemis vaincus suggéraient que ces valeurs ont été atteintes ou seront atteintes en conséquence des guerres victorieuses et grâce au pouvoir vainqueur de l'empereur invaincu. L'annonce de tels rapports a apparu dans la propagande de Gordien III. Ses monnaies du type *VICTORIA AETERNA* présentant la déesse Victoire et le captif servaient à propager une victoire éternelle et la foi au retour de l'époque de bonheur lié à son règne[99]. Ensuite sur les antoniniens de Gallien, du type *VICT AET AVG*, illustrés de la déesse Victoire et du captif barbare[100] les espoires-rêves des effets réels et durables des victoires militaires de l'empereur étaient exprimés. Dans ce contexte il est aussi possible de comprendre les représentations des autres antoniniens de Gallien, avec le sigle *PAX FVNDATA* et la présentation d'un trophée et de deux captifs assis[101]. D'autre part sur les *aurei* de Postume, le souverain comme *restitutor Galliarum* reste debout tenant le pied sur le corps

---

[94] RIC V/1 (Aurelian), n° 316—318; Göbl 1993, n° 252.

[95] RIC V/2 (Numerianus), n° 401; Gnecchi I, p. 11, n° 1, pl. 4,7; Gnecchi II, p. 123, n° 12; K. Pink: *Die Medaillonprägung unter Carus...*, p. 559, n° 14.

[96] RIC V/2 (Numerianus), n° 398—399.

[97] Schulte (Victorinus), n° 56.

[98] RIC V/2 (Victorinus), n° 9, 90; Schulte (Victorinus), n° 28, 54—55.

[99] RIC IV/3 (Gordian III), n° 154—156, 165—166, 337—338. Cf. W. Kaczanowicz: *Gordian III. Ideał władcy okresu początków kryzysu Cesarstwa Rzymskiego w świetle źródeł numizmatycznych.* W: *Rzym antyczny. Polityka i pieniądz.* T. 1. Red. A. Kunisz. Katowice 1993, p. 68—76.

[100] RIC V/1 (Gallienus, Sole Reign), n° 291.

[101] RIC V/1 (Gallienus, Sole Reign), n° 652; Göbl 2000, n° 1635.

1. Médaillon de bronze, Rome, cf. RIC IV/2, p. 152, n° 121
Av./ *MAXIMINVS ET MAXIMVS AVGVSTI GERMANICI*, bustes affrontés de Maximin le Thrace,
lauré et cuirassé et de Maxime nu-tête
Rv./ *VICTORIA GERMANICA*, l'empereur galopant et foulant aux pieds deux barbares,
il est précédé par la Victoire qui tient une couronne et suivi d'un soldat

2. Denier, Rome, cf. RIC IV/2, p. 142, n° 23, pl. 10,8
Av./ *MAXIMINVS PIVS AVG GERM*, buste lauré, drapé et cuirassé de Maximin le Thrace
Rv./ *VICTORIA GERM*, la Victoire debout, tenant une couronne et une palme, à ses pieds un captif

3. Médaillon de bronze (*as* ?), Rome, cf. Gnecchi II, p. 92, n° 46
Av./ *IMP GORDIANVS PIVS FELIX AVG*, buste lauré, drapé et cuirassé de Gordien III
Rv./ *VICTORIA AVG*, l'empereur assis sur une *sella*, couronné par la Victoire, devant lui un soldat
(Mars ?) et une figure debout de face, aux pieds du soldat un captif suppliant à genoux

4. Médaillon de bronze, Rome, cf. Gnecchi II, p. 106, n° 1, pl. 113,4
Av./ *IMP GALLIENVS P F AVG GERM*, buste lauré, drapé et cuirassé de Gallien,
un globe surmonté d'une Victoire à la main de l'empereur
Rv./ *ADLOCVTIO AVGG*, deux empereurs debout, derrière eux le préfet du prétoire,
ils haranguent les soldats ; sur le premier plan deux barbares, assis dos à dos, les mains
attachées derrière le dos

5. Antoninien, Cologne, cf. RIC V/1, p. 72, n° 49
Av./ *GALLIENVS P F AVG*, buste radié et cuirassé de Gallien
Rv./ *VICT GERMANICA*, la Victoire tenant un trophée et une couronne ; sous ses pieds un globe ;
de chaque côté un barbare assis à terre

6. Antoninien, Trèves, cf. RIC V/1, p. 72, n° 54
Av./ *GALLIENVS P F AVG*, buste radié et cuirassé de Gallien
Rv./ *VIRT GALLIENI AVG*, l'empereur en habit militaire tenant une haste et un bouclier,
son pied posé sur un barbare

7. Médaillon de bronze, Rome, cf. Gnecchi II, p. 111, n° 3, pl. 116,5
Av./ *LIC COR SAL VALERIANVS N CAES*, buste nu, drapé et cuirassé de Salonin
Rv./ *PRINCIPI IVVENTVTIS*, le prince debout, en habit militaire, tenant un globe et une haste,
à ses pieds une barbare assise

8. *Aureus*, Rome, cf. RIC V/1, p. 212, n° 9, pl. 5,77
Av./ *IMP CLAVDIVS AVG*, buste lauré de Claude II le Gothique
Rv./ *VICTORIA AVG*, la Victoire tenant une palme et une couronne, entre un captif à genoux
qui lui tend les mains et un autre captif assis, les mains liées derrière le dos

9. Antoninien, Cyzique, cf. RIC V/1, p. 232, n° 251, pl. 6,86
Av./ *IMP C M AVR CLAVDIVS AVG*, buste radié et cuirassé de Claude II le Gothique
Rv./ *VICTORIAE GOTHIC SPQR*, trophée entre deux barbares

10. *Aureus*, atelier gaulois, cf. RIC V/2, p. 405, n° 38
Av./ *IMP C G P ESV TETRICVS AVG*, buste lauré de Tétricus I
Rv./ *VICTORIA GERM*, l'empereur en habit militaire, couronné par la Victoire ;
à ses pieds un captif assis, les mains liées derrière le dos

11. *Aureus*, atelier gaulois, cf. RIC V/1, p. 405, n° 41
Av./ *IMP TETRICVS PIVS AVG*, buste lauré et cuirassé de Tétricus I
Rv./ *VIRTVS AVG,* l'empereur lauré, vêtu militairement debout ; à ses pieds un captif, les mains
attachées derrière le dos

12. Demi-*aurelianus*, Rome, cf. RIC V/1, p. 273, n° 73
Av./ *IMP AVRELIANVS AVG*, buste lauré, drapé et cuirassé d'Aurélien
Rv./ *VICTORIA AVG*, la Victoire tenant une couronne et une palme, à ses pieds un captif assis,
à l'exergue : *B*

13. *Aureus*, Siscia, cf. RIC V/1, p. 276, n° 99
Av./ *IMP C AVRELIANVS AVG*, buste lauré, drapé et cuirassé d'Aurélien
Rv./ *VIRTVS AVGVSTI*, le trophée entre deux barbares

14. Médaillon de bronze, Rome, cf. Gnecchi II, p. 115, n° 1, pl. 119,1
Av./ *IMP PROBVS P AVG*, buste casqué de Probus, tenant une épée et un bouclier
orné d'un cavalier galopant et terrassant un ennemi
Rv./ *ADLOCVTIO AVG*, l'empereur debout, accompagné du préfet du prétoire, entouré de six
soldats qu'il harangue, sur le premier plan deux barbares à genoux et deux autres debout

15. *Aurelianus*, Cyzique, cf. RIC V/2, p. 117, n° 904
Av./ *VIRTVS PROBI AVG*, buste casqué et cuirassé de Probus, tenant une haste et un bouclier orné
d'un cavalier galopant et terrassant un enemi
Rv./ *ADVENTVS PROBI AVG*, l'empereur à cheval, levant la main droite et tenant un sceptre
de la gauche ; devant lui, un captif assis, les mains liées dans le dos

16. *Aureus*, Rome, cf. RIC V/2, p. 32, n° 136, pl. 2,1
Av./ *IMP PROBVS P F AVG*, buste lauré consulaire de Probus, tenant le *scipio* de la main droite
Rv./ *PACATOR ORBIS*, l'empereur lauré et en habit militaire, debout entre deux barbares à genoux
et deux autres debout

17. *Aurelianus*, Rome, cf. RIC V/2, p. 41, n° 223, pl. 2,10
Av./ *PROBVS P F AVG*, buste radié et cuirassé de Probus
Rv./ *VICTORIA GERM*, trophée au pied duquel se trouvent deux captifs opposés, les mains
liées dans le dos, à l'exergue : *RAA*

18. Médaillon d'or, Siscia, cf. RIC V/2, p. 81, n° 601
Av./ *IMP C M AVR PROBVS P F AVG*, buste radié et cuirassé de Probus
Rv./ *VICTORIAE AVGVSTI*, deux Victoires tenant un bouclier gravé *VOT X* à un palmier
auprès duquel sont deux captifs assis, les mains liées derrière le dos ; à l'exergue : *SIS*

19. *Aurelianus*, Serdique, cf. RIC V/2, p. 113, n° 877, pl. 5,2
Av./ *IMP C M AVR PROBVS F AVG*, buste radié consulaire de Probus,
tenant le *scipio* de la main droite
Rv./ *VIRTVS PROBI AVG*, l'empereur galopant, terrassant de sa haste, un barbare dont le bouclier
est tombé sous le cheval de l'empereur, à l'exergue : *KA.Γ*.

20. Médaillon de bronze, Ticinum, cf. Gnecchi III, p. 68, n° 58, pl. 157,5
Av./ *IMP C M AVR PROBVS P F AVG*, buste lauré et cuirassé de Probus
Rv./ *VIRTVS AVGVSTI*, l'empereur à cheval, lançant une haste contre un barbare à terre ;
deux autres barbares terrassés

21. Médaillon de bronze, Siscia, cf. Gnecchi II, p. 120, n° 43, pl. 121,10
Av./ *IMP C M AVR PROBVS PIVS AVG*, buste lauré de Probus, tenant une égide et une haste
Rv./ *VIRT AVGVT NOSTRI*, l'empereur à cheval, tenant une haste et poursuivant un barbare ;
un autre barbare à longue barbe suivant l'empereur ; à l'exergue : *SIS*

22. Médaillon de bronze, Ticinum, cf. Gnecchi III, p. 68, n° 61, pl. 157,6
Av./ *IMP C M AVR PROBVS P [F]AVG*, buste casqué et cuirassé, avec une épée et un bouclier
Rv./ *VIRTVS PROBI AVG*, l'empereur en habit militaire, galopant et lançant sa haste
contre un barbare à terre ; un autre ennemi terrassé ; un soldat précède l'empereur

23. *Aurelianus*, Lugdunum, cf. RIC V/2, p. 153, n° 142
Av./ *CARVS ET CARINVS AVGG*, bustes radiés et cuirassés de Carus et de Carin
Rv./ *VICTORIA AVGG*, la Victoire debout sur un globe, tenant une couronne et une palme ;
de chaque côté du globe, un captif assis les mains liées derrière le dos ; dans le champ : *A*

24. Médaillon de bronze, Siscia, cf. Gnecchi II, p. 123, n° 11, pl. 123,8
Av./ *IMP NVMERIANVS P F AVG*, buste lauré et cuirassé de Numérien
Rv./ *TRIVNFV QVADOR*, deux empereurs dans un quadrige, précédés par la Victoire qui tient
une couronne et une palme ; sur le second plan deux personnages qui accompagnent le char ;
un trophée entre deux captifs barbares ; à l'exergue deux barbares assis dos à dos,
les mains liées derrière le dos

25. *Aurelianus*, Rome, cf. RIC V/2, p. 196, n° 423
Av./ *IMP NVMERIANVS AVG*, buste radié et cuirassé de Numérien
Rv./ *VNDIQVE VICTORES*, l'empereur debout, vêtu militairement, tenant un globe de la main
droite et un sceptre long de la gauche, à ses pieds de chaque côté, un captif, les mains
liées derrière le dos ; à l'exergue : *KAC*

de l'ennemi jeté à terre, devant lui *Gallia* personifiée à genoux[102]. Sur ses *sestertii et dupondii* l'idée *felicitas* est illustrée d'un trophée entre deux captifs assis, les mains liées derrière le dos et de l'arc de triomphe[103]. Michel Christol remarque que ces symboles de victoire se rapportaient aux actions de guerre de Postume et leurs résultats; en effet ils devaient apporter la félicité universelle[104]. Pourtant les mérites d'Aurélien à introduire l'unité et la paix dans l'Empire étaient symbolisées par la présentation de l'empereur et du captif assis sur les antoniniens du type *PACATOR ORIENTIS*[105] et de l'empereur à cheval au galop, brandissant sa haste au-dessus de deux ennemis sur les *aurei* du type *RESTITVTOR ORIENTIS*[106]. Les antoniniens sur lesquels Aurélien portait le titre *restitutor Orbis* répandissaient la représentation de l'empereur et du captif enrichie du personnage féminin avec la couronne à sa main, c'était soit *Orbis* personifié soit la déesse de la Victoire[107]. Dans la propagande de Probus le motif du barbare était lié au vaste programme de paix. Le slogan *ubique pax* est son reflet sur les monnaies mais aussi le contenu de l'inscription: *Quot (sic) saeculo eius universus orbis floreat*[108]. Cette vision de la paix universelle était aussi répandue par les émissions au motif du barbare — ce qui est un certain *signum temporis*. Dans un tel contexte il est possible de comprendre les légendes des monnaies où Probus a été appelé *restitutor saeculi*[109]. L'empereur recevant l'hommage de deux barbares debout et deux agenouillés a été montré sur les *aurei* qui l'appelaient *pacator Orbis* et glorifiaient son oeuvre pacifique[110], et sur les *aurei* et *aureliani* qui par le slogan *VICTORIOSO SEMPER* clamaient l'idée de l'invincibilité perpétuelle de Pro-

---

[102] RIC V/2 (Postumus), n° 82; Schulzki (Postumus), n° 71—72, 74.

[103] RIC V/2 (Postumus), n° 118—119a, 120, 195; Bastien, n° 12—14, 142, 156, 207, 211, 222, 236, 238.

[104] M. Christol: *La Félicité de Postume*. Dans: *Mélanges de Numismatique offerts à P. Bastien à l'occassion de son 75ᵉᵐᵉ anniversaire*. Éd. H. Huvelin et al. Wetteren 1987, p. 107—108. L'image avait été utilisée à l'époque de Valérien I et Gallien, cf. Bastien, p. 66; D. Hollard: *Le prototype des bronzes de Postume „à l'arc de triomphe" enfin retrouvé*. BSFN 1997, t. 52, p. 71—75.

[105] RIC V/1 (Aurelian), n° 231; Göbl 1993, n° 192.

[106] Göbl 1993, n° 365; S. Estiot: *L'or romain...*, fasc. 1, n° 159; cf. H.-G. Pflaum: *Essai de billon d'un aureus d'Aurélien de Lyon au R/RESTITVTOR ORIENTIS et de type inhabituel*. BSFN 1954, p. 299—300.

[107] RIC V/1 (Aurelian), n° 349, 368—369; Göbl 1993, n° 337.

[108] RIC V/2 (Probus), n° 139, 296; CIL VIII 26560 = ILS 8927. Cf. plus largement, L. Polverini: *Utopia della pace nella Vita Probi*. Dans: *Contributi dell'Istituto di storia antica*. Vol. 11: *La pace nel mondo antico*. Ed. M. Sordi. Milano 1985, p. 230—245; T. Kotula: *Brevi milites necessarios non futuros: pensée irénique au temps de l'empereur Probus et sa réception littéraire*. Dans: *Speculum Antiquitatis Graeco-Romanae. Studia Joanni Burian sexagenario oblata*. Praha 1991, p. 207—217.

[109] RIC V/2 (Probus), n° 403—406.

[110] RIC V/2 (Probus), n° 136 (fig. 16), 591.

bus[111]. Enfin les médaillons à la présentation de deux Victoires tenant un
bouclier à un palmier accosté de deux captifs, ou de la déesse Victoire, de l'empereur et du captif qui donnent la formule « *vota x* »; ou « *votis x et xx* »[112].
Ils exprimaient les voeux du règne stable de Probus. Dans le monnayage de
Numérien le motif du barbare a été utilisé aussi bien que ce soit dans une
étendue plus petite et différemment que dans la propagande de Probus, pour
illustrer les prétentions « universalistes » du souverain romain. L'image de
l'empereur et d'un ennemi a été utilisée sur les *aureliani* qui appellaient
Numérien *pacator Orbis*[113]. Les représentations sur d'autres monnaies sont
plus originales. On peut aussi voir deux captifs de guerre à côté de l'empereur,
c'était le schéma traditionnel mais le slogan est unique dans le monnayage
romain au IIIe siècle : *VND(I)QVE VICTORES*[114]. Cette victoire sur les
ennemis de partout a été également accentuée sur le dessin. L'empereur est
vainqueur de tout côté, c'est pourquoi l'un des barbares possède les éléments
de la tenue orientale pendant que l'autre est déguisé en représentant des
peuples du nord.

Sans doute les représentations des barbares, malgré leur grande popularité,
n'apparaissaient pas très souvent sur les monnaies impériales à l'époque de la
crise du IIIe siècle (cf. tableau n° 1). Dans les années 235—284, soixant huit
personnages prétendaient au pouvoir impérial et y prenaient part[115]. Bien que
plus la cinquantaine frappât les monnaies, les émissions au motif du barbare
ont apparu dans le monnayage de dix-neuf d'entre eux. On voit le développement de la pratique d'usage de ce motif et sa de plus en plus grande présence
dans le monnayage impérial de l'époque de la crise du IIIe siècle et aussi la
multitude de fils et même l'universalité des sujets propagandistes clamés. Ce
motif se rapportait toujours à la lutte contre les voisins barbares de l'*Imperium
Romanum* mais de plus en plus souvent il servait à souligner que la puissance
vainqueure de l'empereur qui se faisant voir dans cette bataille c'est la condition principale de la grande renaissance — *restitutio* — de l'État romain.
Dans la propagande impériale des années 235—284 le monde extérieur peuplé

---

[111] RIC V/2 (Probus), n° 143—144, 224; cf. A. C a l ó L e v i: *Barbarians...*, p. 45. Voir AE
1923, 102, l'inscription qui qualifie Probus de *semper invictus*; cf. S. B e r r e n s: *Sonnenkult...*,
p. 194, n. 204.

[112] RIC V/2 (Probus), n° 601; Gnecchi I, p. 10, n° 8, pl. 4,3; K. P i n k: *Die Medaillonprägung unter Kaiser...*, p. 25, n° 42; S. E s t i o t: *À propos du multiple...*, p. 342—344, n° 8.

[113] RIC V/2 (Numerianus), n° 390.

[114] RIC V/2 (Numerianus), n° 422—423 (fig. 25); cf. A. C a l ó L e v i: *Barbarians...*, p. 45.

[115] F. H a r t m a n n: *Herrscherwechsel und Reichskrise. Untersuchungen zu den Ursachen und
Konsequenzen der Herrscherwechsel im Imperium Romanum der Soldatenkaiserzeit (3. Jahrhundert
n.Chr.).* Frankfurt a.M.-Bern 1982, p. 63—65, ici Marinianus, fils de Gallien parmi les souverains
légaux, bien qu'il n'ait pas eu du titre dynastique et aussi Odénath parmi les usurpateurs, en
somme il y a 70 noms.

des barbares est montré comme hostile, il faut lutter contre ses représentants[116], mais cette confrontation est propice pour l'*Imperium Romanum* et pour
l'empereur romain. Telles compositions iconographiques en faisant l'opposition Romains — Barbares, désignent le système bipolaire de l'*Imperium Romanum* — *Barbaricum*. Elles montrent le caractère unique des relations de l'Empire romain aux barbares et manifestent son invincibilité et celle de son chef.

Le monnayage du règne de Maximin le Thrace, de Gordien III et des deux
Philippes se place dans la première étape de l'emploi du motif du barbare dans
le but de lancer l'image de l'empereur invaincu. La façon de construire leurs
portraits propagandistes est différente. L'image militaire de Maximin le Thrace
et de Maxime césar, ou de Philippe l'Arabe et de Philippe le Jeune comme
chefs invincibles et guerriers était enracinée dans la réalité. Il n'est pas de même
pour Gordien III. Dans le domaine d'exposer l'idée de *l'imperator invictus* son
iconographie monétaire était plus outrancière. L'accent trop fort était mis sur
la personne de l'empereur et son pouvoir vainqueur résultant aussi de la
sanction divine. Les années du règne de Valérien I et de Gallien étaient la
césure dans l'apparition des barbares dans le monnayage impérial. Depuis ce
temps-ci l'usage du motif du barbare est beaucoup plus répandu que dans la
première étape de la crise du IIIe siècle. La diversité des légendes des revers
a augmenté bien que leur contenu se rapportât toujours aux batailles menées
contre les peuples qui attaquaient le territoire de l'Empire et aux actions de
l'empereur-chef. Le courant annoncé dans la propagande de Gordien III se
développait. Les correspondances militaires ont pris une dimension universelle
et un caractère exagéré. Les silhouettes des barbares étaient composées aux
modèles qui illustraient le surnom vainqueur de l'*imperator*. Les idées *victoria*
et *virtus* ont été individualisées. On s'est concentré à représenter le personnage
de l'empereur. L'iconographie des monnaies restaient cependant monotone.
Les années 70 du IIIe siècle ont apporté une autre césure dans l'usage du motif
du barbare dans le monnayage impérial. La propagande du dernier tiers de la
crise du IIIe siècle prouve quatre traits dans le domaine d'usage des représentations du barbare : le catalogue des inscriptions des revers a été élargi et les
légendes qui se rapportaient aux événements plus généraux que la guerre sont
devenues plus nombreuses que dans les années précédentes ; un grand nombre
de variantes de monnaies clamaient la vertu d'invincibilité de l'empereur par
les formules *virtus* ou *invictus* ; les dessins étaient plus originaux ; l'exposition
de la sanction divine et de la protection des dieux était une grande importance.

Dans le monnayage de l'époque de la crise du IIIe siècle le motif du barbare
était successivement et de plus en plus souvent utilisé dans la propagande
impériale mais cette croissance résultait non seulement de la politique étran-
gère et des actions de guerre mais du développement de «la théologie de la

---

[116] À l'exception de représentations, décritées ci-dessus, dans le monnayage de Probus.

Tableau n° 1. Le motif du barbare dans

Représentation de revers monétaire	
Légende	iconographie
1	2
Titulature impériale	Empereur et captif
	Sol et captif
	Trophée et captifs
	Victoire et captif ou captifs
	Victoire dans un quadrige, empereurs et Mars, et captifs
ADLOCVTIO AVG(VSTI)	Empereur, soldats et captif ou captifs
ADLOCVTIO AVGG	Empereur, soldats et captifs
ADVENTVS AVG(VSTI)	Empereur à cheval et barbare ou barbares
ADVENTVS AVGG	Victoire, empereurs à cheval, soldats et captifs
ADVENTVS PROBI AVG	Empereur et captif ou captifs
APOL CONS AVG	*Sol*, Apollo, et captif
	Sol et captif
CONSERVAT AVG	*Sol* et captif
CONS PRINC AVG	Empereur, trophée et captifs
DEFENSOR ORBIS	Empereur, Mars, barbares
FELICITA	Arc de triomphe, trophée et captifs
FELICITA(S) AVG (SC)	Arc de triomphe, trophée et captifs
FELICITAS I/AVG	Trophée et captifs
FORT REDVX	Victoire et captif
GERMANICVS MAXIMVS	Trophée et captifs
GERMANICVS MAX TER	Trophée et captifs
GERMANICVS MAX V	Trophée et captifs
GERMANICVS MAX TR P	Trophée et captifs
GERM MAX CARPICI MAX III ET II COS	Victoire dans un quadrige, empereurs et Mars, et captifs
INVICTVS AVG	Empereur à cheval et ennemi
IOVI CONSER	*Sol*, Jupiter, et captif
MARS INVICTVS/MARTI INVICTO	*Sol*, Mars et captif
MARTI PROPVGNATORI	Mars et ennemi
MARS VICTOR	Mars et captif

le monnayage impérial (235—284)

								Souverain										
Maximin le Thrace	Gordien III	Philippe l'Arabe	Philippe le Jeune	Valérien I	Gallien	Salonin	Claude II le Gothique	Quintille	Aurélien	Tacite	Florien	Probus	Carus	Carin	Numérien	Postume	Victorin	Tétricus I
3	4	5	6	7	8	9	10	11	12	13	14	15	16	17	18	19	20	21
			+									+						
									+									
																+		
			+															
			+															
												+						
					+													
					+				+			+						
					+ᵃ													
												+						
									+									
									+									
									+									
									+									
																	+	
																+		
																+		
																+		
+																		
					+													
			+		+													
					+											+		
					+													
		+ᵇ																
																	+	
									+									
									+									
				+														
										+		+						

1	2
ORIENS AVG	*Sol*, empereur et captif
	Sol, Jupiter et captif
	Sol, barbare ou barbares
	Sol dans un quadrige et barbare
PACATOR ORBIS	Empereur et ennemi
	Empereur et barbares rendant hommage
PACATOR ORIENTIS	Empereur et captif
PAX FVNDATA	Trophée et captifs
PRINC(EPS) IVVENT(VTIS) (SC)	Prince et captif ou captive
RESTITVTOR GALLIARVM	Empereur, femme suppliante et captif
RESTITVTOR ORBIS	Empereur, Orbis ou la Victoire, et captif
RESTITVTOR ORIENTIS	Empereur à cheval et ennemis
	Sol et captifs
RESTITVT(OR) S(A)ECVL(I)	Victoire, empereur et ennemi
	Sol, empereur et ennemi
RESTITVTOR S AVG	*Sol*, empereur et ennemi
SOLI CONSERVATORI	*Sol*, empereur, captifs à l'exergue
SOLI INVICTO	*Sol*, Mars, et captifs
	Sol, captif ou captifs
TRIVNFV QVADOR	Victoire, empereurs dans un quadrige, soldats, trophée, captifs, et captifs à l'exergue
VICTORIA	Victoire et captif
VICTORIA AETERNA (SC)	Victoire et captif
VICT AET AVG	Victoire et captif
VICTORIA AVG(VSTI) (SC)	Victoire et barbare ou barbares
	Empereur, trophée et captifs
	Empereur à cheval et ennemi
	Victoire, empereur, soldat et captif
	Trophée et captifs
VICTORIA AVG VI SC	Victoire et captif
VICTORIA AVG VII	Victoire et captif
VICTORI(AE) AVG (SC)	Deux Victoires et captifs
VICTORIAE AVG GERMANICA	Victoire et captif
VICTORIAE AVGVSTI / VOT X	Deux Victoires avec un bouclier inscrit VOT X, et captifs
VICTORIE AVGG / X	Deux Victoires avec un bouclier inscrit X, et captifs
VICTORIA AVGG / AVGVSTORVM (SC)	Victoire et captif ou captifs
	Victoire, empereur et captifs
	Deux souverains, soldat et captifs

tabl. nº 1 (suite)

3	4	5	6	7	8	9	10	11	12	13	14	15	16	17	18	19	20	21
									+									
									+									
									+			+						
									+									
															+			
												+						
									+									
					+													
			+			+								+				
																+		
									+									
									+									
									+									
												+						
												+						
												+						
									+									
									+									
									+									
															+			
																+		
	+																	
					+													
					+		+		+			+	+			+		+
												+				+		
												+						
	+																	
									+			+						
					+													
					+													
																+		
					+													
												+						
														+				
				+	+								+c		+			
														+	+			
+d																		

1	2
VICTORIAE AVGG IT GERM	Victoire et captif
VICT GALLIENI AVG	Empereur et ennemi
VICTORIA GERM(ANICA) (SC)	Victoire et barbare ou barbares
	Victoire dans une *biga* et ennemi
	Victoire, empereur et captif ou captifs
	Victoire, empereur à cheval, et ennemis, parfois soldats
	Trophée et captifs
VICTORIA GERM ou VICTORIA G M	Trophée et captifs
VICTORIA G M	Victoire et captif ou captifs
VICT GER II	Victoire et captif
VICTORIA GOT(T)HIC(A)	Victoire et captif
	Trophée et captifs
VICTORIAE GOTHIC (SPQR)	Trophée et captifs
VICTORIA GOT(T)HICA COS II	Victoire et captif
VICT PART(ICA)	Victoire et captif
VIC POSTVMI AVG	Victoire et captif
VICTORIA PROBI AVG	Victoire, trophée et captifs
VICTORIOSO SEMPER	Empereur et barbares
VIRTVS AVG(VSTI) / VIRTVTI AVGVSTI	Empereur et barbare ou barbares
	Empereur à cheval et ennemi ou ennemis
	Empereur, femme suppliante et captif
	Sol, Hercule et captif
	Sol, empereur et captif
	Mars et captif
	Victoire, empereur, soldats et captif
	Victoire, empereur, trophée, et captif ou captifs
	Virtus, empereur, *Sol*, personnage mâle, enfant et captifs
	Trophée et captifs
VIRTVS AVGG / VIRTVS AVGVS-TORVM	Empereur et barbare
	Empereur à cheval et barbares ou barbares
	Mars et captifs
	Deux Victoires, deux empereurs et ennemis
VIRTVS AVGV(S)T(I) N(OSTRI)	Empereur à cheval et ennemi
	Empereur à cheval, soldat et captif
VIRTVS AVG TRIVMFVM GOT-THICVM	Victoire, empereur à cheval, trophée et captifs
VIRTVS CLAVDI AVG	Empereur à cheval et ennemis
VIR(TVS) GALLIENI AVG	Empereur et barbare
	Empereur à cheval et ennemi
	Empereur à cheval, soldats et ennemis

tabl. nᵒ 1 (suite)

3	4	5	6	7	8	9	10	11	12	13	14	15	16	17	18	19	20	21
				+	+													
					+													
+				+	+							+				+		
														+				
+					+													+
+[c]																		
							+					+						
					+													
				+	+		+											
					+													
											+[f]	+[g]						
							+											
							+	+	+									
										+								
				+														
																+		
												+						
												+						
					+			+			+	+				+		+
	+				+				+		+	+		+				
					+													
									+									
									+									
					+				+		+	+				+		
	+																	
					+												+	
	+																	
					+		+		+									
																		+
														+	+			
														+				
															+			
												+						
												+						
												+						
							+											
					+													
					+													
					+													

1	2
VIRTVS ILLVRICI	Mars et captif
VIRTVS INVICT(I) AVG	*Sol*, empereur et captif
	Empereur à cheval et ennemi
	Empereur à cheval, Mars et ennemi
VIRTVS POSTVMI SC	Victoire, empereur et captif
VIRTVS PROBI AVG	Empereur et captifs
	Empereur à cheval et ennemi ou ennemis
	Empereur à cheval, soldat et ennemis
	Mars et captif ou captifs
	Trophée et captifs
	Victoire et captifs
VND(I)QVE VICTORES	Empereur et captifs
VOTIS DECEN ET VIC	Victoire, empereur et captif

[a] Émission avec Salonin.
[b] Émission de Philippe l'Arabe et Philippe le Jeune.
[c] Émission de Carus et Carin.
[d] Émissions de Maximin le Thrace et Maxime.

victoire». Ce qui probablement explique la lacune dans les années 249—253 quand sur les monnaies impériales les barbares n'ont point apparu. Ce n'étaient pas les défaites essuyées de Goths[117], bien que leur influence ne soit pas exclue mais le développement insuffisant de l'idée de l'empereur invaincu a causé cette absence. Cette interprétation explique aussi l'apparition universelle du motif du barbare dans la propagande des souverains de la dernière étape de la crise, même de ceux dont le règne était court — il n'ont pas donc eu de temps d'avoir des succès militaires, et de ceux dont la propagande n'a pas eu de caractère personnel. Le monnayage de Quintille, Florien et de Numérien y sert d'exemple. Dans le cas de quelques empereurs les représentations décrites illustrent exactement l'idéologie impériale et la tendance dans la propagande qui étaient propres pour la période de leur règne. L'entassement de ces représentations est visible dans le monnayage de Gallien, Postume, Aurélien et de Probus — souverains qui accentuaient la propagande de l'empereur invincible.

La représentation de l'ennemi ou du captif suggère des associations: guerre, bataille, victoire, triomphe. Cela constituait un grand signe de la réussite et de la puissance de l'État romain et de son chef. L'iconographie monétaire au motif du barbare aboutissait donc à un simple schéma de l'affirmation de la puissance romaine. Emilienne Demougeot remarque jus-

[117] Cf. p.ex. F. L a m m e r t: *Zum Kampfe der Goten bei Abrittus im Jahre 251.* „Klio" 1942, Bd. 34, p. 125—126; E. D e m o u g e o t: *La formation...*, p. 402—417.

tabl. n° 1 (suite)

3	4	5	6	7	8	9	10	11	12	13	14	15	16	17	18	19	20	21
									+									
												+						
												+						
												+						
																+		
												+						
												+						
												+						
												+						
												+						
												+						
															+			
												+						

[e] Émissions de Maximin le Thrace, ou de Maximin le Thrace et de Maxime.
[f] Cf. supra note 48.
[g] Cf. supra note 49.

tement à ce propos que ces représentations au III[e] siècle glorifiaient aussi les victoires impériales. Aucun des souverains de l'époque de la crise «n'eut les moyens financiers et politiques d'élever ou de se voir dédier des monuments sculptés relatant, en reliefs historiés, leurs guerres contre des envahisseurs barbares...»[118]. Néanmoins, les monnaies qui par milliers de pièces multipliaient l'image de la victoire, avaient un rôle «des monuments triomphaux» des empereurs romains, pour célébrer leur vaillance et leurs victoires.

Certaines émissions décrites ci-dessus commémoraient les victoires militaires, grandes ou petites, sur les ennemis des Romains. Elles servaient plus souvent à la propagande de la victoire abstraite et des démarches universelles des souverains romains. Très peu nombreuses sont les émissions qui rendent mémorable des actions de guerre concrètes et favorables[119]. De plus en plus la relation entre les actions militaires réelles des souverains et les contenus lancés dans leur propagande se relâchait. Dans ce contexte les représentations décrites présentent l'évolution de la propagande impériale «de la narration au symbolisme». Les diverses représentations dans le monnayage de plusieurs empereurs, surtout de la dernière étape de la crise du IIIe siècle étaient dans cette saisie le résultat de la recherche des idées les plus impréssionnantes à remettre à l'empereur le nimbe du chef charismatique, et le côté «artistique»

[118] Eadem: *L'image...*, p. 128. Cf. G.Ch. Picard: *Les trophées...*, p. 472—481.
[119] Cf. p.ex. E.A. Sydenham: *Historical References to Coins of the Roman Empire from Augustus to Gallienus.* London—San Diego 1968, p. 135—137, 147—150; J.M.C. Toynbee: *Roman Medallions.* New York 1986, p. 159—160.

pouvait décider du nombre de captifs ou d'ennemis barbares confrontés au vainqueur. Cette exagération de la symbolique exprimait mieux le pathétique de la *virtus* impériale.

Il est possible de désigner quelques modèles où les silhouettes des barbares servaient à l'expression iconographique de la vertu *invictus* de l'empereur. Dans le premier, le barbare reste le symbole même du pouvoir vainqueur de l'*imperator*. Il est présent à côté du trophée, qui comprend aussi la symbolique de la guerre et de la victoire militaire. Dans le deuxième modèle, le barbare apparait comme par exemple l'ennemi attaqué par l'empereur — ce qui est un acte symbolique sans rapport à la réalité historique. Dans le modèle suivant, le captif barbare est présenté dans une scène allégorique où l'*imperator* est couronné par une déité ou reçoit un globe du dieu. Dans le dernier modèle, le barbare construit l'image de l'événement historique, par exemple comme prisonnier dans les commémorations de la cérémonie d'*adventus* ou du *processus consularis*, ou du triomphe. Dans chacune de ces saisies le barbare reste l'adversaire, l'image d'un peuple, surtout si la légende comprend une valeur ethnique, ou l'image de tous les peuples extérieurs d'en dehors du monde romain.

Dans l'iconographie des émissions mentionnées, les barbares constituent un élément supplémentaire mais important. Les légendes qui étaient illustrées ainsi en profitaient d'une certaine manière. Cela concerne ces slogans qui se rapportent aux différents domaines de l'activité de l'empereur. La représentation du barbare y a porté une nouvelle signification propagandiste. C'est pourquoi les idées qui sont exprimées par l'iconographie et les légendes monétaires ont gagné un caractère plus lisible et la légende souvent abstraite a gagné un sens plus réel. L'iconographie est aussi importante que l'idée proposée dans les slogans des revers. L'essentiel des légendes ne parvenait pas toujours aux destinateurs des monnaies impériales, les dessins pouvaient être plus lisibles. Donc de telles réunions des formes graphiques et des slogans n'étaient pas dû au hasard. Les légendes monétaires étaient différentes, elles se rapportaient à la victoire militaire, aux rapports du chef à l'armée, aux retours de la guerre de l'empereur, aux possibilités et réalisations du souverain, à la stabilité de son pouvoir, à la prospérité de l'Empire romain. Dans l'iconographie le motif du barbare ammenait tous ces trames à l'idée de l'empereur invaincu. Comme la propagande impériale persuadait au sommet de son développement dans les dernières années de la crise du IIIe siècle l'empereur romain est invincible, il gagne toujours et partout (*victoriosus semper* et *undique victor*). La Victoire est devenue sa compagne constante qui ne le quitte pas, et la source de cette réussite de l'empereur c'est sa puissance surnaturelle, *virtus Augusti*, l'élément essentiel du charisme impérial.

Traduit par Malgorzata Balcerzak

Agata A. Kluczek

CESARZ NIEZWYCIĘŻONY I BARBARZYŃCY
WYOBRAŻENIA BARBARZYŃCÓW W MENNICTWIE RZYMSKIM
W LATACH 235—284

Streszczenie

Motyw barbarzyńcy, mimo niewątpliwie dużej popularności, nie występował powszechnie w mennictwie imperialnym w latach 235—284. Znane są emisje monetarne ponad pięćdziesięciu ówczesnych władców, ale motyw barbarzyńcy był obecny na monetach tylko dziewiętnastu emitentów. Odnosił się do walki militarnej z sąsiadami Imperium, ale z upływem lat coraz częściej służył podkreślaniu, że zwycięska moc władcy, która się w tej walce ujawnia, to jedyny warunek szeroko rozumianego odrodzenia — restitutio — Cesarstwa Rzymskiego. Powszechniejsze występowanie motywu i bardziej uniwersalne odniesienia wyobrażeń monetarnych wynikały jednak nie tyle z polityki zagranicznej i działań wojennych, ile z rozwoju „teologii zwycięstwa". Takie rozumienie tłumaczy występowanie motywu barbarzyńcy w propagandzie władców rządzących krótko, którzy nie zdążyli odnieść sukcesów militarnych nad barbarzyńcami, i tych, których propaganda nie przybrała indywidualnego zabarwienia. Przykładu dostarcza mennictwo Kwintyl-lusa, Floriana, Numeriana. W wypadku Galliena, Postumusa, Aureliana i Probusa, którzy rozwijali propagandę cesarza niezwyciężonego, emisje z motywem barbarzyńcy ilustrują doskonale ideologię imperialną i tendencje w propagandzie charakterystyczne dla ich rządów.

Sylwetki barbarzyńców w ikonografii rewersów monet są wprawdzie elementem dodatkowym, jednak ważnym. Legendy, które tak ilustrowano, dzięki temu zyskiwały szczególny wymiar. Dotyczy to przede wszystkim haseł odnoszących się do dziedzin innych niż wojna. Legendy monetarne są bowiem różne, nawiązują do wiktorii militarnej, kontaktów wodza z armią, podróży cesarza, możliwości i osiągnięć władcy, trwałości jego władzy, pomyślności Imperium. Motyw barbarzyńcy w ikonografii sprowadzał wszystkie te wątki do idei cesarza niezwyciężonego. Jak przekonywała propaganda imperialna w szczytowym momencie jej rozwoju w ostatnich latach kryzysu III w., cesarz jest niezwyciężony, zwycięża wszędzie i zawsze (victoriosus semper i undique victor), Victoria go nie opuszcza, a źródłem jego powodzenia jest nadnaturalny element — virtus Augusti.

Agata A. Kluczek

THE INVINCIBLE EMPEROR AND BARBARIANS
BARBARIAN IMAGES IN THE ROMAN
MINTING OF THE YEARS 235—284 A.D.

Summary

The barbarian motive, despite its unquestionably big popularity, was not common in the imperial coin system between 235 and 284. What is known are the coin issues of over fifty rulers at that time, however, this motive was present on nineteen of them. It was related to the military battle with the Empire's neighbours, but, with years, it more often served the role of pointing out that the victorious power of the ruler revealing itself in this battle is the only condition of a widely-

-understood restoration — *restitutio* — of the Roman Empire. Its more common appearance and more universal references of coin images derived not only and not so much from the foreign affairs and military actions as from the development of the "theology of victory". Such an understanding explains the presence of the barbarian motive in the propaganda of rulers ruling for a short period of time — they did not manage to succeed over barbarians, and those whose propaganda did not take on an individual colouring. To these belonged Quintillus, Florian, and Numerianus. However, in the case of Gallienus, Postumus, Aurelian and Probus, who paid an emphasis on the propaganda of an invincible emperor, the barbarian motive coin issues perfectly illustrate the imperial ideology and tendencies in propaganda typical of their ruling.

The barbarian profiles in the iconography of coin reverses are just an extra yet important element. Legends, which were illustrated in this way, were given a special significance thanks to it. It concerns mainly those slogans referring to the fields other than war. The coin legends are diverse, referring to the military victory, emperor's contacts with the army, emperor's journey, ruler's possibilities and achievements, stability of his power, and success of the Empire. The barbarian motive in the iconography boiled down all these elements to the idea of an invincible emperor. As the imperial propaganda has it, in the peak moment of his development in the last years of the crisis in the 3rd century, the emperor is invincible, wins everywhere and always (*victoriosus semper* and *undique victor*). *Victoria* does not leave him, while the source of his failure comes from *virtus Augusti*, a supernatural element.

DARIUSZ CHOJECKI

Funde
von römischen Münzen in Oberschlesien
angesichts der Berichte
des Königlichen Evangelischen Gymnasiums
zu Ratibor

Berichte des 1819 gegründeten Königlichen Evangelischen Gymnasiums zu Ratibor (heute Racibórz) sind die redlichsten und vollständigsten Quellen über die Funde von römischen Münzen in Oberschlesien, in der ersten Hälfte des XIX Jahrhunderts. Diese Schule hat nicht nur die Jugend gebildet, sondern auch setzte sich auch zum Ziel die Erschaffung eines eigenen Museums, dessen Sammlungen bei der didaktischen Arbeit mit den Schülern behilflich sein sollten. Um die Kollektionen zu ordnen, teilte man sie in thematische Gruppen und so bildete man auch Eigenabteilungen für: Naturgeschichte, Kunst und Altertum, Mathematik und Physik, Geographie, Musik, Denkmalkunst und die uns am meisten interessierende numismatische Abteilung. Die Jahresberichte der Schule haben Informationen über die einzelnen Neuerwerbungen der Eigenabteilungen beinhaltet. Solche Informationen galten ebenfalls für die numismatische Abteilung. In jener Abteilung befanden sich auch Numismatiken aus der Antike, die oft in Oberschlesien gefunden wurden. Carl Linge, der 1782 in Meisen geboren wurde und die klassische Philologie in Lipsk (Leipzig) absolvierte, war der

erste Direktor des ratiborer Gymnasiums.[1] Ihm und dem nächsten Direktor
— Eduard Hänisch verdankt das ratiborer Gymnasium eine Sammlung von
über hundert Münzen. Beide Direktoren begrenzten sich nicht nur zur Beschreibung der Münzen, die in das Gymnasium eingetroffen waren. Besonders
Carl Linge war überhaupt an allen Funden von römischen Münzen in Oberschlesien interessiert, insbesondere auf dem mit Ratibor benachbartem Lobschützerboden. In den Jahresberichten des Gymnasiums aus den Jahren 1822
und 1829 hat er zwei Artikel unter demselben Titel veröffentlicht: *Über die in
Oberschlesien gefundenen Münzen* und sie diesem Fragenkomplex gewidmet.
Der zweite Artikel hat denselben Inhalt wie der erste, er wurde jedoch erweitert
und um Informationen, die der Autor in den Jahren 1822—1828 erhalten hat,
bereichert. Die Art, in welcher Linge sein Untersuchungsthema behandelte,
zeugt von seinem großen Engagement und Interesse an den Funden von
römischen Münzen in Oberschlesien. Für die Problematik der Funde von
römischen Münzen in den drei ersten Jahrzehnten des XIX Jhs. sind diese
Artikel eine unentbehrliche Wissensquelle. Der Autor behandelte das Thema
sehr gewissenhaft, er ließ nicht zu, dass Phantasie und übliche menschliche
Klatscherei redliche, wissenschaftliche Arbeit verhüllten.

Eduard Hänischs besonderer Verdienst hingegen, war die Veröffentlichung
im Jahresbericht des Gymnasiums von 1842 eines Katalogs der römischen
Münzen *De Gymnasii Ratiboriensis Numis Romanis*, die im Besitz des ratiborer
Gymnasiums waren. Diese drei großen Publikationen werden durch kurze
Erwähnungen in jenen einzelnen Jahresberichten ergänzt. Bis 1828 wurden die
Jahresberichte von Carl Linge, die späteren von Eduard Hänisch geschrieben.
Analyse von dieser Literatur erlaubt uns sich näher mit den Funden von
römischen Münzen in Oberschlesien am Ende des XVIII Jhs. und am Anfang
des XIX Jhs. vertraut zu machen.

In dem Artikel *Über die in Oberschlesien gefundenen Römischen Münzen* aus
dem Jahre 1822 beschreibt Linge vor allem römische Münzen, die auf dem
Gebiet von **Głubczyce (Leobschütz)**, in der Nähe von Ort **Bieskau** (heute ein
Teil von **Nowa Cerekiew**) und deren Nachbarsdörfern gefunden wurden. „Das
Dorf Bieskau liegt [...], längst dem Flüsschen Troja [...], zwei Meilen von
Leobschütz, zwei und eine halbe von Ratibor, eine halbe Meile von Katscher,
[...] in der Parochie Marktslecken Deutsch-Neukirch [...]. Die nordöstlich vom
Dorfe gelegenen Felder erheben sich vom Flüsschen Troja aus gegen Knispel,
zu einer sanften Anhöhe, die eine sehr bebaute Bergfläche bildet. Auf dieser
Höhe zwischen den Fusssteigen und den Knispler und Köslinger Feldmarken,
auf unserer Karte von a, b, c, d eingeschlossen, haben die Bieskauer seit
undenklichen Zeiten bei ihrer Feldarbeit die alten Römischen Münzen ausge-

---

[1] C. L i n g e: *Über die feierliche Eröffnung des Gymnasiums zu Ratibor am 2 Juni 1819*. Ratibor
1820, S. 29.

ackert, und sie entweder gleich hinter dem Pfluge, oder wenn unmittelbar nach dem Eggen ein Regen folgte, sie dann gefunden, oder auch wohl beim Flachs-raufen herausgerissen, aber nicht auf einer Stelle, sondern auf mehreren Ackern, nicht auf einmal, sondern zu verschiedenen Zeiten. Auch auf den benachbarten Feldern von Knispel, Zauchwitz und Rosen sind dann und wann einzelne Römische Münzen gefunden worden, und zu Deutsch-Neukirch selbst, als vor vierzig Jahren die alte Kirche erweitert und von Grund aus neu gebaut wurde, beim Grundgraben".[2]

Die Anzahl der gefundenen Münzen auf diesem Gebiet muss sehr hoch gewesen sein, da Linge, der sich auf einen glaubwürdigen Zeugen berufen hat, sie auf einen Scheffel bestimmte. Er führte auch ein denkwürdiges Beispiel an: „Auch der Wirtschaftshauptmann Klass, der vor ungefähr vierzig Jahren die Verwaltung der Deutsch-Neukirsch Herrschaft führte und das herrschaftliche Vorwerk Bieskau gepachtet hatte, soll ein ganzes Bierglas voll gehabt [...]."[3]

Nach einer ziemlich allgemeinen Einleitung beschrieb Linge die größte Privatkollektion, die hauptsächlich aus **Bieskau** stamm. Diese hat dem Justiz-kommissarius Mader gehört. Die unten angeführten Münzen kommen aus-schließlich aus Bieskau. Die Kollektion stellen folgende Münzen zusammen: „1. Zwei goldne. [...] Eine von Vespasian, auf unsere Karte Nr. 9, S. Eckhel T. VI. p. 340. 2. Acht und sechzig silberne von Julius Cäsar bis auf Com-modus. Einzelne: von Julius Cäsar (beschädigt), Nero, Galba, Vitellius, Ves-pasian, Titus, Domitian, auf der Karte Nr. 1, und von Nerva; von Trajan 23, die Kehrseite mit bekannten mannichfaltigen Figuren, eine mit dem Da-nuvius vom J.Chr.105. Sie steht Eckhel T. IV. p. 418, auf unsrer Karte Nr. 6; von Hadrian 15, auf der Kehrseite meist mit einer opfernden Priesterin [...] [eine aus Zauchwitz, sehe unten — D.Ch.]. Von Antoninus Pius 6, von Marc Aurel 3, von L. Aurelius Verus 1, von Commodus 7 und 1 zerbrochene. Von Sabina, der Gemahlin Hadrianus I, [...] von Beiden Faustinen 4, eine davon auf der Karte Nr. 10. Unter diesen sind aber, nach Professor Schramm Angabe, 4 falsche, d.h. nicht von Silber, sondern von Erz und mit einem seinen Hautchen Silber künstlich überlegt. Die Alten machten besonders die Silber-münzen auf diese Art häusig nach. Von den Maderschen werden da-für gehalten eine von Trajan, zwei von Hadrian und eine von L. Aurelius Verus [...]."[4]

---

[2] I d e m: *Über die in Oberschlesien gefundenen Römischen Münzen, Denkwürdigkeiten Ober-schlesiens zu Ankündigung der am 15. 16. und 17 April zu haltenden Prüfung des Königl. Evangel. Gymnasium zu Ratibor.* Ratibor 1822, S. 10.

[3] Ibidem, S. 11.

[4] Ibidem, S. 11—12. Carl Linge hebt bei der Beschreibung der Kollektion von Mader hervor, dass Manche von den Münzen mit den ihnen zuständiegen Nummern an der Karte zu sehen sind. Diese Karte, die zugleich eine Landkarte von Paar Nachbarsdürfern und darunter auch von Bieskau ist, wurde am Ende des Artikels von Carl Linge platziert.

Dies waren jedoch nicht alle Münzen, die in Bieskau gefundenen wurden. Dem Bericht vom C. Linge nach, haben sich noch mehre von den Münzen erhalten. Manche von ihnen hat man unter ziemlich ungewöhnlichen Umständen gefunden. „So fand der Pfarrherr Lauffer zu Deutsch-Neukirch im vergangenen Jahre unter dem Opfergelde eine Silbermünze mit dem Caput laureatum des Kaiser Hadrian und der Legende: Imp. Caesar. Trajan. Hadrianus; auf der Kehrseite: eine stehende weibliche Gestalt unterhalb bekleidet, das Gewand über dem linken Arm geschlagen, in jeder Hand etwas haltend, das nicht mehr erkennbar ist. Die Figur ist vielleicht eine Isis, deren Dienst Hadrian beförderte."[5] — Rentmeister Aschersleben in Ratibor besitzt zwei Silbermünzen von Bieskau, eine von Trajan auf der Kehrseite mit der Trajanssäule und der Legende: „...P.P.S.P.Q.R., vermutlich vom Jahre 114. Eine von Commodus, sehr schön; die Figur auf der Kehrseite ist die Liberalitas; sie ist vom Jahre 181; auf der Karte unter Nr. 5. — Salz-Factor Dagner zu Ratibor hat mehrere seltene Silbermünzen in Silbergaräth so einsetzen lassen, das Vorder- und Kehr-Seite sichtbar sind. Unter diesen befindet sich auch in einer Sahnkelle eine Bieskauer: Caput laureatum des Vespasian mit der Legende: Vespasian. Aug.; das übrige ist erlochen; auf der Kehrseite erkennt man noch eine kniende Figur. — Dr. Albrecht in Ratibor, Sohn des oben erwähnten Kaufmann Albrecht in Deutsch-Neukirch besitzt noch vier Erzmünzen von Bieskau, die aber schon sehr gelitten haben. Die grösste darunter ist von Trajan; die zweite, ein wenig kleiner, wahrscheinlich eine Faustina, hat gar keine Schrift mehr, so auch die dritte, vielleicht eine Faustina; auf der vierten und kleisten ist das Caput Laureatum, eines Kaisers; die Legende ist verschwunden; auf der Kehrseite steht der Sonnengott, die rechte Hand erhebend; Legende: Soli inv(icto). Es kommen von Gallienus Münzen dieser Art. Vor; sie beziehen sich auf die glänzenden Spiele, die damals im Monat Dezember dem Sonnengotte, soli invicto, zu Ehren-gegeben wurde."[6] Wie uns der Bericht aus dem folgende Jahr mitteilt, hat diese vier Münzen Dr. Albrecht zu der Sammlung des ratiborer Gymnasiums übergeben[7]. Drei von diesen Münzen wurden in dem von E. Hänisch 1842 veröffentlichtem Katalog beschrieben. Man sollte aber hervorheben, dass er nicht komplett ist. Es fehlen zahlreiche Ordnungsnummern. Am deutlichsten hat man im Katalog die unbestimmten Münzen nicht platziert, man hat ihnen aber dennoch Nummern gegeben. Demnach musste Hänisch seinen Katalog auf einem anderen, wahrscheinlich handschriftlichen stützen. Die vom Dr. Albrecht dem Gymnasium übergeben Münzen, das sind:

---

[5] E. K o n i k zählt diese Münze fehlerhaft zu Maders Kollektion hinzu, in: *Znaleziska monet rzymskich na Śląsku.* Wrocław 1965, s. 99, Pos. VI.

[6] C. L i n g e: *Über die in Oberschlesien...*, S. 12—13.

[7] I d e m: *Zu der öffentlichen Prüfung aller Klassen des Königlichen Gymnasiums zu Ratibor.* Ratibor 1823, S. 30.

„Trajanus

...AESAR. TRA.... IMP.... Caput Laureatum. Praeterea nihil neque legi neque cognosi potest in hoc numo aeneo primae formae; neque hoc mirum, est enim nostro demum tempore in agris apud Biescaviam vicum inventus, ubi nescio quot saecula glebis et arateo videtur attritus. Ex nostris aeneis primus.

Faustina Junior, M. Aurelii uxor

FAVSTINA. AVGVSTA. Caput mulieris cultu solito.

VENERI. VICTRICI. S.C. Dea seminuda sedens dextra Victoriolam tenet, sinistra cornu copiae [...]. Est ex numis aeneis nostris tertius, inventus in agris Biescaviensibus.

AETERNITAS. AVG. FAVSTINA. Caput cultu solito, facie pulcherrima. In aversa Quamquam supersunt vestigia inscriptionis, ego praeter S.C. Nihil, quod sententiam praebeat, extrico. Mulier solio insidens dextra sceptrum, sinistra cornu copiae tenet. Est numus aeneus, apud nos secundus, inventus in agris Biescoviensibus."[8]

Hiermit enden noch nicht die Funde von römischen Münzen in Bieskau, die 1822 von Carl Linge beschrieben wurden. In einem weiteren Teil des Artikels nennt er folgende: „Auch soll Dr. Furch zu Freudenthal, der in Deutsch-Neukirch geboren, sich immer für diese Altertümmer interessierte, in Bieskau gefundene Römische Münzen und Waffen besitzen. Der Fürstbischöfliche Commissarius und Dechant Lauffer zu Katscher, der ebenfalls viel zu Erhaltung dieser altertümlichen Schätze beigetragen hat; schickte in verschiedenen Sendungen elf Stück dieser Münzen an die Breslauer Sammlung. Kaufmann Scotti zu Ratibor, mit Eifer jede vaterländische Forschung befördernd, sammelte und schickte im Jahre 1818 unter andern, elf Stück ebenfalls in jener Gegend gefundene Römische Münzen dahin. Auch Professor Schramm legte seiner Nachricht über die Heidenberge [...], zwei bieskauer Münzen bei."[9]

Im nächsten Jahr hat das Königliche Evangelische Gymnasium zu Ratibor seinen Besitz um eine Münze von Hadrian vergrößert, die ebenfalls aus dem besprochenen Ort stamm. Der Schenker war der Lehrer Hänisch: „Hr. Oberlehrer Hänisch schenkte 1 Hadrian von Bieskau."[10] Derselbe Lehrer hat während seines Direktorats, wie schon oben erwähnt wurde, einen Katalog von römischen Münzen, die sich im Gymnasium befanden, veröffentlicht. Von den Hadrianmünzen wurde nur eine in Bieskau gefunden. Es ist eine Silbermünze, die im Katalog der in Bieskau gefundenen Münzen unter Nummer 7 zu sehen ist.

[8] E. Hänisch: *De Gymnasii Ratiboriensis Numis Romanis.* In: Idem: *Zu der öffentlichen Prüfung aller Klassen des Königlichen Gymnasiums zu Ratibor.* Ratibor 1842, S. 8, 15.

[9] C. Linge: *Über die in Oberschlesien...*, S. 12—13.

[10] Idem: *Zu der öffentlichen Prüfung...*, S. 30.

„HADRIANVS. AVG. COS. III. P.P. Caput laureatum, sine barba. NILVS. Nilus conspicitur procumbens, sinistra cornu copia tenens [...]. Est argenteus, ex nostris septimus, inventus apud Biescaviam vicum."[11]

Die oben beschriebene Münze ist somit Eduard Hänischs Gabe, um welche sich das Gymnasium 1823 bereichert hat. Im Katalog hat man nur vier in Bieskau gefundenen Münzen platziert. Dr. Albrecht machte die Gabe von vier Münzen (eine von Trajan, zwei von Faustina Junior, eine mit SOLI INVICTO beschriftet), der Lehrer Hänisch von einer Münze, von Trajan. Es sollten also fünf in Bieskau gefundenen Münzen sein. Die Frage, warum die mit SOLI INVICTO beschriftete Münze nicht im Katalog aufgenommen wurde, lässt sich nur schwer eindeutig erklären. Man sollte auch vermerken, dass im ganzen Katalog keine einzeige Münze mit der Aufschrift SOLI INVICTO zu sehen ist. Am wahrscheinlichsten war sie in soweit nicht lesbar, dass sie im Katalog keinen Platz einnehmen konnte.

Soviel hatte Carl Linge 1822 über die Funde von römischen Münzen in Bieskau zu sagen. Kommen wir auf die Kollektion des Justizkommissarius Mader zurück. Die Mehrzahl von diesen Münzen wurde auf den zu Bieskau gehörenden Feldern gefunden. Manche von ihnen wurden aber auf einem anderen Gebiet entdeckt worden:

1. Ein Aureus von Nero auf den zu Dorf **Księże Pole (Knispel)** gehörenden Feldern „Eine von Nero, vom Jahre Christi 56, auf den **Knispeler** Feldern gefunden und sehr schön erhalten; sie ist auf unserer Karte abgebildet unter Nr. 2 Eckhel Doctrina Numorum T. VI. p. 262 führt ähnliche von diesem Jahre an, aber nicht dieselbe."[12]

2. Ein Denar von Hadrian auf den zu Dorf **Sucha Psina (Zauchwitz)** gehörenden Feldern „[...] von Hadrian [...] eine davon auf der Karte Nr. 4, das Jahr derselben ist ungewiss, da vom Jahr 119 an auf allen Münzen dieses Kaisers das dritte Consulat steht; sie ist auf den **Zauchwitzer** Feldern gefunden."[13]

3. Ungefähr zehn Münzen aus Maders Sammlung kommen aus **Rogożany (Rosen)**. „Ungefähr zehn Erz-Münzen. Sie sind der Angabe nach alle bei den Thongruben auf den **Rosener** Feldern einzeln gefunden worden, als: ein Cäsar Octavius von großer Schönheit, den ich aber für unëcht halte, weil er so frisch

---

[11] E. H ä n i s c h: *De Gymnasii...*, S. 11.

[12] C. L i n g e: *Über die in Oberschlesien...*, S. 11.

[13] Ibidem. Sture B o l i n schrieb irrtümlicherweise, dass ein Denar von Trajan, der sich in Maders Kollektion befindet, in Sucha Psina (Zauchwitz) gefunden wurde, sehe *Fynden av romerska mynt i det Fria Germanien* (Lund 1926, S. 79, q). Bolin nach haben weitere Forscher dieser Fehler vervielfacht, z. B. E. K o n i k: *Znaleziska...*, S. 136, K. G o d ł o w s k i: *Materiały kultury przeworskiej z obszaru Górnego Śląska.* „Materiały Starożytne i Wczesnośredniowieczne" 1973, T. 2, S. 292.

erhalten ist, wie ich nie eine antike Erzmünze gesehen habe. Er ist auf der Karte unter Nr. 8 gezeichnet; auserdem von Trajan, Hadrian, Marc Aurel, Septimius Severus, auf der Karte Nr. 3, Alexander Severus, Gallienus, Constantin d. jüng. und Lucilla."[14]

In weiterem Teil seines Artikels vom Jahre 1822 beschreibt Carl Linge noch eine Goldmünze, die zu Maders Kollektion gehörte. Diese wurde in **Grudynia Wielka (Gross-Grauden)** gefunden: „So ist auf einem Felde zu Gross-Grauden, eine Meile von Leobschütz nach Cosel zu, eine Goldmünze vom Kaiser Julius Verus Maximus gefunden worden und in die Madersche Sammlung gekommen. Sie ist auf unsrer Karte unter Nr. 7 abgebildet und merkwürdig, [...] mit der Inschrift Pietas Aug. Und den instrumentis pontificalibus, wovon sich in der Kaiserlichen Sammlung zu Wien ein Exemplar befindet."[15]

Eine weitere Münze, die Maders Sammlung vergrößerte, wurde in Głubczyce **(Leobschütz)** gefunden: „Zu Leobschütz wurde beim Schlemmen des Hospitalteiches ein Trajan gefunden und in die Madersche Sammlung gebracht."[16] Dies ist schon die letzte, uns bekannte Münze, die in Maders Besitz gekommen ist.

Die weiteren, von Linge genannten Funde, wurden schon außerhalb Głubczyce gemacht: „Bei **Troppau** fand Professor Enz hinter dem Park bei dem sogenannten Gypsbrünnel eine Silbermünze von Aurelian und sorgte für würdige Aufbewahrung derselben in dem Troppauer Museum. — Bei **Slawikau**, 1,5 Meile von Ratibor, wurde auf einem Felde der Kaminiza eine Silbermünze gefunden, auf deren Vorderseite der Kopf Trajans, auf der Kehrseite ein gerüsteter wahrscheinlich Römischer Krieger steht; Besitzer derselben ist Administrator Kegel."[17]

Nach einem Jahr wurde diese Münze dem Gymnasium übergeben und kam ebenfalls in seine Sammlung: „[...] desglechen 1 Trajan, in Slawikau gefunden, und einige der in Kyowitz ausgeackerten Hohlmünzen, vom Hrn. Administrator Kegel in Slawikau."[18] Diese Information hat Linge 1828 in scinem Artikel wiederholt[19]. Hänischs Katalog nach war es aber kein Denar von Trajan, sondern einer von Hadrian:

„Hadrianus

IMP. CAESAR. TRAIAN. HADRIANVS. AVG. Caput vel potius protome laureata, sine barba, facie satis pingui et mento paene rotundo.

---

[14] C. L i n g e: *Über die in Oberschlesien...*, S. 12.

[15] Ibidem, S. 13—14.

[16] Ibidem, S. 14.

[17] Ibidem, S. 14.

[18] C. L i n g e: *Zu der öffentlichen Prüfung...*, S. 30.

[19] I d e m: *Über die in Oberschlesien gefundenen Römischen Münzen*. In: *Zu der öffentlichen Prüfung aller Klassen des Königlichen Gymnasiums zu Ratibor*. Ratibor 1828, S. 62.

P. M. TR. P. COS. III. Mulier stans dextra porrecta nescio qiud, sinistra hastam tenet [...]. Numus argenteus, ex nostris sextus, inventus non procul a Ratiboria prope Slavicaviam vicum."[20]

Das Vorkommen zweier Kaisernamen auf der Kopfseite der Münze hatte Carl Linge wahrscheinlich verirrt. Die Beschriftung lässt aber keine Zweifel, die in Slawikau gefundene Münze war ein Denar von Hadrian. 1822 nannte Carl Linge weitere Ortschaften, in denen Funde von römischen Münzen gemacht wurden. In der Nähe von Ratibor, in **Wojnowice (Woinowitz)** stieß man auf unbestimmte Münzen, unweit von Cosel, in **Słowięcice (Slawentzitz)** hat man eine Münze von Antonius Pius gefunden. Weitere unbestimmten Münzen hat man unweit von **Racibórz (Ratibor)**, in **Czernica (Czernitz)**, in **Strzelce Opolskie (Gross Strehlitz)**, in **Toszek (Tost)**[21], unweit von Gleiwitz und in **Szymiszów (Schimischow)** gefunden. Unweit von **Strzelce Opolskie** entdeckte man auch unbestimmte römische Münzen: „Auch in **Woinowitz**, eine Meile von Ratibor, in der Nähe von Sudoll, sollen, nach der Aussage des Landrath v. Kölichen und Kaufmann Bordollo zu Ratibor, vor vielen Jahren Römische Münzen gefunden worden sein, was von grosser Wichtigkeit ist. — Selbst bis über die Oder verirrten sich diese Fremdlige, obwohl sehr sparsam; denn in **Slawentzitz**, ungefähr zwei Meilen von Cosel, wurde vor mehrern Jahren ein Antonin gefunden; auch sind mir außerdem noch **Czernitz** und **Gross-Strehlitz** als Fundorte Römischer Münzen genannt worden; **Tost** und **Schimischow** sind schon in Kruses Budorgis aufgeführt."[22]

1823 vergrößerte sich die Kollektion des ratiborer Gymnasiums um jene fünf römischen Münzen aus der Gegend von **Szymiszów**: „Zu einer Münzsammlung ist ein glücklicher Anfang gemacht hauptsächlich der Bemühung des Hrn. Justizrath Taitrzik verdanken wir die Entstehung derselben; denn durch seine Vermittelung erhielten wir 5 römische Kaisermünzen, in der Gegend des Annaberge gefunden, vom Hrn. Justitiarius Schneider zu Schimischow."[23] In **Strzelce Opolskie** gefundene und 1822 von Linge beschriebenen, unidentifizierten Münzen wurden im Artikel vom 1828 von demselben Autor näher besprochen: „Endlich ein Philippus, Faustina und Vespasian, aus dem Nachlass des Kaufmann Matros zu Gross-Strehlitz herrühred, dem sie von Landleuten für Waaren an Zahlungsstatt gegeben worden."[24]

Ein weiteres, dem ratiborer Gymnasium übergebenes Kollektionsstück, war eine in der Nähe von **Strzelce Opolskie**, in **Dolna (Dollna)** gefundene

---

[20] E. H ä n i s c h: *De Gymnasii...*, S. 10.
[21] Diese Münze beschrib E. K o n i k: *Znaleziska...*, S. 144.
[22] C. L i n g e: *Über die in Oberschlesien...*, S. 14.
[23] I d e m: *Zu der öffentlichen Prüfung...*, S. 30.
[24] I d e m: *Über die in Oberschlesien gefundenen Römsischen Münzen*. In: *Zu der öffentlichen Prüfung...*, S. 63. Die Beschreibung von diesen Münzen befindet sich in der Arbeit von K. G o d - ł o w s k i: *Materiały kultury...*, S. 377.

Münze von Domitian, über die 1828 Linge schrieb: „Unserer Ratiborer Sammlung schenkte Justitiarius Schneider in Schimischow fünf Silbermünzen aus jener Gegend, als einen Domitian, vortrefflich erhalten, auf dem Felde bei Dollna durch die Leute des dasigen Pfarrer Nawe gefunden."[25] Hänisch beschrieb im Katalog diese Münze folgend:
„Domitian
IMP. CAES. DOMIT. AVG. GERM. P. M. TR. P. VII. Caput laureatum.
IMP. XV. COS. XIIII. CENS. P. P. P. Pallas stans dextra hastam tenet sinistra post tergum flexa. Cusus est hic numus eodem anno 88 p. C. N., quo ludi saeculares acti. Est ex nostris argenteis primus, inventus prope Dollnam, vicum haud procul a Strehlitia Majore, urbe Silesiae superioris situm."[26]

Wir lesen beim Linge über einen nächsten Fund nach: „Auf den südöstlich von diesem Dorfe gelegenen Feldern sind nach Angabe der Eigenthümer öfters ähnliche Münzen gefunden worden. Ferner eine Crispina aus dem Nachlasse des Pfarrer Schneider zu Wyssoka, die ihm als Opfergeld wahrscheinlich von einem Einwohner des benachbarten Dorfes Dollna gegeben worden ist."[27] So beschrieb Linge zwei Funde im Dorf **Dolna**: einen Denar von Domitian und eine Münze von Crispina. In den gegenwärtigen Bearbeitungen wird die Münze von Crispina ausgelassen.

Zu einem größeren Fund kam es auch in der Nähe von Annaberg, in **Zakrzów (Sackrau)**. Auch dieser wurde 1828 von Carl Linge beschrieben. „Von der grössten Wichtigkeit aber ist der Fund, den zu Sackrau, ebenfalls im Angesicht des Annaberges, der Müller Kaschura machte, als dies Dorf noch dem Vater des jetzigen Besitzers gehörte. Er fand nämlich einen ganzen eisernen Topf voll Römischer Silbermünzen; sie sind aber alle zerstreut worden bis auf 16 Stück, welche die Frau Gräfin v. Strachwitz, damals noch auf Sackrau, erhielt und unsrer Sammlung schenke."[28] Da man diese Münzen dem ratiborer Gymnasium weiterschenkte, wurden sie natürlich auch in Hänischs Katalog eingeschrieben. Das waren die folgenden Münzen:
„Nero
IMP. NERO. CAESAR. AVG. P. P. vel P. M. Caput laureatum. In aversa est aquila alas concutiens inter duo signa militaria. Est ex nostris numis argenteis duodecimus, integerrimus, inventus apud Sacraviam, vicum non procul a monte St. Annae situm.

Trajanus
IMP. TRAIANO. AVG. GERM. DAC.... Caput laureatum.

---

[25] C. L i n g e: *Über die in Oberschlesien gefundenen Römischen Münzen.* In: *Zu der öffentlichen Prüfung...,* S. 63.
[26] E. H ä n i s c h: *De Gymnasii...,* S. 8.
[27] C. L i n g e: *Über die in Oberschlesien gefundenen Römischen Münzen.* In: *Zu der öffentlichen Prüfung...,* S. 63.
[28] Ibidem.

...Q...DAR... Homo sellae insidens dextra nescio quid porrigere vel projicere videtur, sinistra hastam tenet. Etiam hic numus in Silesia superiore apud Sacraviam, vicum sub radicibus montis St. Annae situm, est inventus. Ex argenteis nostris est undevicesimus [...].
IMP. TRAIANO. AVG. GER. DAC. P.M.TR.P.COS.V.P.P. Caput laureatum.
ARAB. ADQ. S.P.Q.R. OPTIMO. PRINCIPI. Mulier stans dextra ramum, sinistra calamum tenet, adstat ad ejus pedes struthiocamelus [...]. Ex est argenteis nostris nonus, inventus prope Sacraviam, vicum sub radicibus montis St. Annae situm.

Ejusdem consulatus quinti, qui incidit in annos 104—111 p. C. n., eodem loco inventus est alius numus argenteus, ex nostris duodevicesimus, in cujus antica legitur TRAIANO, cetera obliterata sunt; in aversa: COS V. P. P. S........C. i. e. Sine dubio S. P. Q. R. OPTIMO PRINC. Praeterea conspicitur figura hominis obscurata.

... ..AIANO. AVG. GER. DAC. P. M. TR. P. COS. VI. P. P. Caput laureatum.
S. P. Q. R. OPTIMO. PRINCIPI. Homo nudus, cingulo tamen circumdatus, incedens, dextra hastam tenens. Est hic numus ex argenteis nostris undecimus, inventus prope Sacraviam, vicum in radicibus montis St. Annae situm. Cusus videtur inter annum 112 et 114 p. C. n.

... . AVG. GERM. DAC. Trajani caput laureatum.
PARTHia. CAPTA. vel PARTHico. p. m. Cos. VI. p. p. s. p. q. r. Imperator stans dextra hastam, sinistra parazonium tenet [...]. Est ex argenteis nostris decimus et septimus, inventus ad Sacraviam vicum.

Hadrianus
IMP. CAESAR. TRA... ..DRIANVS. AVG. Caput laureatum.
P. M. Tr. p. COS. III. Insidet figura sellae dextra spices, sinistra hastam tenes. Ex literis. Quae in infima numi parte scriptae sunt, mediae tantum legi possunt: P. T. Est argenteus, apud nos decimus et tertius, inventus prope Sacraviam, vicum sub radicibus montis St. Annae situm.

Ejusdem generis videtur esse numus argenteus octavus, ad Sacraviam vicum inventus, qui in antica habet caput imberbe laureatum cum inscriptione HADRIANVS ...., in aversa feminam sellae insidentem, dextra ramum sive tale quid, sinistra cornu copiae tenentem; dedes imposti sunt prorae navis [...].

Antoninus Pius
ANTONINVS. AVG. PIVS. TR. P. Caput laureatum.

Praeter duas literas Q. S. In aversa nihil legi potest. Mulier, nescio an Minerva dea, stans angui erecto cibaria manu porrigere videtur. Est numus argenteus, apud Sacraviam vicum inventus, ex nostris vicesimus.

ANTONINVS. AVG. PIVS. P. P. Caput laureatum.
COS. IIII. Sella curulis cum fascibus superimpositis. Est numus argenteus, ex nostris decimus et quartus, inventus prope Sacraviam vicum.

Faustina Senior, Antonini Pii uxor.
Antica est eadem. In aversa legitur CERES. Dea stans dextra spices, sinistra facem tenet. Sunt numi argentei quartus et decimus et sextus, quorum posterior inventus est apud Sacraviam vicum.

[Unter dieser Position hat man zwei Münzen von Faustina Senior mit den Nummern 4 und 16 registriert, die aus Sackrau stammen. Sich auf dem Bericht von Bolin stützend, nennen Eugeniusz Konik und Kazimierz Godłowski nur eine Münze von Faustina Senior. Godłowski stützt sich auf Dr. Hufnagel, der in den dreißiger Jahren des XX Jhs. die Gymnasialmünzen erforschte und er gibt noch zu diesem Schatz eine Münze von Faustina Junior dazu. Es könnten demnach im Sackrau nicht zwei, sondern nur eine Münze von Faustina Senior gefunden worden sein. Die zweite Münze war von Faustina Junior — D.Ch.].[29]
Marcus Aurelius
M. AVR. ANTON. CAES. PONTIF. Caput vel potius protome nudis capillis.
PRINCIPI. IVVENTVTIS. Caesar paludatus stans prope tropaeum daxtra bacillum vel ramum, sinistra hastam tenet. Est ex numis nostris argenteis decimus, inventus prope Sacraviam vicum.

Lucius Verus
L. VERVS. AVG. ARM. PARTH. ..... Caput radiatum.
Tr. P. VI. IMP. IIII. COS. II. Mulier stans dextra nescio quid offert, sinistra cornu copiae tenet. Est numus argenteus, ex nostris vicesimus secundus, inventur prope Sacraviam vicum."[30]

Vierzehn von sechzehn in Sackrau gefundenen und dem ratiborer Gymnasium übergebenen römischen Münzen wurden von Hänisch beschrieben. Die zwei übrigen Münzen fehlen in der Bearbeitung, weil sie am wahrscheinlichsten unlesbar waren.

1833 bereicherte sich das ratiborer Gymnasium um zwei weitere römische Münzen, die in **Walidrogi (Schulenburg)**, in Kreis Opole (Oppeln) und in **Racibórz Miedonia (Niedanie)** entdeckt wurden. „[...] Herr Referendarius Graf von Ballestram eine bei Colonie Schulenburg bei Oppeln gefundene Silbermünzen von Antoninus Pius; der Tertianer Beständig eine auf den Feldern von

---

[29] S. B o l i n: *Fynden av romerska mynt...*, S. 74, E. K o n i k: *Znaleziska...*, S. 165, K. G o d - ł o w s k i: *Materiały kultury...*, S. 332.
[30] E. H ä n i s c h: *De Gymnasii...*, S. 5—14.

Niedanie bei Ratibor gefundene Silbermünze, deren Schrift schon unleserlich geworden ist [...]."[31] Beide Münzen hat Hänisch in sein Katalog aufgenommen.

„Antoninus Pius

ANTONINVS. AVG. PIVS. P. P. TR. P. nescio utrum VII. an III. Caput laureatum.

CO.... ..... Mulier stans sinistra serpentem ab ara adsurgentem ex patera pascit, sinistra cornu copiae effundit. Est ex numis argenteis nostris tricesimus nonus, inventus ad Schulenburg, vicum haud procul ab Oppolia situm.

Faustina Junior, M. Aurelii uxot.

DIVA. FAVSTINA. AVG. PII. AVG. FIL. Caput cultu solito.

CONCORDIA. Mulier sedens, quae quid manibus teneat, cognosci jam non potest. Est ex numis argenteis nostris quadragesimus, inventus in agris Niedaniensibus haud procul a Ratiboria urbe."[32]

Die aus Niedanie stammende Münze ist also ein Denar von Faustina Junior. K. Godłowski, der sich auf Hufnagels Forschung stützt, gibt eine andere Beschriftung der Münze an. Hufnagel ist aber ein Fehler unterlaufen[33].

Außer diesen, zählen noch andere römische Münzen zu der Kollektion des Gymnasiums, die auf den Feldern von **Nowa Cerekiew (Deutsch-Neukirch)** gefunden wurden.

„Trajanus

IMP. (Hic deest numi pars a Judaeo quodam, qui eam mihi vendidit defracta, ut videret, utrum argenteus esset an non.) VA. TRAIAN. AVG. GERM. Caput laureatum. In aversa conspicitur quidem figura stans flexis brachiis, sed quae reliqua ibi fuerunt, ea in agris apud Deutsch-Neukirch urbem, ubi hic numus inventus est, detrita sunt omnia. Est ex argenteis nostris Quadragesimus sextus.

imp. caes. ner. TRAIANO. optimo. aug. germ. dac. Caput laureatum.

PARTHICO. P. m. tr. p. coS. VI. P. P. S. P. Q. R. Mulier stans dextra extensa gladium, sinistra cornu copiae tenet [...]. Est ex argenteis nostris quadragesimus tertius, inventus in agris apud vicum Deutsch-Neukirch.

Faustina Senior, Antonini Pii uxor.

FAVSTINA. AVGVSTA. Caput laureatum.

In aversa inscriptio plane deleta est, mulieris figura adhuc conspicitur. Est ex numis argenteis nostris quadragesimus quintus, inventus apud vicum Deutsch-Neukirch.

---

[31] Idem: *Zu der öffentlichen Prüfung...*, S. 34.
[32] Idem: *De Gymnasii...*, S. 13, 15.
[33] K. Godłowski: *Materiały kultury...*, S. 374.

DIVA. AVG. FAVSTINA. Caput mulieris cultu solito.

AVGVSTA. Mulier galeata stans dextra sceptrum, sinistra nescio quid tenet. Est numus argenteus quadragesimus septimus, inventus prope vicum Deutsch-Neukirch.

Septimius Sewer

L. SEPT. SEV. PERT. AVG. IMP. X. Caput laureatum.

SALVTI AVGG. (i. e. Severi et Caracallae). Figura seminuda solio insidens dextra in ara sacrificare videtur sinistro brachio solio imposito. Est ex numis argenteis nostris quadragesimus quartus; [...]. inventus est prope Deutsch-Neukirch vicum [...]."[34]

Wie schon oben erwähnt wurde, informierte uns bereits 1822 Carl Linge über die Funde von römischen Münzen in Deutsch-Neukirch. Wir wissen aber nicht darüber bescheid, wer und wann diese Münzen gefunden hat, auch nicht wann sie zu der Gymnasialkollektion dazukamen. Man weiß ebenfalls nicht, ob sie wie uns Linge informierte, bei dem Umbau der dortigen Kirche gefunden wurden, oder ob wir es mit anderen Funden zu tun haben. Die Gymnasialberichte schweigen darüber.

In Hänischs Katalog ist noch eine im Wald, am rechten Ufer der Oder, in der Nähe von Racibórz gefundene Münze zu sehen. Es ist ein Denar von Traian.

„Trajanus

IMP. CAES. NERVA. TRAIAN. AVG. GERM. Caput laurcatu.

P. M. TR. P. COS. III. P. P. Mulier stans sinistra cornu copiae, dextra Victoriolam tenet. Est hic numus anni centesimi p. C. n., ex argenteis nostris quinquagesimus. Inventus esse dicitur in silva, quae est in dextra Viadri ripa non procul a Ratiboria."[35]

In der Umgebung von Racibórz hat man auch einen Denaren von Antoninus Pius gcfunden, welcher ebenfalls in Hänischs Katalog zu sehen ist.

„ANTONINVS. AVG. PIVS. P. P. Caput laureatum.

TR. POT. COS. III. LIB. IIII. Mulier stans dextra labarum, sinistra cornu copiae tenet. Conf. Eckhel. 1. 1. VII, p. 17. Est ex numis argenteis nostris tricesimus secundus, emtus ille ab artifice aerario hujus urbis, qui eum ab agricola aliquo emerat, unde probabile est, eum esse in nostra vicinia inventum."[36]

Die letzte, in der Umgebung von Racibórz gefundene und in Hänischs Katalog platzierte Münze, ist ein Denar von Faustina Senior.

„DIVA. AVG. FAVSTINA. Caput cultu solito.

---

[34] E. Hänisch: *De Gymnasii...*, S. 8, 9, 10, 13, 14, 17.
[35] Ibidem, S. 9.
[36] Ibidem, S. 12.

AETERNITAS. Mulier velata stans. Est numus argenteus, apud nos tricesimus primus, emtus ab artifice aerario hujus urbis, quare veri est simillimum eum in nostra regione esse inventum."[37]

Abschließend sollte man noch zwei in **Górny Śląsk (Oberschlesien)** gefundene Münzen erwähnen. „Noch könne ich, um die angegebene Zahl der in Oberschlesien gefundenen Münzen zu vergrössern, von zwei sehr interessanten Consularmünzen sprechen, mit welchen Kaufmann Albrecht, in Deutsch-Neukirch geboren, unsere Sammlung beschenkt hat, so wie von den Römer-münzen, welche Kaufmann Scotti, zu Gross-Strehlitz, und andere Privatleute in Ratibor, durch die Umstände begünstigt, gesammelt haben [...]."[38] Die von Kaufmann Albrecht geschenkten Münzen sind wahrscheinlich in Hänischs Katalog platziert worden. Das Problem ist, dass dort drei Konsularmünzen zu sehen sind und Albrecht hat nur zwei geschenkt. Diese drei Münzen wurden unter den Nummern 24, 48 und 25 registriert. Da Albrecht einmalig eine Gabe von zwei Münzen machte, könnte man annehmen, dass ihnen aufeinander folgende Nummern gegeben wurden. Dieser Denkweise nach schließend sind Alrechts Gaben:

„Gens Calpurnia plebeja
Caput Apollinis laureatum, pone X, infra F.
L. PISO. FRVGI. H. Eques, a cujus collo fasciae, quae mihi videtur esse, vento retro agitantur, equo citato invehitur [...]. Es apud nos ex numis argenteis vicesimus quartus [...]

Gens Fonteja plebeja
Caput geminum, quale fere Jani esse solet, sed sine barba; in area ab altera parte est H, ab altera X.
C. FONT. ROMA. [...]. Ex numis argenteis nostris est vicesimus quintus. [...]."[39]

So viele Informationen über die Funde von römischen Münzen in Oberschlesien beinhalteten die Jahresberichte des Königlichen Evangelischen Gymnasiums zu Ratibor. Die meisten betrafen den mit **Racibórz (Ratibor)** benachbarten Lobschützerboden, es fehlt aber nicht an Informationen über Funde aus den von Ratibor entfernten Regionen. Dank ihrer Redlichkeit sind Eduard Hänischs und Carl Linges Berichte vollkommenste Wissensquellen über die uns interessierenden Funde. Da jegliche Archivdokumente aus jener Zeit fehlen, bleiben den heutigen Forschern die Gymnasialberichte als einzige Wissensquelle zum Thema. Die oben besprochenen Informationen über die dem Gymnasium geschenkten, römischen Münzen sind nicht die einzigen, die

---

[37] Ibidem, S. 15.
[38] C. L i n g e: *Über die in Oberschlesien gefundenen Römischen Münzen*. In: *Zu der öffentlichen Prüfung...*, S. 63—64.
[39] E. H ä n i s c h: *De Gymnasii...*, S. 3—4.

Zu
der öffentlichen Prüfung
aller Classen
des Königlichen Gymnasiums zu Ratibor
den 1sten und 2ten April,

und

dem Redeactus
den 3ten April

laden ergebenst ein

Director und Lehrercollegium.

———

Inhalt.

Pinzgeri, Doctoris, Gymnasii Prorectoris et superiorum ordinum Praeceptoris
imi de linguae Graecae in Gymnasiis tradendae ratione oratio.

hulnachrichten. Vom Director Hänisch.

Ratibor 1830. Gedruckt bei F. Langer.

1. Die Titelseite dieser Beschreibung aus dem Jahre 1830

die Berichte enthalten. Leider fehlt in weiteren Fällen der Fundort. Wir
können nur annehmen, dass unter ihnen auch aus Oberschlesien stammende
Münzen sind. Katalog der in Oberschlesien gefundenen Münzen, dessen
Anfertigung auf den Berichten des Königlichen Evangelischen Gymnasiums zu
Ratibor gestützt ist:

Bieskau (heute ein Teil von Nowa Cerekiew):
Zahlreiche Funde von römischen Münzen, darunter:
— eine Goldmünze — 1 Vespasian,
— Silbermünzen — 1 Julius Caesar, 1 Nero, 1 Galba, 1 Witellius, 2 Ves-
   pasian, 1 Titus, 1 Domitian, 1 Nerwa, 23 Trajan, 16 Hadrian, 6 Antoninus
   Pius, 3 Marc Aurel, 1 L. Aurelius Verus, 8 Commodus, 1 Sabina, 4 von
   beiden Faustinen,
— Bronzemünzen — 1 Trajan, 2 Faustina Junior, 1 Münze mit SOLI
   INVICTO beschriftet,
— Eisenmünzen mit Silber beschichtet — 1 Trajan, 2 Hadrian, 1 L. Aurelius
   Verus.

Księże Pole (Knispel):
— eine Goldmünze von Neron vom Jahre 56

Sucha Psina (Zauchwitz):
— ein Denar von Hadrian

Rogożany (Rosen):
— ungefähr 10 Bronze- oder Kupfermünzen, darunter: 1 Caesar Octavius,
   1 Trajan, 1 Hadrian, 1 Marc Aurel, 1 Septimius Severus, 1 Alexander
   Severus, 1 Gallienus, 1 Constantin II, 1 Lucilla.

Grudynia Wielka (Gross-Grauden):
— eine Goldmünze von Juliusz Verus Maximus

Głubczyce (Leobschütz):
— eine Münze von Trajan

Opawa (Troppau):
— eine Silbermünze von Aurelius

Sławików (Slawikau):
— eine Silbermünze von Hadrian

Sławięcice (Slawentzitz):
— eine Münze von Antoninus Pius

Szymiszów (Schimischow):
— fünf römische Münzen

Wojnowice (Woinowitz):
— unbestimmte römische Münzen

Toszek (Tost):
— unbestimmte römische Münzen

Czernica (Czernitz):
— unbestimmte römische Münzen
Strzelce Opolskie (Gross-Strehlitz):
— 1 Faustina, 1 Philippus, 1 Vespasian
Dolna (Dollna):
— 1 silberner Domitian,
— 1 Cryspina
Zakrzów (Sackrau):
— 16 römische Silbermünzen, darunter: 1 Nero, 5 Trajan, 2 Hadrian, 2 Antonius Pius, 2 Faustina Senior (oder 1 Faustina Senior, 1 Faustina Junior), 1 Marc Aurel, 1 L. Verus.
Walidrogi (Schulenburg):
— Silbermünze von Antoninus Pius.
Racibórz-Miedonia (Ratibor Niedanie):
— Silbermünze von Faustina Junior, M. Aurelii uxot.
Nowa Cerekiew (Deutsch-Neukirch):
— Silbermünzen — 2 Trajan, 2 Faustina Senior, 1 Septimius Sewer.
Racibórz (Ratibor):
— eine Silbermünze von Trajan, eine Silbermünze von Antoninus Pius, eine Silbermünze von Faustina Senior.
Górny Śląsk (Oberschlesien):
— zwei Silbermünzen — Gens Calpurnia plebeja, Gens Fonteja plebeja.

Dariusz Chojecki

ZNALEZISKA MONET RZYMSKICH NA GÓRNYM ŚLĄSKU, ODNOTOWANE W SPRAWOZDANIACH ROCZNYCH GIMNAZJUM KRÓLEWSKO-EWANGELICKIEGO W RACIBORZU

Streszczenie

Artykuł dotyczy znalezisk monet rzymskich na Górnym Śląsku odnotowanych w sprawozdaniach rocznych Gimnazjum Królewsko-Ewangelickiego w Raciborzu. Uczelnia ta powstała w 1819 roku. Nauczyciele gimnazjalni stworzyli w jej murach różnorodne kolekcje, niektóre o charakterze muzealnym. Miały one służyć jako pomoce dydaktyczne w pracy z młodzieżą. W sprawozdaniach gimnazjalnych zamieszczano informacje dotyczące nowych nabytków.

Wśród kolekcji znalazły się również numizmaty, w tym monety rzymskie. Sprawozdania gimnazjalne traktują także o nich. Informacje dotyczące nowych nabytków gimnazjum są na ogół bardzo lakoniczne. Wiemy, kto monetę przekazał do gimnazjum, ale tylko w nielicznych przypadkach zapisano nazwisko znalazcy i miejsce, w którym doszło do odkrycia. Zazwyczaj brakuje także opisu monety. Wieloletni trud kolekcjonerski nauczycieli wieńczy opublikowany w 1842 roku katalog monet rzymskich będących własnością gimnazjum.

Bardzo szczegółowy opis znalezisk monet rzymskich na Górnym Śląsku przedstawił dyrektor gimnazjum Carl Linge. W dwóch artykułach zamieszczonych w sprawozdaniach z 1822 i 1828 roku zaprezentował całą swą wiedzę dotyczącą znalezisk i kolekcji monet rzymskich na tym obszarze. Niektóre spośród tych monet trafiły do zbiorów gimnazjum. Sprawozdania raciborskiej uczelni są najdokładniejszym i najkompletniejszym źródłem traktującym o znaleziskach interesujących nas numizmatów na Górnym Śląsku w pierwszej połowie XIX wieku.

Autor niniejszego artykułu poddaje analizie zawarte w sprawozdaniach informacje o monetach rzymskich. Końcową część tekstu stanowi katalog monet rzymskich uwzględniający miejsce ich odkrycia.

Dariusz Chojecki

FINDS OF THE ROMAN COINS UPPER SILESIA RECORDED IN THE ANNUAL REPORTS OF GIMNAZJUM KRÓLEWSKO-EWANGELICKIE IN RACIBÓRZ

Summary

This article concerns the finds of the Roman coins in Upper Silesia, recorded in the annual reports of Gimnazjum Królewsko-Ewangelickie in Racibórz. This school was founded in 1819. In its building, the gymnasium teachers created different collections, some of which were of a museum type. They were to serve the purpose of teaching aids when working with the youth. The gymnasium reports included information concerning the new finds.

Also, the collection comprised numismatists, the Roman coins included. The gymnasium reports treat of these too. The information dealing with the new finds is usually very laconic. What is known is who gave the coin to the gymnasium, but both the place and the name of its finder is revealed in rare cases. Ordinarily, the coin description is left out too. The teacher's collection pains of many years are crowned in a gymnasium-owned catalogue of the Roman coins published in 1842.

A very detailed description of the finds of the Roman coins in Upper Silesia was presented by Carl Linge, a headmaster of the gymnasium. In the two articles inserted in the reports from 1822 and 1828, he shared all his knowledge about the finds and collection of the Roman coins in this area. Some of these coins belong to the gymnasium collections. The reports from Racibórz constitute the most-detailed and complete source of the finds of numismatists in Upper Silesia in the first half of the 19th century.

The present article analyses the information on the Roman coins included in the reports. The closing part of the work constitutes a catalogue of the Roman coins taking into account the place of their discovery.

Redaktorzy
BARBARA MALSKA, JERZY STENCEL,
KATARZYNA WIĘCKOWSKA

Komputerowe przygotowanie
okładki i wklejek oraz redakcja techniczna
MAŁGORZATA PLEŚNIAR

Korektor
MIROSŁAWA ŻŁOBIŃSKA

ISSN 0208-6336
ISBN 978-83-226-1638-3

Wydawca
Wydawnictwo Uniwersytetu Śląskiego
ul. Bankowa 12B, 40-007 Katowice
www.wydawnictwo.us.edu.pl
e-mail: wydawus@us.edu.pl

Wydanie I. Nakład: 350 + 50 egz. Ark. druk. 9,5 + wklejki.
Ark. wyd. 13,5. Przekazano do łamania w sierpniu 2007 r.
Podpisano do druku w lutym 2008 r. Papier offset. kl. III, 80 g
Cena 22 zł

Łamanie: Pracownia Składu Komputerowego
Wydawnictwa Uniwersytetu Śląskiego
Druk i oprawa: EXPOL, P. Rybiński, J. Dąbek, Spółka Jawna
ul. Brzeska 4, 87-800 Włocławek